Praise for *Walking Alongside:*
*The **Essence** Of Parish Nursing*

"After working with Barb for many years on the Pastoral Care Team of our Church, I am not at all surprised by the thoroughness, competence, comprehensiveness, and overall excellence of her written work. As a parish nurse, Barb brings a unique set of skills to our team. In short, Barb makes a real difference in the kind and quality of care that is offered to our members and to the wider community. I am convinced that her book will make a significant difference as well.
I wholeheartedly commend this book to parish nurses, clergy and faith communities alike as they seek to provide the best possible care for their members."

—The Rev. Don Downer
Associate Pastor
Holy Trinity Church, Thornhill

"Walking Alongside reflects Barbara's unwavering commitment to parish nursing. As a pioneer in the field, she has a vast amount of experience to share. Speaking from her personal experiences is what makes this book such a treasure for those people trying to get their head around the concept of parish nursing. The mixture of heartfelt writing and practical tips makes this book a must for people who hope to become parish nurses."

—Mol　　　　　　　　　　　　　　Λ.Ed.
　　　　　　　　　　　　　　　　culty
C　　　D0813268　　　, BC.

"This book is well researched and will be a useful resource for both the novice and experienced Parish Nurse. A must for Church Libraries."

—Glennis Harris RN
Parish Nurse

"My exposure to parish nurse work over the past 15 years has been very positive and definitely beneficial in making health care decisions for extremely complex situations in a timely, professional manner. I think the 'to do list' provides the meat of the book and would be useful for the practitioner. The quotes provide a spiritual backdrop."

—Joe Marshall
Family Physician
Thornhill, ON

"Barbara is a pioneer of parish nursing, and was practicing in Canada when Granger Westberg formalized the concept in the late 1980's. She is therefore, qualified to write this practical tool for parish nurses. As well as telling her inspiring personal story she shares valuable advice. These are evidenced based nursing interventions, especially helpful to beginning parish nurses.
This book is a needed addition to the growing collection of parish nursing resources. It is a 'church-tested' recipe for a successful parish nursing ministry."

—Gloria Wiebe RN
Parish Nurse since 1998
St.James' Anglican Cathedral
Toronto, Ontario.

Walking Alongside:

The *Essence* Of Parish Nursing

Walking Alongside:

The *Essence* Of

Parish Nursing

/ ʔ o 3 o /

Barbara Caiger, R.N.

RECEIVED

JUL   2006

SENECA LIBRARIES
KING CAMPUS

Edited by

Margaret Black, R.N., BScN., Ed.D.

WITHDRAWN

PROPERTY OF
SENECA COLLEGE
LIBRARIES
KING CAMPUS

vi

© Copyright 2006 Barbara Caiger, R.N.

Author portrait by Kris King Media

All rights reserved. No part of this publication may be reproduced, stored in a retrieval system, or transmitted, in any form or by any means, electronic, mechanical, photocopying, recording, or otherwise, without the written prior permission of the author.

Note for Librarians: A cataloguing record for this book is available from Library and Archives Canada at www.collectionscanada.ca/amicus/index-e.html
ISBN 1-4120-5385-4

Printed in Victoria, BC, Canada. Printed on paper with minimum 30% recycled fibre. Trafford's print shop runs on "green energy" from solar, wind and other environmentally-friendly power sources.

PUBLISHING™
Offices in Canada, USA, Ireland and UK
This book was published *on-demand* in cooperation with Trafford Publishing. On-demand publishing is a unique process and service of making a book available for retail sale to the public taking advantage of on-demand manufacturing and Internet marketing. On-demand publishing includes promotions, retail sales, manufacturing, order fulfilment, accounting and collecting royalties on behalf of the author.

Book sales for North America and international:
Trafford Publishing, 6E–2333 Government St.,
Victoria, BC V8T 4P4 CANADA
phone 250 383 6864 (toll-free 1 888 232 4444)
fax 250 383 6804; email to orders@trafford.com
Book sales in Europe:
Trafford Publishing (UK) Limited, 9 Park End Street, 2nd Floor
Oxford, UK OX1 1HH UNITED KINGDOM
phone 44 (0)1865 722 113 (local rate 0845 230 9601)
facsimile 44 (0)1865 722 868; info.uk@trafford.com
Order online at:
trafford.com/05-0280

10 9 8 7 6 5 4 3

Contents

Foreword by Rev. Canon Dr. Linda Nicholls
Preface
The Author

Part One:
The Foundation

Part Two:
The Practice

Part Three:
The Parish Nurse As Educator

Part Four:
Cultivating Solutions For Human Challenges

Part Five:

Lay Pastoral Visiting

Part Six:
Family Violence and Emotional Trauma

Part Seven:
Grief and Loss

Part Eight:
Life Challenges
(Supporting Individuals and Families)

Part Nine:
The Parish Nurse as Role Model

Part Ten:
Success Stories

Part Eleven:
The Voice of Experience

Appendix

Foreword

It is a great pleasure to commend this book to you. Over the past thirteen years I worked with Barbara Caiger as one of the Anglican ministers in pastoral ministry. Her journey of discovery of the richness of this ministry was mine also. Repeatedly we saw the benefits of this pastoral team for individual parishioners, their families and the entire parish, with the parish nurse as an integral and essential component. Staff benefitted from the care and support of the parish nurse – Barb's teddy bears often had staff visitors as well as the parishioners – including me! Vulnerable seniors without extended family had an advocate and were well supported in their needs. Educational events brought community members into the church and opened our doors to their needs.

It was a tremendous privilege to journey with Barbara in pioneering this ministry in our community. She searched for and found or developed the resources and networks she needed and established the credibility of the ministry to such an extent that local health care providers – doctors, nurses, community agencies – breathed a sigh of relief when they knew she was part of the whole team of care.

The chapters that follow are distilled from the experiences of Barb's ministry, tested and proven in the hurly-burly of a large, active suburban church. I pray that they will be a catalyst for others to discover the rich benefits of parish nursing ministry.

As a parish priest my personal desire is to always have a parish nurse on the ministry team!

May God richly bless you as we were blessed in discovering parish nursing as a vehicle for sharing the love and healing compassion of Christ!

The Rev. Canon Dr. Linda Nicholls

Dedication

To the memory of my mother, Betty King, who taught me the meaning of unconditional love.

To the memory of my father, Jim King, who modelled integrity and service to others.

To my husband and best friend, Chuck, who encouraged me to follow my dream.

Preface

*I am a part of all that I have touched
and all that has touched me.*

Thomas Wolfe

We are at a time in history where our health care systems are challenged, medical staffing is reduced, and technology is creating a distance between practitioners and patients. How can we provide health care that attends to the physical needs of people, while addressing their emotional and spiritual dimensions as well? How much longer can our health care system carry on with the interminable wait lists for critical interventions? How do consumers learn to take more responsibility for their own health care? The recent concerns about our health care systems urge us to examine ways for faith communities to reclaim the ministry of healing and wholeness.

Scope of This Book

This is a book about promoting healing and wholeness in faith communities. As a parish nurse with fifteen years experience, I have learned some profound lessons about the human condition. I share these lessons through stories, illustrations, and personal experiences. I recognize that each faith community, with its own unique identity, will exhibit different manifestations of common issues. Beneath those external wrappers, the basic needs of human beings cross cultural, economic, and geographical boundaries. I challenge the *conventional wisdom* that often impedes the best possible resolution of age-old problems.

Intended Audience

This book is for nurses, family physicians, faith communities, and their leaders. If you are an educator in health care, you can use these principles to enhance the scope of your knowledge about a growing community resource. If you are a volunteer coordinator in a faith community, there are tips for you. People organizing health education workshops can learn some pitfalls to avoid. Families caring for aging relatives and friends will gain insights that they may not have considered.

The Approach

This book is written from the perspective of a professional nurse working in a faith community. The stories and examples are drawn from fifteen years of experience in a parish nursing role. These illustrations are composites of real-life situations, to protect the privacy of individuals.

I have learned many lessons from the people who invited me into their lives, and from the ministers with whom I have worked. Life, itself, is a teacher, and I have developed insights through personal experiences. In my role as a *nurse in a church,* I am challenged to use my imagination when travelling through *uncharted waters.* I use my faith to strengthen my decision-making and I respect each person as an autonomous individual and a child of God.

I select courses and resources to fill the gaps in my understanding. I have built up a comprehensive library to substantiate and/or challenge ideas and approaches I am considering. In this book I aim to simplify practical strategies by using stories to illustrate the salient points.

Overview of the Contents

Part One comprises the first six chapters. Chapters 1 and 2 describe the origins of my position as parish nurse and the underlying principles of my ministry. Chapters 3 to 6 examine the attributes needed to be an excellent parish nurse, strategies for building trust and gaining credibility, ways to create an inviting work space and the tools required for the job.

Part Two includes Chapters 7 to 22 and discusses the practice of parish nursing. A code of ethics for nurses and nursing principles are covered in Chapters 7 and 8. In Chapter 9 you will learn about assessment and analysis while Chapter 10 discusses planning, implementing, evaluating and documenting parish nursing practice. Chapter 11 reinforces the value of working in partnership, as a valued member of a pastoral team. Chapter 12 is one of the most important chapters, as listening is fundamental in almost any situation you can imagine, not just in parish nursing. Chapter 13 looks at the aspects of faith in the role. Parish nurses should be committed members of a faith community, and be willing to grow in their faith. Chapters 12 and 13 are the bedrock undergirding Chapters 14 to 16, where topics such as decision-making, conflict resolution, and advance directives are discussed.

Chapters 17 and 18 are together because they look at the different ways that people perceive illness, and the impact of chronic health challenges. Each of us has our own way of dealing with these trials, but we need to be able to understand how other people deal with them. Chapter 19 describes how I help people get the most out of visits to their doctors. Chapter 20 follows in this vein, as people often need someone to advocate for them when they encounter today's healthcare system. Older people were raised with the notion that *the_doctor would look after them* but today people have to take responsibility for their own health care. Chapter 21 examines one model of intervention, a case study from my practice. This chapter is just that, one model, but the principles of autonomy and independence are consistent with any parish nursing interventions. Chapter 22, the final chapter in Part 2 reveals some of the merits of a *teddy bear ministry.* If you think that teddy bears are just for children, this chapter may change your thinking!

Part Three looks at the role of the parish nurse as educator. One of the goals of parish nursing is to transform a faith community into a place of healing and wholeness. Chapters 23 to 26 examine different aspects of that objective, from individual learning and health promotion, to executing a major educational event for the community. Chapter 25 outlines approaches for working with a Health and Wellness committee.

Part Four consists of Chapters 27 to 34. Chapter 27 is an overview of different configurations of family groups, and the challenges associated with them. Chapters 28 to 31 identify needs and strategies for dealing with the issues related to families with children, teens, family groups consisting of adults (including singles), and older adults. In these chapters, I tackle the more common trials and tribulations, and offer techniques for family meetings, and support for extended family members who may not live in the community. Chapter 34, the last chapter in this section identifies various ways for parish nurses to make use of their skills and talents for the benefit of the wider community. Strategies include offering educational opportunities for ministers in faith communities without a parish nurse. It is beneficial to connect with neighbourhood organizations, such as schools, other churches, and children and youth groups to expand the awareness and benefits of parish nursing.

Part Five is about a lay pastoral visiting program. Chapters 35 to 38 provide an overview of the visiting program, the role of the parish nurse, training of volunteers for visiting, and the pitfalls to avoid. Lay pastoral visiting is a means of solidifying the ministry of one person to another and should be visible in the faith community. It is important to note that some people's skills are better utilized in other areas of service.

Part Six examines the painful topics of family violence and the resulting emotional trauma. Chapter 39 gives an overview of the causes and effects of these difficult situations, while the next three chapters focus on different ages and situations. Family violence can occur in any age group, culture, or economic stratum. It can be difficult to offer support to the victims of abuse and, at the same time, show compassion for the perpetrator. In the majority of cases, the people acting out against others have, themselves, been victims of neglect, violence, or abuse.

Part Seven's Chapters 43 and 44 offer insights into normal grief, and useful tools for working through common, but difficult, times in life. Included are some successful strategies and useful resources for offering guidance, and a helping hand along the way. The outline of a *grief and growth* course can be used as a starting point for creating a suitable program for each unique audience.

Part Eight confronts some of life's biggest struggles. Chapter 45 is an overview of the ways people adapt to catastrophic events and situations. Chapters 46 and 48 address specific conditions. Caring for people with dementia or a life-threatening illness causes incredible strain on caregivers. These situations are compounded, as the individuals receiving the care are loved ones of the caregivers. Acknowledgement of this *double hit by* an outsider can open the door to dialogue with, and ultimately, assistance for the caregiver. Chapter 47 takes a different approach and looks at the burden of mental illness while examining determinants of mental health, and strategies for mental health promotion. Chapter 49 puts forward some education and support options to consider in planning a program for caregivers. Chapter 50 is a complex story of the magnitude of issues, and challenges faced by some families on a daily basis. *Only when you have walked a mile in another's moccasins...*

Part Nine is a challenge to nurses, ministers, care-givers and others to reflect on how well they are looking after themselves. Has setting limits on the constant demands on your time been difficult for you? If so you may discover some useful strategies for caring for yourself. Chapter 52 reveals a few of my personal challenges.

Part Ten is about stories of success in my role as parish nurse. Chapter 53 tells how writing a week-ly bulletin article made a difference in people's perceptions of the parish nurse role. Chapter 54 gives the history of successful groups that were initiated to satisfy a need. Chapter 55 summarizes a successful mentorship over a ten-month period. I learned as much from the woman I mentored as she learned from me.

Part Eleven covers the concluding two chapters of the book. A writer can always find more sub-jects to cover, but at some point a book must draw to a conclusion. Under the umbrella of *The Voice of Experience*, Chapter 56 reveals some heartwarm-ing examples of how little things do mean a lot. Sometimes the smallest gift holds the greatest value. Chapter 57 is, I believe, aptly named *And The Greatest of These is Love...* It is what matters most in parish nursing! When people feel the love of God radiating from another human being, many adversities are more easily managed. Walking alongside, demonstrating the love of God is the *essence* of parish nursing.

An appendix, a comprehensive reference section, and index complete the book.

Acknowledgements

*There will come a time when you
believe everything is finished.
That will be the beginning.*

Louis L'Amour

When a new concept is emerging, many people can be involved in the process. After several years in my position as a *nurse in a church,* my friend Wendy Dimmock, a registered nurse, attended a discussion group that was looking at parish nursing. I had not heard of the concept but, when we examined the parameters of the position, we learned that this was exactly what I was doing. Wendy encouraged me to explore this further and the result was to change the name of my position to parish nurse from pastoral assistant. The secular world found the concept easier to grasp with the word *nurse* in the title. I am grateful to Wendy for facilitating that transition, and for her consistent support along the way.

Another friend, Sister Valerie Clarke, pointed out that the skills and experience I was accumulating, as a pioneer in the field in Canada, should be shared with others. While the time to do this by writing a book did not seem to be the "right time", the thought percolated away in the background. From time to time Val would check in to see if I was at least starting to jot down some ideas. Those gentle nudges encouraged me to seriously consider the challenge.

Allan, a health care professional, helped me to believe that I had something unique to offer and urged me to get on with it. He assisted in brainstorming concepts and drafting outlines. Those seeds planted earlier were being fed and watered, and were starting to germinate!

My editor (a nurse and educator) volunteered for that role, as she was keen to be part of creating a useful Canadian tool for practitioners, ministers, educators and faith communities. Dr. Margaret Black has been a wonderful supporter and has the ability to get right to the point when I have glossed over it. Her gentle, focused, and encouraging editing kept me on track and helped me to see the gaps in my writing. She generously suggested options for consideration when I needed to rethink my presentation of the material.

Christopher Blackburn, indexer and assistant editor provided invaluable, and thought provoking insights. His quiet, steady assistance in getting the manuscript to press is much appreciated. I am grateful for the talents of Victor J. Crapnell, the graphic artist who designed the cover and demonstrated patience in working with me to achieve my objectives.

Dr. Ernest Griffin was a much-loved mentor who would have been so proud to witness the publishing of my book. I regret that he did not live to see it.

My colleagues and friends Rev. Dr. Linda Nicholls and Rev. Don Downer were strong proponents of my decision to undertake the writing of this book. I am thankful for family and friends who have been willing to listen and offer suggestion for alternative ways of approaching topics. My life-long friend, Linda McIntyre walked with me on the path when I found the going rough. My friends Marg Stanford, Charlene Campbell-Schaefer, Carolyn and Bob Groves, Helen and George Brcko, Michele Custoreri, Dorothy Davis, Cathy Pearson, Elaine Ainlay, Kathi McGuirl, Linda Robertson, Ron Purcell, Perlita Delaney, Kathy Abbott, Mary Beth Bozanin, Vivienne Hansford, Molly Chisamore, Trish Robichaud and Joe Marshall provided encouragement at various times throughout the process. My friends in the Sarah Group have been supportive and encouraging, as have my "coffee buddies" Susan Hogeboom, Joan Virtue and Brenda Olsen.

I am grateful to family members (who must be tired of hearing about *my book)* for allowing me to think out loud and test ideas. These include my sons Mark and Ian and their wives Kara and Robin, my brothers Steve and Tom and their wives Sandy and Marion, and my sister-in-law Marjorie who always shows a keen interest in how things are progressing, and has been willing to listen when they were not going well. Particular appreciation goes to my son, Ian who made use of his extensive technology expertise to rescue me when I was lost, and to my nephew, Kris King who utilized his professional photography skills for my portrait.

In a successful and lasting relationship the partners love, respect, and honour one another.

They share common goals and nurture one another in individual pursuits. My husband, Chuck has been incredibly generous and tolerant while I have followed my dream. To him, my most sincere thank you.

The Author

Protrait by Kris King Media

Barbara Caiger R.N.

Barbara has worked in different areas in nursing including ICU, IV Team, Neurology ICU, and most recently has spent 15 years in Parish Nursing.

Her background in volunteer experience includes chairing parent organizations at her children's schools, working with troubled girls and young women with Big Sisters and Children's Aid, Beaver leader in the Scouting movement, and developing and teaching babysitting courses in British Columbia and Ontario.

Barbara volunteered with St. John Ambulance and taught *Healthy Aging for Seniors* in Toronto. She developed and taught programs for Homemakers (now Personal Support Workers) before colleges offered these courses. Her experience on several Boards of Directors of agencies working with the elderly and people with disabilities enabled her to see the broader picture while not losing sight of the clients' specific needs.

Part One:

The Foundation

One

In The Beginning...

*Do not go where the path may lead,
go instead where there is no path
and leave a trail.*

Ralph Waldo Emerson

Beginnings are not always planned. Sometimes they just evolve. Such was the case in the beginning of my ministry as a *nurse in a church*. I was studying gerontology at Ryerson Polytechnic University, volunteering as a lay pastoral visitor in my own church, and chairing the board of directors of a community agency providing support services for seniors. I was on a steep learning curve.

I had developed a program to train *homemakers* (now personal support workers) to work with older people in their homes, before that type of training was available in educational facilities. While running these courses for different support agencies, I was a volunteer instructor for St. John Ambulance, teaching *Healthy Aging for Seniors* in subsidized housing facilities in Toronto. I was on a path... but I really didn't know where it was leading me. I had originally planned to do corporate work in retirement planning, but as my interest in that field waned, my uncertainty about my future increased. I made an effort to know more of the members in the church and offered to teach the *Healthy Aging* course at the church. That turned out to be a wonderful experience as the women (no men attended) developed strong friendships with one another. These women became more confident in managing their lives in a healthy way, and took pride in their newfound knowledge and assertiveness. They regretted seeing the end of the program looming before them and wanted to continue meeting. The Tuesday Group was created that day. That was 1986.

For more on the Tuesday Group please see Chapter 54.

That same year the church was seeking a leader for the lay visiting team and, as I had a number of ideas about ways to improve the program, I offered to do the job. The following year a fundraising campaign within the local Anglican churches created an opportunity to submit a proposal for consideration by our congregation. In the 80's, older people were not valued as contributing members of society (and often, the church). As a volunteer I felt that I lacked authority to make changes. With the convergence of those factors and my interest in increasing the profile of older people in the church, I proposed the position of a *nurse in a church* with a focus on the elderly. I planned to highlight ministry with seniors using their many gifts, and to promote meaningful roles and activities for them within the church. I planned also to focus on intergenerational activities. When the congregation selected my proposal as their number one priority, I applied for the job and the rest, as they say, is history...

Please see Chapter 35 on The Visiting Program.

An Innovative Staff Position in the Church

I started in the position as *pastoral assistant* in 1988, working two days a week for a stipend. At the time, I was unaware of the work being done by the Rev. Granger Westberg in the United States. I started with a clean slate and no resources. In the professional community I was viewed as a curiosity as there appeared to be no history of an arrangement such as this. Because I was developing the job as I went along, it was sometimes difficult for people to understand my role. It was difficult for me too! Prior to learning about Dr. Westberg, I began receiving calls from other churches inquiring about my program.

Evolution of New Programs

By the end of the first full year in the position, we had started a number of new programs. *The Tuesday Group* blossomed and was becoming an integral part of the church. The local Alzheimer Society called the church about a gentleman whose wife was in an Alzheimer day program, asking if we had a group activity for older men. This man was looking to reconnect with the church. We did not have such a group at the time, but we soon had *The Tuesday Men* up and running with a membership of ten. I did eventually have the privilege of meeting Dr. Westberg in Chicago at a Parish Nursing Conference where we talked about how each of us had worked toward developing this new ministry.

As I became better acquainted with the older men and women and learned more about their challenges, I began to connect with their families. It was evident that there was a need for education and support for the families and caregivers. I developed and taught a six-week program entitled *You and Your Aging Relatives.* Response to this program was positive and led to other people coming to seek advice and support.

Please see Chapter 49 on Caring for Caregivers.

Increasing Awareness of and Appreciation for the Nursing Role

The clergy were beginning to understand what the scope of a nurse in a church could be, and increasingly consulted me on suitable strategies to use in situations involving older people. This was a *two-way street* though, as I requested advice on handling the faith and pastoral care issues. While becoming more familiar with the health-related concerns of parishioners, I began building an information file. I was given a small budget to work with and was encouraged to use my discretion. I gathered books and other resources on the support services and care facilities in our community. Books and articles on grief, dementia, and gerontology were among those gathered in the early stages of my developing an extensive resource library. When people inquired about specific illnesses or situations, I found appropriate information for them. Other resources were selected for the education of lay pastoral visitors; topics such as the link between faith and health, how to be a good visitor, and visiting in a care facility were selected. I offered these resources to people with a need for them, and I informed others through articles in the newsletter and Sunday bulletin. To increase my own knowledge, I visited local agencies to learn about their work and became familiar with respite and day programs that were becoming available. I attended conferences and workshops on palliative care, grief support, gerontology, and faith and health issues.

Strategies Used for Increasing Awareness

At the beginning it was difficult for people to understand why a church would have a nurse on staff because we were travelling through uncharted waters. As much of my work was pastoral support, helping people to see the link between faith and health, helping them explore options available in moving to care facilities and gaining access to support services in the community, I was not able to talk about these confidential issues. I used two strategies to increase awareness of the potential benefits of the role.

The first strategy I used was a program provided by the Ministry of Community and Social Services (that was 1989) to improve the knowledge and understanding of the challenges for older people. I encouraged participation by the staff, lay pastoral visitors, and other volunteers working with older people. The program, entitled *Through Other Eyes,* required individuals to don swim goggles modified to impair their vision, ear plugs to reduce hearing, rubber gloves, weights on their legs, and to use a cane, while carrying out a list of prescribed tasks. The tasks were activities that people would normally do in and around the church. Media coverage by several newspapers and television stations helped to educate the community as well as the congregation. Participants in the program experienced first hand the difficulties some people encounter. All experienced frustration but gained sensitivity. This was a successful strategy. The congregation was pleased to see that their church was taking a lead in identifying barriers for people.

The second strategy was less successful. I invited some people to act as a *Seniors' Advisory Committee* to work with me in developing a tool for surveying the congregation, and in planning intergenerational activities. I was naïve to think that I could put a group together without some team-building activities and specific guidelines. What didn't work was that the members did not become a cohesive group with a natural leader emerging. In addition, I was not clear as to what my own expectations were, so we did flounder.

A beneficial outcome of that fiasco was that I had broadened the base of people who more clearly understood my role and the potential for growth. We did not develop a useful tool, but there was support for developing intergenerational activities.

Early Accomplishments

Even though there were numerous hurdles to clear at the beginning, I was able to achieve many of the things I had set out to complete and some others I didn't plan.

- The Tuesday Ladies and the Tuesday Men's groups were filling a need for lonely, isolated people.

- Parishioners were requesting my presence at doctor's visits.

- I was able to advocate for appropriate services and care in the community for several individuals.

- Improving lay pastoral visitor education gave new self-confidence to the visitors and enhanced the ministry to homebound parishioners.

- New programs such as *You and Your Aging Relative, Through Other Eyes,* and *Age in Action Sunday,* along with several intergenerational activities served as primary communicators themselves.

Two
Walking Alongside

The greatest good you can do for another is not just to share your riches, but to reveal to him his own.

Benjamin Disraeli

When I began my ministry as a *nurse in a church* I had only a vision of what the ministry could be. There were no guidelines, no framework. The opportunities for ministry were many and it was important for me to establish some priorities and develop strategies and guiding principles. I adopted *Walking Alongside* as my motto. In previous nursing positions in acute care facilities and in teaching roles, I learned that people wanted to keep control of as much of their lives as possible. Individuals, who are acutely ill, as in a post-operative situation, have a need for maximum care in the early stages. Each of us sometimes needs to be sustained by others until we are able to restore our equilibrium. But it is important to encourage their natural wish to do things for themselves as soon as they are able. When people are beaten down by life's challenges, it is human nature to want to help them. Helping does not mean taking over!

I have concluded that people do not want someone to take over their lives; they just need support along the way. Most individuals would like somebody to listen. I have discovered that by taking the time to listen to the pain of others, I provide an opportunity for them to reflect on their problems and determine appropriate solutions. My role as supportive listener increases people's confidence in their decision-making abilities. I acknowledge the positive aspects identified by clients and offer some hope, while being sensitive to their emotional state. False or exaggerated hope is not helpful and usually unwelcome. *Walking along-*

side encapsulates for me the ethics of nursing practice: treating people with dignity and respect while encouraging autonomy and independence in decision-making.

Please see Chapter 8 on Ethics.

My Guiding Principles for Walking Alongside

The Walking Alongside image is, in my mind, of two people travelling over rugged terrain, side by side, with one lending a hand when the other loses balance. I use this image as the guiding principle for my parish nursing ministry. The nurse's role is one of gathering information, assisting with understanding of illness, and the implications of decisions about treatment, but not pulling or pushing the client who is making those decisions. That picture of walking alongside is foremost in my mind when I am working with people. Albert Camus, a noted philosopher and Nobel Prize winner (1957) for literature, captures the concept in his quotation:

> *Don't walk in front of me; I may not follow. Don't walk behind me; I may not lead. Just walk beside me and be my friend.*
>
> Albert Camus

Encompassing this image is the presence of God on the journey. Through prayer and meditation I seek God's guidance and support in my ministry. I pray for wisdom and sensitivity to the needs of the other person as I walk alongside through the difficult times. I keep in mind the passage from The Gospel Of Matthew, Chapter 25, verse 40, "Truly, I tell you, just as you did it to one of the least of these who are members of my family, you did it to me" (Holy Bible, NRSV.1990.) which shows us how to serve God through serving others.

Three
What Makes a Good Parish Nurse?

Love is patient; love is kind;
love is not envious or boastful or
arrogant or rude.
It does not insist on its own way; it is
not irritable or resentful.
And now faith, hope and love abide,
And the greatest of these is love.

1 Corinthians.13: V. 4, 5, and 13.

It is important for a parish nurse to understand and clearly communicate how the interrelationship of spirit, body, and mind affects health, wellness, and healing. When thinking about wellness, we have to include all aspects of a person's health in our assessment. People can be emotionally and spiritually healthy while living with a chronic or terminal illness. They may have come to terms with their disease or impending death and put their lives in God's hands. This deep faith can lead to opportunity for healing the broken parts of their lives and result in a feeling of peace.

Alternatively, a conflict or long-standing, unresolved anger can trigger physical illness such as chronic headaches, back pain, and digestive disorders, or spiritual illness that may manifest itself in a loss of hope. The physical suffering and spiritual distress can worsen the emotional anguish, possibly resulting in complete breakdown. The parish nurse can help individuals learn to channel energy from anger into more healthy and productive activities. One option might be to participate in an anger management program. Another could be to meet with the clergy or a counsellor to address the root causes of the anger and conflict. It may be important to consider prayer, meditation, yoga, tai chi, or Pilates to augment the other strategies.

Relating To Others

One of the major functions of a parish nurse in the early 21st century is to interface with other health care professionals in the community. Whether accompanying someone to see a doctor or advocating with a health agency for more care for a parishioner, a professional, non-threatening manner is constructive. Learning to advocate for others requires that the nurse become aware of the available options and be assertive in stating her case. Assertiveness does not exclude flexibility, of course. In negotiating with other professionals for the benefit of the parishioner, the nurse should be willing to compromise. Recognizing when to *battle* and when to back off are skills learned through experience.

The parish nurse should attempt to get to know, and be known by, the parishioners. People who were once regular attendees may withdraw from church activities, but as many people attend church irregularly, this may go unnoticed for some time. At a point where the person becomes spiritually unwell and really needs support, the staff may not know until there is an illness or injury that brings him or her to their attention. Knowing the congregation and maintaining open lines of communication with the clergy helps the nurse to be aware of situations where her skills as a support and referral resource might be useful. On the other hand, attending Sunday services and writing articles for the bulletin and the church newsletter to inform people of the services available can increase the congregation's awareness of the parish nurse role.

Personal Qualities

A love of God, a passion for people, and a concern about the well-being of others are primary qualities required to be an exemplary parish nurse. Natural curiosity and a desire to learn are valuable characteristics to possess. A growing spiritual depth and maturity are essential in order to be authentic in the role. The parish nurse should be sensitive to the needs of others and non-judgemental in her interactions, while maintaining a pleasant and welcoming demeanour. As a member of a pastoral team, the nurse ought to be able to recognize when she, herself, needs support and to elicit it from other members.

Problem Solving and Coping Skills

A first rate parish nurse helps a person explore alternative solutions, create a menu of options, and make his/her own decisions with support. It is the nurse's responsibility to ensure that people understand the potential implications of the decision. Encouraging people to make their own decisions, particularly if you do not agree with them, is one of the most difficult skills to develop, but learning to trust others' decision-making abilities is important.

Please see Chapter 8 on Code of Ethics.

Listening and Communication Skills

It is absolutely essential that a parish nurse have good listening and communication skills. Listening is a big part of the parish nursing role. I am reminded repeatedly of that when people leaving my office remark on how much I have helped, when all I have really done is listen. Listening and really hearing, with some probing questions and perceptive feedback, can help people hear themselves and begin to make changes and improvements in their lives. In some respects it is like holding up a mirror for them. When advocating for a client with other health care professionals, skilful communication is more likely to result in the desired outcome.

Please see Chapter 12 on Listening.

Speaking and Writing Skills

Having the ability to speak well in public and to write coherently goes a long way to making the educator role an easier one. Whether running a support group, sponsoring an educational program, or writing articles for the church bulletin and newsletter, being able to communicate without a lot of jargon makes your ministry more effective. It is important to capitalize on the communication opportunities as they present themselves and ensure that what you are trying to say is clearly understood. One effective way to promote understanding of the parish nursing role is to participate at Sunday services by delivering the homily.

Teamwork Skills

Parish nursing is about teamwork. In an ideal situation, the parish nurse and the clergy work together. In my work I am seen as an integral part of the pastoral team. This works if you keep open lines of communication, as the nurse and the clergy may look at things from somewhat different perspectives and can support one another in dealing with difficult situations. Our pastoral team meets formally on a weekly basis and in a confidential environment keeps the rest of the team up to date on current activities. We do not reveal things that we have been asked to keep confidential, and we do ask permission to share information with the clergy or the nurse. At times there is a role for one of the others to be involved, and we do refer people to one another. For example, I have often been made aware of someone who is having difficulty getting out to church and I have indicated that the clergy are willing to take communion to people at home. In the Anglican tradition, Holy Communion is often very important to people, but some may be shy about requesting communion at home.

Please see Chapter 11 on Team Ministry.

Priority-Setting and Boundary-Setting Skills

In a parish nursing role it is necessary to develop skills in setting limits. The ability to set priorities is vitally important, as the needs are always greater than the time available to deal with them. Wisdom about appropriate levels of involvement in people's lives is another skill developed over time. The nurse cannot attempt to fit people into a mould with a simple solution that fits a category. Individuals arrived at where they are as a result of a unique series of events and experiences, so each is just a little different. I remember one of my gerontology professors saying that people become more of what they already are, as they age. Over time, with the variety of life experiences, people become more individualistic, not more the same. The role of the parish nurse is to help people to be the best that they can be, not what we think they should be.

Professional Requirements

Parish nurses should manage their practices according to the Standards of Practice of the governing body in their particular geographical area; and the Parish Nursing Standards developed by the Canadian Association for Parish Nursing Ministry. In Ontario, the parish nurse is licensed under the governing body, The College of Nurses of Ontario. A combination of education, a baccalaureate in nursing, plus a parish nursing course and pastoral care training are useful in developing the skills for parish nursing. Life experience and some work in a community setting enhance the formal education.

Please see Chapter 7 on Nursing Principles.

I believe that an effective parish nurse is one who is well prepared academically and experientially, and possesses the personal qualities and skills needed to demonstrate the love of God, the outreach of the church, and a genuine desire to serve others.

Four

Building Trust and Gaining Credibility

A healthy therapeutic relationship always begins with trust.

Arnold & Boggs, 1995

Gaining the trust of parishioners is essential to being an effective parish nurse. Using the *Canadian Oxford Dictionary (2000)* definition of the word *trust* as "faith or confidence in the loyalty, veracity, reliability, strength, etc. of a person" (p. 1131), that may seem like a formidable task. I began the process of building trust with parish members even before I was a parish nurse. One of my earliest experiences in working with people in the church was as a volunteer with St. John Ambulance, teaching a *Healthy Aging for Seniors* course. I introduced the program to a group of older people, all women, who had responded to advertising in the parish. Most of the women were widowed and lived alone.

Taking Pride In Learning

The group seemed to have a certain level of trust in me, by virtue of my status as an R.N. In the first of six sessions, the women were hesitant to reveal much about their health issues, and I was accepting of that. With the relaxed environment, as well as the opportunity to speak and be heard, the women became more confident in themselves and their abilities to manage their own health. They had lived through an era where it was believed that the *doctor will take care of you* and that you did not take responsibility for your own health care. Part way through the program a physician asked one woman who was much more assertive as a result of a session on *Visiting Your Doctor* what had happened to her since her last visit. I guess that he noticed her growing self-confidence. This tiny, eighty-year-old woman replied with pride, "I have been attending lectures!"

Since I was a relative newcomer to the parish, interacting with these long-time worshippers gave me a group of supporters to help build trust on a larger scale. A very positive outcome was that this group, who enjoyed being together and were disappointed when the program ended, wanted to continue meeting. While the format and the people have changed over the seventeen years, The Tuesday Ladies' group still exists today.

Building Trust

Trust is built on consistency, continuity of experiences, and familiar and predictable behaviours (Erickson, 1963). Characteristics of a trusting relationship include honesty, caring, respect, faith, and hope, but a healthy therapeutic relationship always begins with trust. (Arnold & Boggs, 1995). The lessons I learned about building trust in a group like The Tuesday Ladies' Group provided me with a firm foundation as I moved into other roles in the church, and eventually into the parish nurse role. I had volunteered as a lay pastoral visitor and had not felt the support I needed to be effective. When I was asked to take a leadership position in the lay visiting program, I initiated a collaborative working relationship with the other visitors, sharing our knowledge and experience. The lay pastoral visitors felt empowered, and my strategies helped people to see that I followed through on what I promised to do.

Please see Chapters 35 to 38 on Lay Pastoral Visiting.

The Challenge of Gaining Credibility

Gaining credibility is more difficult than building trust. The credibility issues come to the forefront when a new idea or concept is presented. If people are unfamiliar with the concept of parish nursing, it takes time and effort to *sell* the idea. When a parish is considering hiring a parish nurse, there is often a profusion of myths and uncertainties. The most-often expressed concern is that the nurse will be duplicating services already in existence. Questions like "why do we need a nurse?" and "what can a nurse in the church do?" are common. People struggle with the concept even after the role is explained. Nursing as a profession has been identified with hands-on caring for the sick, but as the practice has evolved, a more holistic approach to health and health care is emerging.

The Changing Focus of Health Care

Maintaining a treatment-only focus on health care has proven to be too costly, and people have not been made accountable for their lifestyle decisions. Governments are beginning to see the benefits of preventive medicine. Health Canada Online (2004) acknowledges in its strategy, *Achieving Health for All: A Framework for Health Promotion*, that while there are many challenges ahead, there have been some positive changes over the past ten years.

Today there is an expectation that individuals should take charge of their own health. That concept can be overwhelming to some people, particularly the elderly who have lived their lives with the belief that the doctor will look after them. A parish nurse has many opportunities to guide people who have to take responsibility in areas that were previously looked after by others.

Historical Roots of Health Care And The Church

In spite of the fact that the role of a nurse in the church is fairly new in today's world, the concept of religious healers is not new. Historically, parish nursing is rooted in the early efforts of the religious sisters and deaconesses who worked in churches promoting healing of body, mind, and spirit. The Bible speaks about the interrelationship of the body and soul. In *Luke 9: 2* (NRSV, 1990), Jesus reminded his disciples that their job was not just to preach the "Word of God" but also to heal the sick.

Rationale For A Parish Nursing Ministry

The objective in setting up a parish nursing practice is to transform the faith community into a source of health and healing, to build on people's strengths, and to guide them in caring for themselves and each other within the context of their faith and their relationship with God and the community. A definition of health used by the Miriam

Dobell Healing Centre (2003), "Health is equilibrium; it is harmony among physical, mental, spiritual and community aspects within every human being," could be prefaced by *we believe that* and used as a guiding light for a parish nursing ministry.

There Is More To Wellness Than Not Being Sick

Granger Westberg (1990), in his book, *The Parish Nurse*, acknowledges that the scientific community has recognized the limitations of looking only at physical health as a determinant of wellness. It is important to look at the person's environment, relationships, and mental and spiritual health before wellness can be assessed. Are we thinking too much about *not getting sick*? Clark & Olson (2000) suggest that there is confusion between *health promotion* and *disease prevention*. They endorse Labonte's (1993) definition of health promotion as, "any activity or program designed to improve social and environmental living conditions such that people's experience of well-being is increased" (p.40). Disease prevention is perceived as "being problem-oriented, with an emphasis on slowing, changing, or eliminating disease process" (Labonte, 1993, p. 99). The change in thinking defines more clearly that health promotion is a community responsibility, not just an individual one.

Unfamiliar Concepts Require Time For Acceptance

Resistance to the concept of parish nursing is often due to insufficient understanding of spirit, mind, and body medicine. Health promotion concepts are becoming more accepted but parish nurses are faced with challenges, nevertheless. Parish nurses can choose various methods to educate parishioners, while coaching them to adopt behaviours that link the faith traditions with the concepts of wellness, healing, and health promotion (Clark & Olson, 2000).

While a parish nursing ministry is a valuable resource, it takes time to become established in a church. Building bridges between the parish, the community, and the nurse takes time, exposure, determination, and dependability. To be successful, parish nurses should become involved in some community organizations and link with others, while identifying the key players in the system. Tapping into parish resources through a survey or questionnaire, and increasing the nurse's profile within the congregation by preaching, teaching, and writing articles for the newsletter and church bulletin are some strategies to consider.

The nurse can speed up acceptance of the role by offering programs targeting specific groups. Providing education or support groups, bringing in a pharmacist to offer advice about medications, holding a blood pressure clinic during Heart and Stroke month, and asking young parents how the church can support them are some strategies we have used. Any activity that responds to the recognized needs of the congregation gives the nurse more credibility.

*Strategies for Building Trust
and Gaining Credibility*

- Determine the needs and expectations of the parish

- Build bridges in the community

- Be transparent about the role and objectives

- Identify the key players in the parish

- Select a small group with a particular focus and offer a program to meet their needs

- Foster a cooperative atmosphere

- Watch for opportunities to respond to even a small need

- Be consistent and respectful

- Offer to visit people in their homes

- Listen and encourage

- Be persistent

It is often the small things that make a difference in someone's life. A person may be struggling with a problem and not know where to turn. The parish nurse has many opportunities to be present, to listen, to walk alongside when people need a shoulder to lean on, and if the nurse is visible, sincere, welcoming, and consistent, parishioners will learn to trust the nurse, and the parish nurse role will gain credibility.

Five

Create an Inviting Space

Only in quiet waters do things mirror themselves undistorted. Only in a quiet mind is adequate perception of the world.

Hans Margolius

In a quiet, restful environment, people can slow down the hectic pace of their lives and think more clearly. A parish nurse requires an office where a pleasant, private environment with a conversation area where two or three can speak face to face, can be created. The room colour should be calming and there should be comfortable chairs conducive to relaxing. I have found it useful to position the desk facing the corridor and visible to those passing by. Leaving the door open makes it convenient to smile at or acknowledge people. The door can be closed if privacy is needed.

People may drop into the church to leave an envelope or something else in the office, not consciously planning to talk to the parish nurse or a minister but under the right circumstances may *open up* about something that is bothering them. An ideal location for the parish nurse's office is near the main office. The nurse can encourage people by greeting them and inviting them in for a minute or just inquiring about how they are. Perhaps a relative or friend has been troubled; asking how that person is doing may be a good way to begin a discussion.

Welcoming Ideas

Someone may want to talk but be hesitant about making a formal request for an appointment. Anything that causes a person to stop in front of the office can provide an opening. Having an interesting door decoration and changing it often gives people a reason for stopping. The parish nurse then has an opportunity to initiate conversation.

Using stuffed animals around the office seems to soften the environment. Because I use teddy bears in my ministry, many adorn my office; some of my own and others returned to me after the person who received the bear died. Since I only give out new bears, those old friends have stayed with me. On one of the chairs closest to the door I keep a large teddy bear named Ed. People choose whether they want to hold the bear or not. There are situations when a person has something very difficult to talk about and, if there is a teddy to hold on to, it can feel less intimidating.
Please see Chapter 22 on Teddy Bear Ministry.

Live Animals Can Be Good Company

Calm, friendly, live animals can be both supportive and perceptive. I have on numerous occasions taken my dog, Emma, to work. Emma is very welcoming and seems to have a sense when someone needs her and sits close to that person, where she can be stroked. People do find it soothing to have something to do with their hands while talking.

It is important to create an environment that feels safe and comfortable. Having an armchair that tends to surround a person helps people feel less exposed. When talking about difficult and often painful subjects, people need to feel safe in order to *let down their guard*. I have learned, through many years of creating opportunities to engage people in conversation, how the serenity of a quiet place and a casual invitation to come in encourages the sharing of some of the deepest and most troubling concerns. The parish nurse is privileged to be part of these intimate conversations and requires good listening skills to make the most of these opportunities.

Please see Chapter 12 on Listening.

Six

Your Tool Box

The very first step towards success in any occupation is to become interested in it.

Sir William Osler

Congratulations!
Today is your day!
You're off to Great Places!
You're off and away!
You have brains in your head.
You have feet in your shoes.
You can steer yourself
any direction you choose.
You're on your own. And you know what you know.
And YOU are the person who'll decide where to go.
You won't lag behind, because you'll have the speed.
You'll pass the whole gang and you'll soon take the lead.
Wherever you fly, you'll be the best of the best.
Wherever you go, you will top all the rest.
You'll get mixed up of course,
as you already know.
You'll get mixed up
with many strange birds as you go.
So be sure when you step.
Step with care and great tact
and remember that Life's
a Great Balancing Act.
Just never forget to be dexterous and deft.
And never mix up your right foot with your left.
And will you succeed?
Yes! You will, indeed!
(98 and ¾ percent guaranteed.)
KID YOU'LL MOVE MOUNTAINS!!
Dr Seuss (as cited in Durbin, 1998)

If parish nursing is seen to be a health pro-motion, risk reduction, disease prevention nursing role that focuses on the care of the whole person, holding the spiritual dimensions to be central to the practice, what tools or gifts do you bring to the task? Moving from a traditional nursing practice into parish nursing should perhaps be regarded as merely a change of venue. Reclaiming and recall-ing the tools we used in traditional practice gives us the confidence to be effective in the new envi-ronment. We are not alone and we do not come with an empty toolbox.

Spencer Johnson, M.D. in his book, *The Pre-cious Present* (as cited in Durbin, 1998), suggests that the precious present is a gift you give your-self, acknowledging who you are at this time, with gifts or tools just waiting to be rediscovered. You may choose a formal tool to assist your journey in the process of rediscovery. Another option is to reflect quietly upon your training and experience to this point in your life, noting which tools were successful and which need some refining.

Working in a church as a parish nurse is dif-ferent from working in other clinical settings, as a personal commitment to a faith community is a requirement. When you examine the job descrip-tion for parish nursing (see appendix), the broad range of skills and tools comes into focus.

Basic Listening And Communication Skills

Both verbal and written communication skills should be well developed to facilitate group leadership, education sessions, one on one consultation, public speaking, advocacy, and health promotion articles and activities.

Physical skills are not the focus of parish nursing, as the ministry is not about hands-on nursing care. A broad general knowledge of nursing skills is beneficial as there may be opportunities for educating clients facing anxiety-producing procedures. Up-to-date reference books about nursing skills, medical procedures, lab and diagnostic tests, and medications are important accessories when giving explanations to clients. It is helpful to be physically fit and conscious of your own health and well-being in order to be able to do the job effectively. Driving skills are a benefit.

Creative Expression and Mental Skilfulness

These skills include the use of intuition, memory, creative thinking, and forward thinking, conceptualizing, integrating and improvising, as the situation dictates.

Analytical Proficiency

Analytical skills help us to plan, assess, implement, and evaluate interventions. These are the basic principles for planning nursing care.

Humanitarian Attitude

Humanitarian traits such as kindness, compassion, gentleness, and an interest in social justice issues are necessary for coaching and encouraging, listening attentively and objectively, explaining and teaching, and advocacy.

Leadership and Management Expertise

Proficiencies in leadership and management are required for initiating ideas, developing strategies, planning steps for meeting goals and objectives, designating and following through with supervision of activities. Mediating and coordinating also require good leadership skills.

Commitment to Personal Spiritual Growth

An essential component for an effective parish nursing ministry is the commitment to personal spiritual growth. As we strengthen our faith we can learn to integrate other skills with our belief system (Durbin, 1998).

The skills or *tools* outlined above are always a work in progress. It would be surprising if we could claim levels of excellence in all of them. We can do our utmost to grow and develop in the role. The parish, the community and we, ourselves, benefit from our personal growth and skill development.

AND WILL YOU SUCCEED! YES! YOU WILL, INDEED!

Dr. Seuss (as cited in Durbin, 1998)

Part Two:
The Practice

Seven

Nursing Principles

The foundations, which we would dig about and find are within us, like the Kingdom of Heaven, rather than without.

Samuel Butler

First and foremost, in a helping profession the helper should recognize the potential for self-determination in all people. It is important that registered nurses in a parish nursing role, usually an independent practice, follow the guidelines and standards established for the profession.

During my practice in the province of Ontario, clear guiding principles have been developed and updated by The College of Nurses of Ontario. The Professional Standards (CNO, 2002) provide a framework for the skills, attitudes, and judgement required to practice safely and professionally in Ontario. The principles and standards of practice are applicable whether a nurse works in an institution or in private practice. In an institution, the organization's policies add another layer of regulations, and there is increased visibility when working with several colleagues. Understanding and implementing the nursing standards when working in a self-regulating environment is fundamental. The guidelines and standards provide an essential foundation in independent practice where nurses are faced with ethically and legally ambiguous situations. Parish nurses are largely dependent on their own integrity.

The Canadian Association for Parish Nursing Ministry (CAPNM, 2003) has developed a guide for core competencies as well as Standards of Practice for parish nursing ministry. The Professional Standards for the practice of parish nursing include accountability, continuing competence, facilitation of spiritual care, ethics, knowledge, health promotion, knowledge application, leadership, and relationships.

Accountability

Each nurse is accountable to the public and is required to adhere to the standards of practice as outlined by the governing body for the geographical and practice areas. In 1988 when I began my practice, there were no guidelines for parish nursing, so following the standards of practice for the nursing profession gave me direction. As nurses, we are responsible for our actions and the consequences of those actions.

Part of that responsibility includes:

- explaining the role of the nurse to the clients.

- documenting parish nursing activities according to professional standards.

- working within our capabilities and seeking appropriate assistance when needed.

- maintaining our levels of competence to meet the needs of clients.

- evaluating the quality and effectiveness of the practice and implementing changes as needed.

- taking action in situations where client safety is compromised.

- promoting client self-care and well-being through teaching and advocacy.

Continuing Competence

The competencies for different areas of nursing require particular skills; like all nurses, the parish nurse is responsible for ensuring that her abilities are appropriate for the position. Participating in a Quality Assurance program such as the Ontario College of Nurses' QA program helps identify opportunities for learning.

Parish nurses can improve their levels of competence by:

- taking steps to increase self-awareness and skills in self-assessment.

- engaging the ministry team to assist in the development of a learning plan and participating in evaluating the outcomes.

- investing time and energy to improve knowledge and skill levels.

- inviting feedback on competency from parishioners.

- seeking help to gain the knowledge required for improving competence when faced with unfamiliar situations.

- appointing a committee of qualified volunteers to assist in skills evaluation and identifying opportunities for improvement.

Facilitation of Spiritual Care

The parish nurse develops skills in pastoral and spiritual care by:

- engaging in spiritual growth activities for promoting personal spiritual growth.

- seeking hopefulness, meaning, and purpose in his/her own life.

- incorporating spiritual practices to support health and wholeness in work with clients while being sensitive to their spiritual values.

- providing encouragement for spiritual discussion by listening, supporting, and showing empathy to clients.

Ethics

Ethical nursing care means respecting client choice and maintaining confidentiality and privacy while preserving the sanctity of life. The parish nurse is obliged to act with honesty and integrity and promote the well being of clients and the staff team. The College of Nurses of Ontario has developed a comprehensive ethical framework, which identifies fairness, truthfulness and the importance of maintaining commitments, privacy and confidentiality, and respect for life as key values (CNO,

2002). While all of these principles are significant, client choice and client well-being are primary objectives. It is essential for nurses to be clear about their own ethical values and, when difficult situations arise, consult with team members.

Please see Chapter 8 on Code of Ethics.

Knowledge

Continuous learning is the responsibility of any professional nurse. No specific educational program for a nurse employed by a church existed until the early 1990's. Because parish nursing does not include hands-on bedside nursing, other skills such as grief counselling, pastoral care, and conflict resolution should be enhanced. The responsibility for gaining the appropriate knowledge is part of the nurse's accountability to her clients and her profession.

Ways to broaden knowledge and skills include:

- monitoring the changing roles and opportunities for parish nurses in the health care system and learning from them.

- improving abilities to advocate for clients in an increasingly strained health care system.

- acquiring skills in pastoral care, spiritual assessment, and theological principles.

- pursuing ongoing education in areas of

health promotion, group facilitation, conflict resolution, and grief counselling.

- learning the policies and religious practices
of the church and demonstrating a willingness to participate.

- researching and exploring options available in the community to assist clients and
promote personal growth.

Health Promotion

*Parish nurses recognize opportunities for health
promotion by:*

- encouraging a holistic approach as a goal
for optimal health and wellness.

- identifying needs and developing plans for
interventions and utilizing community resources.

- educating congregations about the primary
causes of illness and teaching them ways
to take responsibility for maintaining and
improving their own health.

- acknowledging the power and place of spirituality in health promotion.

Knowledge Application

A significant part of gaining knowledge is the
application of the knowledge in practice. The research and information database in parish nursing

is a developing resource. More educational programs are becoming available as a profession in its infancy matures.

Some strategies for application of knowledge in parish nursing include:

- advising clients of community resources for their particular needs.

- planning activities and programs for people with similar requirements.

- sharing what you have learned with staff members who would benefit from the information.

- sharing knowledge with parishioners through articles, educational programs, and displays.

- using new assessment tools when describing a client situation.

Leadership

The parish nurse has many opportunities to be a leader. In assuming leadership roles, nurses have to show respect for others, and trustworthiness in their activities.

The parish nurse can demonstrate leadership by:

- modelling professional beliefs and values.

- advocating for parishioners.

- providing information for clients.

- taking action to resolve conflicts.

- collaborating with other health care professionals for the well-being of clients.

- developing innovative solutions for complex situations.

- participating in associations, groups, and
  committees relating to the role.

Relationships

Establishing and maintaining trusting, respectful, and collaborative relationships with clients,
staff, and community professionals is essential for
gaining respect. Developing good listening skills
and showing empathy helps to build trusting relationships.

*The parish nurse can work toward building
solid relationships by:*

- showing an interest in, and a respect for,
  clients.

- ensuring that client needs remain the focus
  of the relationship.

- creating a safe environment where confidentiality is honoured.

- developing collaborative partnerships with
  clients and their families to achieve the best
  outcomes for clients.

- identifying abusive situations; preventing where possible; reporting appropriately with the client's consent (unless the client is a child).

- becoming more self-aware. The nurse's needs must be met outside of nurse-client relationships.

- maintaining boundaries between therapeutic, professional relationships and non-professional, personal relationships.

When a parish nurse works in an independent practice and is faced with difficult decisions, the principles and standards of the profession provide guidance for making those decisions. The associations developing the standards can offer assistance in interpreting the principles when necessary. It is the responsibility of the parish nurse to ensure that the practice complies with the standards of the profession. The nurse should also make certain that he/she is covered by appropriate insurance, through the professional association, and/or the employer, to deal with all potential liabilities in an independent practice.

> *The beginnings of all things are weak and tender. We must therefore be clearsighted in beginnings.*
>
> Montaigne

Eight
Code of Ethics

*Integrity is having the courage to
go with the truth as you know it,
a heartfelt response with care and
consideration for others.*

John-Roger

Any situation involving vulnerable persons and a power imbalance between themselves and a health professional is open to the abuse of power, however unintentional. Thus, in the role of parish nurse, it is important to have principled guidelines to ensure an ethical practice. Both the nursing professional organizations and most Christian denominations have developed ethical guidelines within which the parish nurse is expected to practice. The Code of Ethics for Registered Nurses states the ethical standards for nurses in Canada. (Canadian Nurses Association [CNA] 2002). According to the CNA, the code "gives guidance for decision-making concerning ethical matters, serves as a means for self-evaluation and self-reflection regarding ethical nursing practice and provides a basis for feedback and peer review" (2002, p.1).

The College of Nurses of Ontario (CNO) requires nurses to consider ethical issues in their relationships with clients. *The Professional Standards* document on ethics (CNO, 2003) states that nurses must be clear about their ethical values and use them as guidelines in their practice. These values include fairness, accountability, client choice, privacy and confidentiality, respect, and truthfulness (CNO, 2003). Nurses should follow the *behavioural directives* outlined in the CNO document when confronted with difficult situations. Attending education sessions and consulting with colleagues will help nurses to become clear about their own ethical values.

Other sources of guidance include the Canadian Association for Parish Nursing Ministry's (CAP-NM) Standards of Practice (2003), and the denomination's guidelines in relation to sexual abuse and harassment. The Anglican Church of Canada in the Diocese of Toronto has a policy for sexual misconduct (Diocese of Toronto, 2001) and a screening program for staff and volunteers (2003). All staff and volunteers are required to have police criminal record checks.

Values

With more autonomy in nursing and changing patterns of health promotion and health care, supervision is reduced at the same time as complex care needs are increasing. Research in genetics and the emergence of new technologies gives rise to new ethical dilemmas. Global issues concerning end of life decisions, care of the elderly, and the materialization of recent infections (SARS, for example) raise new questions in a rapidly changing environment.

Values, as defined by the CNA, are "beliefs or attitudes about the importance of a goal, an object, a principle or behaviour" (CNA, 2002). People may possess opposing values and not be aware of it until faced with difficult situations. Nurses should endeavour to support and demonstrate ethical behaviours outside of their workplace as well as within. *The Code of Ethics* is designed to guide nurses in nursing practice, but it can be used as a standard when political issues arise in the community. Parish nurses interacting with community agencies, other professionals, and government services have an opportunity to be role models in ethical practice.

The Code of Ethics for Registered Nurses (CNA, 2003) States That the Primary Structures Pertaining to Ethical Practice Include:

- Safe, competent and ethical care

- Health and well-being

- Choice

- Dignity

- Confidentiality

- Justice

- Accountability

- Quality practice environments

Safe, Competent, and Ethical Care

Providing safe and competent care in a parish nursing ministry draws from the ethics of nursing practice as well as the ethics of the religious facility in which the nurse is working. Parish nurses should be clear about their values and be able to identify value conflicts, if they exist. Safe and competent care in parish nursing practice (hands-on nursing care is not part of the mandate) is as relevant as in any other area of nursing. An example of safe competent care can include providing accurate information about a diagnosis or procedure, and community resources that may be of assistance when a person is dealing with a new reality.

Health and Well-being

Health promotion strategies in parish nursing ministry should speak to the social, political, and environmental issues that influence health as well as to the impact of illness. The parish nurse assists people in striving for wellness and balance in all areas of health: spiritual, social, physical, and mental well-being. Individuals suffering from a terminal illness should be provided with palliative care supporting a dignified and peaceful death. It is important to gain understanding of the values and perspectives of all individuals, especially when they differ from our own values. The ethical values outlined for nurses include the role of the nurse in addressing community issues, promoting changes in health care services for improved access and service provision, and in research issues.

Choice

Parish nurses assist individuals in making good health care decisions by helping them obtain the information they need to make their own decisions. Building trusting relationships with clients improves the likelihood of satisfactory, productive, and comfortable communication. Individuals' choices must be understood, expressed, and advocated for by the parish nurse. People's wishes must be respected if they are unwilling to make decisions or make decisions against the suggestions of health care professionals. Self-determination is a right of every person. Coercion is not acceptable.

There are limits to client choice, though. If a client is making a choice that would endanger other persons or self, or that is clearly against the law, it is ethical to inform the client that the nurse must report the situation (CNO, 2003). The CNO states that clients may be competent to make decisions in one area but not in others. The CNO supports client decision-making in those areas where they are capable of making a decision. When clients are deemed incompetent to make decisions, a substitute decision-maker must be consulted. The substitute decision-maker has the legal right (in Ontario) to make decisions on the client's behalf.

Dignity

Parish nurses should respect the inherent worth of each person as an individual and treat all persons with dignity. That means being sensitive to their needs and choices while advising them of the social, emotional, spiritual, and physical challenges they may encounter. A parish nurse ought to seek opportunities to advocate for the respect and dignity of persons within the church, the healthcare system, and the community. Living and dying with dignity are appropriate and desirable objectives for a parish nurse to pursue for clients

Confidentiality

Nurses safeguard information learned in the context of a professional relationship and ensure that it is shared outside the healthcare team only with the person's informed consent, as may be legally required, or where the failure to disclose would cause significant harm (CNA, 2002, p. 8).

When revealing information about individuals, with or without their consent, it is important to minimize the negative impact on them. Confidentiality should be maintained in pastoral relationships, and shared with the pastoral team only with the client's permission. Parish nurses have many opportunities to work with other health care professionals for the benefit of the client. Confidentiality must be maintained within these boundaries as well.

Justice

A parish nurse upholds the principles of fairness and impartiality when dealing with members of the parish. The nurse advocates for appropriate and ethical health care and fairness in healthcare allocation. Justice issues focusing on broader health concerns such as the environment, world hunger, violation of human rights, homelessness, and violence are concerns for the church and the parish nurse. The nurse can help to keep these issues before the congregation and identify opportunities for others to become involved in justice issues.

Please see Chapter 20 on Advocacy.

Accountability

Parish nurses are accountable for their actions and practice in accordance with the *Code of Ethics for Registered Nurses as* outlined by the Canadian Nurses Association (2002). Following the guidelines, professional standards, and the laws and regulations supporting ethical practice, parish nurses have the responsibility to conduct themselves with honesty and integrity in all they do. The Canadian Association for Parish Nursing Ministry (CAPNM) has developed clear guidelines for the practice of parish nursing in Canada. As well, each province has its own professional regulatory body. Identifying situations beyond the scope and skills of the nurse is crucial. Nurses are accountable to the profession, the clients, and the community.

Quality Practice Environments

A parish nurse, working in a church, needs to have an appropriate space allocated in order to maintain confidential files, and for private conversation with clients. In a healthy work environment there will be mutual respect among the team members. The parish nurse is responsible for informing the administration of the requirements for a quality practice environment. If space constraints are a problem, the nurse must look for creative solutions.

Please see Chapter 5 on Creating an Inviting Space.

Please see Chapter 11 on Team Ministry.

There are many ethical issues in a parish nursing practice. When someone is in a vulnerable position and the parish nurse is able to offer support and interventions that make a big difference, the person may feel compelled to offer a gift or money to the nurse. As in any professional nursing situation, it is inappropriate to accept gifts from clients. I believe that there are times when accepting a small gift such as a little pot of flowers, a hand-knitted dish cloth, or a Christmas decoration made by the individual is of benefit to the donor. The person may feel rejected if the nurse refuses something small that has been chosen or made especially for the nurse. Nurses have some discretion and should consider the self-esteem of the individual.

Examples of Ethical Issues from My Practice

Situation #1

An elderly gentleman I will call Mr. S. loved to drop in to visit and often tearfully thanked me for listening. One day he arrived with a single rose corsage for me to wear. What a beautiful gesture! I proudly wore the corsage and when people asked about it, I replied, "somebody loves me" which is what the gentleman said to me. For Mr. S., being able to offer a small token of his appreciation was important. Can you imagine how he would have felt if I had refused it?

Situation #2

An elderly, widowed gentleman without any family in the country had not designated powers of attorney for property or personal care. He was worried about this and asked if I could fill the role. I knew that was inappropriate and explored with him whom he might request to fill the roles. He had relatives in two other countries, but nobody close. The relatives agreed to act as powers of attorney for personal care.

To assist with his financial matters, I looked at what options might be available and introduced the gentleman to a financial advisor at a reputable trust company. At the first meeting, I helped the man clarify what he needed from the financial advisor. From that point on, the financial dealings were between the gentleman and the trust company. Through his lawyer he appointed the trust company as his power of attorney (substitute decision-maker) for property. I was aware of the importance of distancing myself from his finances.

The issue of a power of attorney (substitute decision maker) for personal care was more complex as the gentleman had no family close enough to be physically present when needed. The clergy and I decided that if the powers of attorney for personal care agreed, in my role as parish nurse, I would keep them informed about his situation. If he needed more help, I would let them know and carry out their wishes. We received written permission to that effect. *It is imperative that decision-making is kept out of the hands of the parish nurse!* The objective for the parish nurse is to assist clients in selecting powers of attorney and creating a living will.

Please see Chapter 16 on Advance Directives.

Situation #3

Ethical issues are complex when people are not managing well and believe that the decisions they are making are in their best interest. If the person has not been declared incompetent and is unwilling to accept help, the parish nurse can be faced with a frustrating situation. There is a struggle between wanting to keep people safe and respecting their decisions. I have experienced more than one situation where a person appeared competent in a doctor's office and did well on a verbal test but was unable to plan meals, take medications correctly, remember appointments, or pay bills. In one case, I knew that the person was not safe living on her own but there was nothing I could do until something happened to change the situation. The client could have benefited from in-home help but, until she agreed, it could not be implemented. Alternatively, she could have agreed to move into a care facility where her husband was living, or her situation could have worsened until a crisis occurred, at which point her competency could have been challenged. Until then we were in a stalemate.

In my role as parish nurse I was in contact with the physician, the pharmacist, the home care case manager, the powers of attorney, a family member, and the client herself and I could only keep others informed of my observations. The lady trusted me and I didn't want to break that trust, but I also needed to keep her safety in mind. There was a very fine line to walk. At this point, we are still in a holding pattern.

Every situation requires an individual assessment by the nurse to determine appropriate ethical behaviour. Our nursing associations and church policies define for us the standards for ethical practice. As nurses, it is our responsibility to ensure that we are familiar with the standards, and practice accordingly.

Nine

Assessment
and Analysis

*Accuracy of observation is the
equivalent of the accuracy
of thinking.*

Wallace Stevens

When I first meet with a parishioner who has come to see me in my office, I encourage the person to take the lead in conversation, and I work at creating a non-threatening environment. My objective is to develop a relationship of trust, so I believe that maintaining eye contact and allowing the person's agenda to unfold uninterrupted fosters more comfortable dialogue. I may begin with an open-ended question or a general statement, but if the conversation is progressing, I will listen attentively.

Possible Conversation Starters

- "You appear tired today, Mr. Jones".

- "Mrs. Smith, I am delighted to see you; tell me how things have been going for you".

- "Sally, I noticed that you were looking sad when I saw you last week. Tell me how you are today".

- "I am so pleased that you came in; how may I help you"?

Considerations When Doing a Proper Assessment

- The physical, emotional, and spiritual health of the person

- The individual's perception of the reason for coming

- The factors leading up to the decision to talk about the concerns

- The person's ability to reflect on possible solutions

Assessment tools can be useful in determining status in different areas. I prefer to become familiar with the tools so that I do not interrupt the flow of the conversation as we are speaking. I make some notes that I flesh out later and pose questions within the context of the dialogue. There are times when it is appropriate to ask questions and fill out assessment tools, but I try to minimize anything that may feel threatening to the parishioner. As stated, my objective at this point in the relationship is to develop trust.

Features of a General Physical Assessment

- Observe the outward appearance for neatness, appropriateness, and hygiene. If a person is untidy and unkempt, that could be an indication of low self-esteem, excessive stress, or perhaps physical or emotional illness.

- Remain sharp-eyed for any injuries that may be observable: bruises, cuts or scrapes, and find a way to tactfully inquire as to their origin.

- Look for any difficulty in breathing, apparent discomfort, tremor or twitching, pallor or flushing. Offer to check the blood pressure if there is a past history of problems, or if mentioned.

- Observe the body language. Is it consistent with the spoken words? Is there a different message that needs to be addressed?

Facial Expressions

Examine the facial expressions carefully and form an opinion about the person's emotional status:

- Are the muscles of the jaw tensed?

- Is the person frowning or scowling?

- Is the facial expression consistent with the topic being discussed?

- Is the skin colour pale or flushed?

- Does the tone of voice or the volume indicate emotional turmoil?

- Is the person on the verge of crying?

Spiritual Assessment

As part of the assessment process, I take note of the factors that might indicate the spiritual status of the individual. The spiritual dimension includes a person's beliefs, emotions, behaviours, and practices, and the person's interpretation of his illness (Smucker, 1997).

Please see Chapter 17 on The Meaning of Illness.

Possible questions for completing a spiritual assessment might include the following:

- What beliefs give meaning and purpose to this person's life?

- Will the current problems cause conflict with the person's ability to continue with his/her belief practices?

- Is there guilt being expressed about the difficulty? Or self-blame?

- Is there a sense of hopelessness being suggested?

- Does the person express, or allude to, feelings of support or abandonment by God?

- Would a referral to the clergy be beneficial for this person?

Planning Further Meetings

To end an initial meeting, I usually ask if there is anything else that we need to talk about. The real reason for coming in to talk may be revealed, if it wasn't earlier. If the time available is not sufficient to deal with all the information, I will suggest another meeting. This gives me time to note what has been observed in the initial meeting and then prepare for the next one. I make every effort to set a firm date and time so that topics raised are addressed in a timely fashion. In many cases, by the next meeting the individual, having spoken about the difficulties, has been able to think more clearly about them and may have come to some resolution. Our discussion of this resolution can validate the process for the person, or there may be some opportunity for modification. Visiting a person at home gives the parish nurse a better opportunity to assess how well an individual is coping overall.

Home Visits

When I am invited into someone's home, I observe:

- the cleanliness and tidiness of the surroundings.

- the condition of plants, if there are any.

- if there are signs of incontinence.

- if the person appears to be well nourished.

- the person's mental and emotional ability to make good decisions.

- how safe the individual appears to be (loose tiles, scatter mats, obstructions, and barriers).

In addition to making these observations I ask some questions in the course of the conversation.

I enquire about:

- how the individual manages with shopping and meal preparation.

- whether the person feels isolated, and if family and friends visit.

- any support services that may be required.

- fears that the person may have about the situation.

Limits on Responsibilities

While assessment is an important task, the parish nurse can only observe and suggest options that could make some improvements in the health and safety of an individual. It is up to the person whether any changes are initiated, or even considered. The role of the parish nurse is to educate and support, not attempt to control a person's life.

It is the parish nurse's responsibility to involve others when a person exhibits signs of cognitive impairment, is at risk, and appears incapable of making good decisions. The nurse also needs to inform the client that the family and the doctor will be contacted (CNO, 2004). By enlisting the family and the doctor when a person is at risk, the nurse is taking appropriate steps to reduce the risks. If there is no family, the person's substitute decision maker (power of attorney) for personal care should be notified of the situation. The nurse can help the substitute decision maker identify possible alternatives and their implications.

If a person is capable of making good decisions and chooses to live at risk, as long as others are not in danger, the nurse has to leave things as they are. People do have a choice in how they live and some people do choose to live in unsafe circumstances. The nurse can monitor the situation and offer suggestions, but that may be all that can be done.

Ten

Planning, Implementing, Evaluating and Documenting Parish Nursing Care

Everything should be made as simple as possible, but not simpler.

Albert Einstein

In any nursing encounter, keeping a record of the process is an essential part of the procedure. In the case of an individual or a family, it is important to have those people involved taking an active role in developing objectives (Clark & Olson, 2000).

The Components Of A Care Plan In A Parish Nursing Situation Should Include The Following:

- Defining the health-related issues that the family is working on at the time (events in the process)

- Determining what outcomes the family sees for the future (what they are working toward)

- Exploring the ways that family members are coping with the present situation and the activities they are involved in to achieve their goals (the tasks and activities)

- Recording the successes and/or failures of the approaches used (the outcomes and responses)
  (According to Laforet-Fliesser & Ford-Gilboe as cited in Clarke & Olson, 2000 P 257).

A nurse is required to maintain clear, concise, and accurate documents to record professional activities (CNO, 2003). These documents have to be relevant, timely, and completed only after giving care.

Core Standards For Documentation (CNO, 2002)

- Clear, succinct, and comprehensive

- Accurate and factual

- Relevant

- Reflective of observations

- Completed during or after care is given

- Chronological

- Permanent and legible

- Client-focused

- Confidential

The confidentiality of the client has to be maintained and documents stored securely (Privacy Act, 2002). For more detailed information on documentation, contact your nursing association and request the documentation practice standards. The method of charting that I use is based on client concerns and behaviours identified during the assessment process.

Complete Assessment Documentation Is Imperative

- Make note of date and time of visit or phone call

- Identify client concerns

- Note any change in condition or behaviour

- Record any significant event (falls, disorientation, missing doctor appointments)

- Describe health issues observed or mentioned by client or family member

From the notes, I develop a care plan involving the client and family member unless client refuses to have family present. We discuss who needs to be involved and how the plan will be implemented. Recording the plan, outcomes, and evaluation of the outcomes is an important part of the documentation. I have developed my own forms, methods, and systems consistent with the documentation practice standards of the College of Nurses of Ontario (2002).

Please see Appendix for Intake and Progress Note Forms.

A Case History From My Practice

Mr. and Mrs. R., a couple in their nineties, were managing reasonably well at home in their apartment even though Mr. R. had several falls in spite of using a walker. Mrs. R. made meals and did laundry, while family and friends helped with shopping. The couple was driven to worship services and other events at the church by volunteer drivers.

I had made numerous attempts to visit this couple in their home, but each time they cancelled the appointment. When I saw Mr. R. at church I noticed that he was becoming quite frail. He complained of a sore shoulder but denied falling. According to his daughter, he had fallen several times. The daughter contacted me to visit the couple while she was there so that they would not cancel the visit. She assured me of her parents' consent.

At the initial visit I used an intake sheet to collect pertinent information. I recorded date, names, and birth dates of the couple, address, and phone number as well as next of kin. I asked Mr. and Mrs. R. if they had designated powers of attorney for health and property. They said that the daughter was responsible for health, while their son would look after the finances. We discussed current health issues. Both were experiencing increasing difficulty in walking. In spite of using a walker, Mr. R. was falling frequently. I asked whether the couple would like the clergy to visit or wished to have home Communion. Both offers were declined.

Questions And Documented Responses

- What is the most important issue for you?

  Response: (Mr. & Mrs. R.) "We want to stay in our home."

- What do help do you need to stay in your own home?

  Response: (Mrs. R.) "I need help with meals. I am too tired to make meals all the time."

- Would having Meals on Wheels help? Frozen meals are delivered and you can heat them in your microwave.

Response: (Mrs. R.) "I have never tried the frozen meals so, I might like them."

- Mr. R., what do you feel that you need in order to continue living in your home?

Response: (Mr. R.) "Well, I am having more trouble getting into the bath tub. I have been told by my doctor that I should have some safety things in there, but my son hasn't had time to put them in yet."

- It seems to me that safety is an issue here. What about your medications? Are you able to manage those on your own?

Response: (Mrs. R.) "Yes, I can manage mine, but I can't keep his straight, and he can't either."

- Your doctor can ask the pharmacist to package your medications differently to make it easier to manage. Would that be helpful?

Response: (daughter) "I think that would be really helpful and I would feel better that their medications are being taken appropriately. One of the problems is that Dad won't let people in here to help."

- Mr. R., if it is important for you to remain in your own home, what are you prepared to accept in order to be safe here?

> Response: (Mr. R.) "I don't like having people coming and going in my house, but if my wife needs help, I will go along with it."

- Mr. and Mrs. R., would you agree to my contacting the home care case manager to have her come and talk to you about what you need and what you are willing to accept?"

> Response: (Mr. and Mrs. R.) "Yes."

Mr. and Mrs. R. believed that they had been living independently and were unwilling to accept help (except from the daughter). The daughter was wearing down because she was the only one they would allow into their home, and she had her own health issues. The first major steps in taking action had been initiated. I was invited to go to their home, and I was given permission to contact the home care (Community Care) case manager. It was important to note the results of these initial interventions.

Notable Interventions

- The case manager visited and assessed their needs (The daughter and I were present at this interview).

- The case manager arranged for the pharmacist to put their medications in *blister packs* to reduce the confusion about whether or not the pills had been taken.

- A personal support worker was assigned to assist both Mr. and Mrs. R. with personal care.

- Mr. and Mrs. R. agreed to have safety bars and bath seat professionally installed.

- The case manager recommended starting applications for long-term care.

- The case manager and the personal support workers recorded activities and outcomes in the chart in the home.

I kept in touch with Mr. and Mrs. R. and noted their responses to the new interventions. The daughter's perceptions and comments were noted as well. As with nursing in any setting, ongoing evaluation and revision of the plan as necessary is an integral part of client care.

Maintaining appropriate documentation not only meets legal requirements, but also helps the parish nurse keep track of clients' ongoing progress. It is nearly impossible to remember numerous clients' status at any point in time. Accurate record keeping is an effective tool for assessing and evaluating interventions and outcomes.

Eleven

What is Team Ministry?

Coming together is a beginning.
Keeping together is progress.
Working together is success.

Henry Ford

As part of the pastoral team, a registered nurse with the training and life experience of a professional nurse adds to the collective knowledge of the team and enhances the ministry of the church. The parish nurse views health issues from a different perspective and provides insights that may not be part of the minister's understanding. As the nurse develops links within the health care system and the community, that information becomes a valuable resource to the clergy.

Pastoral Meetings

I have had the privilege and benefit of working with two clergy. We have scheduled pastoral meetings once a week, giving us time to seek advice on difficult issues. From the people I visit, I may identify a need for a visit from one of the other team members, and the clergy request my advice and expertise on issues that fall within my area of expertise. Our collegial relationship allows for our being comfortable suggesting that one of the other members of the team has more knowledge in a particular area. Our experience of sharing the pastoral duties of visitation at home, hospital, and other care facilities seems to be an ideal recipe for success. There are opportunities for supporting one another in this ministry while using the skills of the most appropriate person.

Stages Of Team Development

The nurse ought to realize that becoming part of an established ministry team has its challenges. As is the case in any group formation, there are stages of development that a group or team must go through in order to become a functional entity. In 1965, Brian Tuckman made an attempt to synthesize data on group development (as cited in Samson & Marthas, 1971). Tuckman's theory emphasizes that in the early stages of working together, group members are sorting out who people are and what skills they bring to the team. This is called the *forming* stage. The next phase is the *storming* phase, where allegiances between some members may develop, resulting in conflict, polarization, and disagreement over methods and strategies. Once the conflicts are resolved, the group begins to develop norms and moves toward being a cohesive group. This stage is called the *norming* phase and it is followed by the *performing* phase where the group functions well and accomplishes tasks without a lot of conflict, since the guidelines for making decisions have been worked out. Some may feel that pastoral teams do not have to go through the phase where disagreement over task and personal issues occurs, but church staff members are like other people. Avoiding this phase can result in a dysfunctional, less effective team. Awareness of the stages of team development can be beneficial for the nurse who understands that early phases can be difficult.

Strategies for Building Effective Team Ministry

- Build a strong pastoral team committed to the ministry and to each other

- Acknowledge and respect the skills of other team members

- Develop a strong governing body, committed to this ministry

- Speak honestly with team members

- Communicate openly with parish members

- Demonstrate harmony to the parish

- Reassure parishioners that their personal information will be revealed only with permission to other team members

The Parish Nurse In The Worship Service

The pastoral role of the clergy includes the performance of rituals associated with a particular faith group. In most denominations there are opportunities for the parish nurse to be part of the worship service in the role of preacher. Having the nurse preach occasionally keeps the parish nurse in front of the people and strengthens the link between faith and health, by showing the nurse in the *faith* role. Examining the scriptures for links to health promotion and the healing ministry gives the nurse, in the role of preacher, an opportunity to illustrate those links between faith and health. An ideal time for the parish nurse to participate in Sunday worship is when healing services are occurring.

Support From Clergy

Early in the planning stages of a parish nursing ministry, the clergy should be committed to, and supportive of, this ministry. If they are not on board, it will be an uphill and often futile battle. I have seen several different situations where the ministry has started with a lot of enthusiasm and then failed. In one instance, the existing cleric was supportive but moved to another church. The new minister did not understand the concept, and while he said he supported it, he really did not. In another case, the ministry started with grants and fanfare, but the minister and governing body did not plan for funding beyond the first year. The nurse continued as a volunteer for a while, but the pastoral team had not built a strong connection and the project failed. There had been some very good things happening, but there needed to be unity between the nurse and a core group of people, including the minister.

To avoid potential misunderstandings with the clergy, the parish nurse has to be clear about how the role fits into the church system. The nurse can do this by demonstrating proficiency in educating parishioners about taking responsibility for their own health, through seminars, articles in newsletters and bulletins, and by meeting with individuals or small groups. I have learned that sharing my knowledge and resources with the clergy helps them understand the illnesses of people they are visiting. As a result of fresh insights, the ministers feel more comfortable in the pastoral role. The clergy advise, support, and encourage me in areas where I have less knowledge.

I have a keen interest in the well-being of the whole staff, not just the pastoral team, and inquire as to how things are going in their lives, making time available to listen and offer support when appropriate. Another component of the wellness objective is for me to challenge staff members when it appears that their overall health is being compromised, as a result of their not taking care of themselves. There are times when asking people "why would you do that?" or "are you taking on too much?" causes them to stop and reflect on the benefits and risks of the planned activity. It is important that the parish nurse offer challenges in a respectful and concerned manner. Staff members have a right to live and work as they choose. The challenge from the nurse should be seen as one of caring, not an effort to control.

An Effective Pastoral Team

Being identified with the pastoral team gives credibility to the role of parish nurse and helps parishioners make the connection between faith and health. In my practice there was a man who was very ill with cancer. He had been a very committed Christian, and his illness was causing his faith to waver. He was suffering a great deal of stress about this when he found that he was unable to pray as he had previously. In our discussions one day he told me how this *spiritual distress* was affecting him. He was feeling unsettled, guilty, and generally disturbed about this state of affairs. I asked him if he would like to have one of the ministers come to see him more often, and he thought that might be helpful. I reminded him that others could pray for him when he could not. This reassurance appeared to give him some comfort. We joined hands, and I prayed with him, requesting God's guidance and support through this difficult period.

The gentleman was appreciative of the offer for the clergy to take communion to his home, as he was unable to get out to church at that time. The clergy were willing to see him on a weekly basis and appreciated my making them aware of his current status. In our discussion at a pastoral meeting, we decided to ask the gentleman if he would like a pastoral visitor who could offer support beyond what staff could provide. When the minister visited and offered this, the gentleman was pleased and gratefully accepted.

A pastoral staff team that can work together, sharing their individual talents and ideas, increases the effectiveness of the collective ministries to the parish. With the input of one or two others, a broader range of options can be developed.

Twelve
Listening

You cannot truly listen to anyone and do anything else at the same time.

M. Scott Peck

Who listens? Who takes the time to really listen to someone? In the hustle and bustle of our world, with the phenomenal growth in the use of electronic mail (email) and cell phones, people are becoming more isolated, in spite of increasing attempts at communication. Superficial conversations on cell phones proliferate. Nobody is really ever out of reach, and yet statistics show that in the 21st century, there is an increasing number of Canadians affected by mood disorders.

Mental Illness – Frequency And Causes

Approximately 20% of Canadians will personally experience a mental illness in their lifetime (Health Canada, 2002). A number of factors seem to affect how many people will have mental illness. One is the support of family and friends. Divorced or separated people are more likely to have a depression than those who are married. Twice as many females as males report depression. Of those with serious physical health conditions, a significant number will develop a major depressive disorder, as outlined in *A Report on Mental Illness in Canada* (Health Canada, 2002). While it is only a small part of the solution to mental illness, isolation and loneliness contribute to the problem, resulting in the need for more devoted, sincere listeners.

People can develop distorted thinking patterns, a notion that occurs over and over again until, in their mind, it becomes a truth. If there is no opportunity to explore these thoughts and perceptions with someone, how are they ever to be challenged?

Think for a moment of the teenage girl who weighs 115 pounds and thinks she is fat. I am not speaking about a person who is suffering anorexia or bulimia. I am speaking about an average teen that may not express her feelings but may have these negative thoughts about herself, nevertheless. These negative thoughts about her weight can mushroom into something bigger that includes her hair and her overall appearance. Buying into these negative thoughts can be devastating to the point of affecting self-esteem and causing larger problems.

The Value Of Listening Skills

A supportive listener can encourage her to speak about her insecurities and, over time, validate her as a person. As she feels better about herself, the appearance issues may diminish. Honest, sincere affirmation of her appearance at appropriate times will help her to think differently about herself, especially if she has come to trust you, the listener.

The gift of listening is incredibly valuable when the nurse is available to spend time with an individual and *really* listens. The opportunities may occur serendipitously, and a perceptive parish nurse will recognize an opportunity and offer to listen. To be present to another person allows the person to speak from the heart and to express the thoughts that have been occurring. The nurse should possess first-rate communication skills and be able to reflect back what was heard. By listening carefully, the parish nurse may uncover some unexpected information, as in the example below.

An Example From My Practice

Mr. E. stopped by my office on the pretence of inquiring about my vacation. I sensed by the way he appeared that there might be something bothering him. He seemed somewhat agitated. He was living at home, caring for his wife who had a diagnosis of Alzheimer's disease. Previously he had refused to have any help. I invited him into my office for a chat.

Nurse: "Hi Mr. E., how nice of you to drop in. How are things going with you?"

Mr. E: "Oh, the usual, I am getting my garden in. I just wanted to say hello and see if you enjoyed your holiday."

Nurse: "Thanks for asking, I had a nice vacation. How are you managing at home with your wife? Are you able to carry on or are you needing some help?"

Mr. E: "Well, bathing her is quite a challenge as she doesn't want to have a bath. I have to yell at her and push her into the bathroom and she screams the whole time. I get the job done, though."

Nurse: "It sounds like it is quite a struggle for you to keep her clean."

Mr. E: "Yeah and she messes her pants now so I have to put diapers on her and she fights me all the way."

Nurse: "Mr. E., it sounds to me like caring for your wife on your own is becoming too much for you. Would you consider letting me get in touch with the social worker at the Alzheimer Society to get you some help?

Mr. E: "You know I should be able to do this myself. I don't want to have a whole crowd of people coming and going in my house."

Nurse: "You have managed so well for so long, but I sense that you are wearing out and that your wife needs more help than one person can give. Your wife might be able to go to a day program and that would give you a break. I would be prepared to meet with you and the social worker, and we can tell her how you feel about having a lot of people coming in. Will you let me call her for you?"

Mr. E: "I feel like I'm letting her down but yes, I am pretty tired as she is up in the night and thinks it is morning."

If I had not taken the time to listen, I would

have missed an opportunity to *hear* this man, who had pulled together the courage to seek help. Certainly my antennae went up when I heard that he *had to push her into the bathroom.*

Please see Part 6 on Family Violence and Emotional Trauma.

Good listening skills such as making eye contact, listening with a focus on the person speaking, observing body language, listening to the tone of voice, and reading between the lines are essential for a parish nurse. In the example from my practice, it was important to be sensitive to the person and support him where he was. Having experienced support from me over a period of time, the gentleman came to trust me. When people feel that they have let someone down, they do not want to debate the issue. That is how they feel! Affirming what they have done and offering some respite does not negate their feelings.

Good Listening Skills – Core Concepts

- Maintain eye contact. This helps you focus on the person.

- Listen carefully to the spoken words and the tone of voice.

- Be sensitive to how the person is feeling.

- Do not argue with what people say they are feeling.

- Observe the body language. Is it consistent with the words?

- Try to understand how it is for that person.

- If someone begins to cry, offering a tissue too rapidly can shut down the expression of true feelings.

We all experience times when we feel needy, and if someone is prepared to listen without distraction, we can benefit immensely. It seems that when someone listens attentively, maintaining eye contact (if culturally appropriate), and *being with us in the moment*, we are like two pilgrims on the journey of life, both moving in the same direction.

> *The little child whispered, "God, speak to me." And a meadowlark sang. But the child did not hear. So the child yelled, "God, speak to me!"*
> *And the thunder rolled across the sky. But the child did not listen. The child looked around and said, "God let me see you." And a star shone brightly. But the child did not notice. And the child shouted, "God show me a miracle!" And a life was born. But the child did not know. So the child cried out in despair, "Touch me God, and let me know you are here!" Whereupon, God reached down and touched the child. But the child brushed the butterfly off and walked away, unknowingly. Take time to listen. Often times, the things*

we seek are right underneath our noses.
Don't miss out on your blessing because
it isn't packaged the way that you expect.

Anonymous

Thirteen

What Does Faith have to do with it?

*I believe in the sun
even if it isn't shining.
I believe in love even
when I am alone.
I believe in God even
when He is silent.*

World War II refugee

Faith has a great deal to do with parish nursing ministry. As Christians, we believe in the unconditional love of God for all people. As parish nurses, we demonstrate the love of God to those we serve. But there are other aspects of faith: faith in others and in the client's decision-making process, faith in our abilities and ourselves. Growth in all facets of faith enhances our effectiveness as parish nurses.

It is important to have faith in others and their abilities for self-determination. The perceived power associated with the role of parish nurse may seem intimidating to some parishioners. Through positive interactions with the parish nurse, where individuals feel that the nurse has listened to them, the development of mutual respect is possible. As the nurse and the individual come to have faith in one another, there is potential for moving in a true direction. Because the parish nurse typically sees people when they are vulnerable, it is critical that the nurse learns to "look out the other person's window; try to see the world as the patient sees it" (Yalom, 2002, p.18).

Feedback on what you think you are hearing clarifies for the individual that you do understand what is being said. By supporting people's choices, you are showing faith in their decision-making abilities. Offering other possibilities while being supportive does not take anything away from a person. Assisting people in creating a menu of options demonstrates that you trust their ability to make the right decisions.

An Example From my Practice Demonstrates Some Aspects of Faith

Mr. and Mrs. K., a couple in their mid eighties, were living at home and managing quite well. Mr. K became ill with cancer and died, leaving this vulnerable lady, with impaired hearing and vision, alone in her house. Mrs. K's son wanted her to move to a retirement home, but she was very much opposed to this. When Mrs. K. was on her own, determined to stay at home, my role was to assist in setting up support services to help her to stay there. I had faith in her ability to manage at home with appropriate help, and encouraged her son to have faith also.

In spite of the home care services, my visits, the assigning of a lay pastoral visitor, and family involvement, Mrs. K. was lonely... but still insisted on keeping her home. While acknowledging her wishes, it seemed appropriate to suggest that she could go on a *vacation* to a retirement home, to test it out. She agreed to do that. After staying for the allotted two-week period, she returned home. It was not very long before she was ready to move there. By not being forced to make unwanted decisions, and by receiving support as she worked through the issues herself, she was able to embrace the possibilities and move ahead.

After moving into the retirement home, relieving herself of the day-to-day worries of shopping, meal preparation, and the care and maintenance of her home, her accelerating anxiety level began to subside. Then she could more easily cope with keeping an eye on her finances. In our congregation a retired chartered accountant volunteered to help Mrs. K. with her income taxes. A nice, supportive relationship developed. The lay pastoral visitor, who had been visiting when she was at home, was able to take Mrs. K. out for pleasurable activities rather than always having to do some errands. My faith in the process of supporting Mrs. K. through her own decision-making journey was warranted.

Eventually Mrs. K. became ill with cancer. The lay visitor was away when Mrs. K was admitted to palliative care at the hospital. When the lay visitor learned that Mrs. K. was in hospital, she was apprehensive about visiting as she was unsure of how effective she would be. Faith in myself and in my instincts led me to offer to go with her. The lay visitor jumped at the chance and it turned out to be the most heart-warming experience. Mrs. K., even in her weakened state, was so pleased to see her visitor. Before we left, we joined hands and prayed, asking for strength and courage to face the difficulties ahead, and for peace. Mrs. K. died the next day. A great opportunity to show the love of God could have been missed that day. Have faith in your instincts. My experience has shown that they are most often right!

In Summary

- Have faith in the person's decision-making process.

- Try to see the world through the other person's eyes.

- Trust your own instincts.

- Allow the process to unfold at the client's rate, not yours

- Bolster the relationship with the visitor, by supporting but not pushing to the forefront. The parish nurse role is to support and encourage the lay visitor to develop self-confidence and skills in dealing with serious life events.

- Our Christian faith is the guiding light for our parish nursing ministry. The Bible provides us with the spiritual resources necessary to uphold and sustain us in our work.

Some Comforting Bible Passages (NRSV, 2002)

When you pass through the waters I will be with you; and through the rivers, they shall not overwhelm you, when you walk through the fire you shall not be burned and the flame shall not consume you. (Isaiah 43:2)

For I am sure that neither death, nor life, nor angels, nor principalities, nor things present, nor things to come, nor powers, nor height, nor depth, nor anything else in creation will be able to separate us from the love of God in Christ Jesus, our Lord. (Rom. 8:38-39)

Cast all your cares on Him, for He cares about you. (1 Peter 5:7)

The practice of parish nursing is about having faith in people to make good and appropriate decisions about their lives. It is a privilege to *walk alongside* people as they fully embrace their possibilities.

> *Faith is free and available to all people at all times. It only requires that one fully embrace possibility, and the ultimate value is in the depth of the embrace.*
>
> Patch Adams MD

Fourteen
Assisting With Decision Making

Adversity has the effect of eliciting talents, which in prosperous times would have lain dormant.

Horace

When an older person is faced with significant decisions to make in the midst of infirmity and confusion, families can become overwhelmed with their perceived responsibility for making decisions for their parents. Adult children may believe and behave as if the parent/child role has been reversed. This can have an adverse effect on older persons who may do everything in their power to sabotage decisions and actions initiated by the adult child. What families may forget is the fact that, although the parent may be struggling at present, he/she is not totally incompetent. Under these circumstances, the parish nurse can help the family member understand that the parent, in not complying with the adult child's decisions, is trying to hold on to whatever control can be preserved. The parent may have lost a partner, many friends, the ability to drive, and therefore some independence, and may be afraid of losing anything more. The older person may not even recognize his/her persistent negative behaviour. Sometimes the family members are imposing their own values on the older adult.

A recent example of this occurred when a daughter decided that she would do her mother's laundry as her mother was not doing it. Each time the daughter brought the clean laundry back, the mother would complain: the sheets were not folded the way she liked, the fabric softener had an unpleasant smell, the clothing had been destroyed by the dryer (*she never put those in the dryer*). The daughter was feeling upset, as the mother did not appreciate what she was doing for her. In my view, what the mother was really saying was "I want to do my own laundry and you have taken that away from me."

When the parish nurse becomes aware of a situation like this, she can ask the daughter if she thinks that the mother is complaining because she wants to do her own laundry, even if it isn't done on the schedule that the daughter thinks is suitable. To be fair to the daughter though, if the laundry is piling up and this is a change from the normal pattern, it may be an indicator that the mother's health is deteriorating. An offer to assist with the laundry rather than take over doing it, would give the daughter an opportunity to observe how the mother is able to cope with ordinary tasks. The pre-existing family relationships and communication patterns will have an impact on how the tensions can be handled. The daughter may have to back away and later try a different approach if her assistance is not being welcomed.

The Role of the Parish Nurse

- To examine the situation from the older person's and the daughter's perspectives and create possible scenarios to explain an event

- To communicate with the older person and ask how she is feeling about her decision-making abilities

- To help the daughter explore new ways of

helping her mother make decisions for her-self, rather that just taking over

- To offer to meet with the parent and the adult child to facilitate resolution of the conflict (An objective third party may be able to mediate in a family discussion while encouraging each person to listen to the feelings of the other)

There may be times, such as in the case of de-mentia or severe depression, when older persons are not capable of making their own decisions. These circumstances can be very difficult, as the adult child may feel uncomfortable going behind the parent's back. If a daughter or son holds the Power of Attorney, the assumption is that there has been some discussion on the wishes of the older person. The parish nurse should inquire of the family member if, in fact, those discussions have occurred. If not, the nurse can assist in ex-ploring the values of the older person and identify possible options supporting those values.

Possible Questions to Consider

- In similar situations, how would your par-ent have handled this type of situation?

- What decision do you think your parent would make if he/she were able?

- In your relationship with your parent, has it been your practice to be involved in his/her decision-making?

- What approach do you think would be acceptable to your parent?

Usually, people want to retain control over their lives. Through aging and increasing limitations, maintaining a degree of independence can be challenging. By working with the older person and the family member to identify new solutions to old problems, the parish nurse encourages both people to be creative in their thinking. The nurse can foster the sense of *teamwork* so that both parent and adult child begin to feel that they are working toward a common goal.

Please see Chapter 46 on Coping with Dementia.

Please see Chapter 16 on Advance Directives.

Fifteen

Helping Parishioners Resolve Conflict

*It takes courage to do what
you want.
Other people have a lot of
plans for you.
Nobody wants you to do what
you want to do.*

Joseph Campbell

Conflict can be defined as a state of opposition; a fight or struggle; the clashing of opposing principles; and the opposition of incompatible wishes or needs in a person (Oxford, 2000). As humans with the ability to make choices, we are forced to deal with opposing principles throughout our lives. Parish nursing ministry involves working with people in situations of conflict. Conflict should not always be viewed as negative. People do have to sort out what values are really important to them and make decisions that coincide with those values.

A common pattern of conflict that many people face occurs when they have to make decisions with respect to housing and care in their later years. Where should I go? With whom should I live? Do I move to live near my son because he wants me to be closer, or do I remain where I am, with my friends and familiar surroundings?

Another instance where conflict often arises concerns driver's licences. The older person may believe (or at least assert) that he or she is still capable of driving. The adult child may have observed the declining ability of the parent and feel that driving should no longer be an option. Conflict occurs for the adult child concerning the safety of the parent and others and the desire for the parent to remain independent.

The children of separated or divorced parents with opposing views on many issues can live in a conflicted state for most of their childhood if these issues are not resolved. For example, one parent may not want a child to be involved in the church, while the other parent is strongly in favour of it. On Dad's weekends, the children are not allowed to attend church school, whereas on Mom's weekends they are able to be there and like it. The children may resent being deprived of something they enjoy.

Adult children with aging parents and a young family are often in conflict over the allocation of time and energy for their parents and their own families. Often referred to as *the sandwich generation,* these people are forever struggling with conflicting issues. "I know Mom really wants to go shopping today, but my daughter wants me to watch her swimming class." "Dad needs help with something that has broken down, but I need to do some work at my own place." "I promised to go out for the day with Mom, but my son needs help getting ready for a weekend camp. I know Mom will be so disappointed." The issues seem endless...

What Is The Role Of The Parish Nurse?

The parish nurse can, by listening and reflecting what she has heard, help people work through their conflicting options. When I encounter someone who is having an internal struggle about whether to do one thing or another, I help the person consider and list the positive and negative aspects of each possible resolution. I do not make the decision, but assist with pointing out potential consequences of each decision. As an objective observer, I may put forward ideas that the other person has not identified.

Situations involving conflict can be opportunities for parish nurses to bring together people with similar concerns, for education and support: a parenting support program with qualified facilitators; a *sandwich generation* support group to share *strategies*; a weekly tea time for isolated young mothers; an interesting work project for people forced into early retirement. As parish nursing is a ministry of the whole parish, providing occasions for people to reach out to others supports that mandate.

I have observed people with deep nagging concerns that are beyond the normal day-to-day living become unwell physically, emotionally, and spiritually. Headaches, digestive disorders, backaches, depression, anger, and isolation are the more common manifestations I have seen. When I become aware of the struggles of parishioners, I ask if I can be of any assistance. If the person chooses not to talk about the difficulty, I respect that. I do *leave the door open* for future discussion.

I believe that parish nurses have many opportunities, using their own resources and those of the church and community, to support people in making the decisions they need to make. In so doing, nurses help them move toward a healthier state of being. I have learned that walking alongside, offering support and encouragement as people grapple with their issues, restores their confidence in their ability to resolve conflict in their lives. If the decision in the end is not the right one, the person will learn from those mistakes. Personal control over our own lives and being permitted to make our own mistakes is what makes us human.

Steps to Conflict Resolution

- Clarify the conflict to be resolved

- Identify with the person what values are important to him/her

- Assist the person in determining what the possible solutions might be

- Help the person recognize the positive and negative aspects of each solution

- Question solutions that are not consistent with the stated values

- Check that the person can live with the outcome, as there will be more stress if an unsatisfactory solution is selected

Sixteen

Advance Directives

You cannot prevent the birds of sorrow from flying over your head, but you can prevent them from building nests in your hair.

Chinese proverb

A parish nurse should understand the importance of powers of attorney for property and personal care, and educate her faith community about them. All the provinces in Canada have some form of legislation or pending legislation, to deal with end of life decisions about care. Advance directives are called many different names, such as instructional directives or proxy directives, and there are different aspects to them. Advance directives generally consist of appointing a person to act on your behalf, should you become incapable of doing so yourself, and providing a document outlining your wishes.

In Ontario, the *Substitute Decisions Act, 1992 (Govt Of Ontario, 1996)* was passed to respond to the need for designating persons authorized to make decisions regarding property and personal care for persons deemed incapable of making those decisions. Bill 19, The *Advocacy, Consent and Substitute Decisions Statute Law Amendment Act, 1995* was proclaimed in March of 1996 (Govt. of Ontario, 1996). The intent of this legislation is to simplify the laws about substitute decision-making and reduce government interference in the private affairs of individuals. The act encourages people to empower family members and friends to act on their behalf, should the need arise. The assumption is that all persons should have the right to make decisions about their own health care, including the right to approve or refuse treatments that will sustain life (CNA, 1994). The co-sponsors of the *Joint Statement on Advance Directives* believe that all involved in health care have a duty to *uphold the client's right to self-determination* (CNA, 1994).

In the past, living wills were used as advance directives, but there were some problems with them. Dr. William Molloy states that these living wills dealt only with the withdrawal of treatment, did not always have input from health care professionals who could help people understand the implications of their decisions, and contained nebulous phrases like "heroic measures" and "reasonable recovery" (Molloy, 1993). People were making decisions without understanding what they were doing. Advance directives are an effective way of maintaining autonomy when we may not be able to make decisions for ourselves, but careful thought and planning are essential. Comprehensive documentation and dialogue with the substitute decision-maker ensures a greater likelihood of a person's wishes being acted upon.

The Code of Ethics for Nurses (CNA, 1998) can be used as a guide when assisting clients considering healthcare decisions. The basic values and associated responsibility statements included in the Code are relevant when assisting and educating persons grappling with these issues. The basic values of health and well-being, choice, and dignity are the guiding principles providing the framework for using the advance directive tools. For parish nurses, knowledge of spiritual assessment skills is important in order to fully integrate all aspects of a person. Sometimes conversations with clergy can result in clarity from a faith perspective for persons making difficult decisions concerning treatments and end-of-life decisions.

Implementation Of The Process For Assisting People With Advance Directives Includes:

- taking into account the health and well-being values of the individual. Nurses can assist clients to achieve their optimum physical, spiritual, social, and emotional health status throughout their lives. Whether clients are physically well, are ill or injured, or in the process of dying, the parish nurse supports the individual with dignity.

- respecting the choices of clients and providing an environment where people feel free to express their deepest fears and concerns.

- encouraging clients to appoint a substitute decision-maker to ensure that their wishes are understood and followed, should they become incapable of making those decisions.

- exhibiting sensitivity when dealing with client's needs, values, and choices. Respect includes honouring, and advocating for, client's expressed wishes, as long as those wishes do not infringe upon the rights of others or go against the defined laws of the jurisdiction.

- recognizing that many life-sustaining treatments are linked to technology, so the parish nurse must ensure that the clients understand the implications of using, or withdrawing, these treatments (CNA, 1998).

- being aware that cultural sensitivities are essential, as the perceptions of illness, death, personal autonomy, and control can vary between cultures. To illustrate this point: many African Americans see illness as a test of faith; Korean Americans do not find autonomy empowering; and some Asian cultures believe that death occurring outside the home means that the person's soul will be wandering without a place to rest (Tennstedt, 2002). Elderly Japanese Christians, because of the history of Canadian governmental discrimination, may distrust and fear formal authority (Waxler-Morrison, Anderson, & Richardson, 1990). Some Vietnamese Canadians hold doctors in high esteem. Nurses are seen only as persons carrying out the doctors' orders, so may not be taken seriously on their own (Waxler-Morrison, Anderson, & Richardson, 1990).

It is important for parish nurses to remember that advance directives, powers of attorney for health and personal care, and/or substitute decision-makers can be called into play in situations other than end-of-life decisions, and people need to be made aware of what they are agreeing to do, when they take on that responsibility. A health care directive cannot authorize an illegal activity.

In Saskatchewan legislation ensures that people following the instructions in a directive will not be liable when acting in good faith (Nilson, 1997).

Reasons Why People Should Complete An Advance Directive, As Outlined In Vital Choices (Molloy, 1993)

- To become educated about the choices in the health care system

- Because it defines areas in which decisions should be made

- So that people can individualize their health care

- To give people time to think about what options they would choose and to provide an opportunity to talk about it with family members and doctors

- So that planning for potential future is- sues is done in a safe environment prior to needing it, and people can retain control of health care decision-making

Through my personal and professional expe- rience, I have seen the powers of attorney (POA) for personal care called upon to make decisions regarding consent for surgery and for changes in treatment. A POA for personal care can be re- quired to make decisions about a person's living conditions, such as no longer living in his/her own home, but moving to a safer environment. A POA can be asked to take responsibility for providing appropriate clothing, transportation for treatment, and ensuring that people have food. If the POA for personal care does not have the POA for property, then that other person has to be involved, and consulted on any financial commitments. It can become a very complicated and time-consuming activity. Powers of Attorney are legally in effect as soon as they are signed, but do not supersede the donor's wishes until the donor becomes incompetent. Having said that, many physicians get around declaring an individual *incompetent* by designating the person *incapable of making good decisions* so that the POA for personal care becomes a collaborative member of the team, advocating for the client and ensuring that his/her wishes are heard.

In most cases a family member is willing to assume the POA responsibility, but that, too, can have problems if the person does not want family members making those decisions. Parish nurses should work with people to explore the feelings associated with the family dynamics. There may be opportunities for resolution and healing. Some family members may not want to consider making decisions for a relative because they are unable to face mortality. The parish nurse has a great teaching opportunity to help family members understand that creating an advance directive and appointing powers of attorney is a way of maintaining some control over one's life in difficult times. We cannot change the fact that human beings are mortal creatures and life does end. As suggested in the Chinese proverb at the beginning of this chapter, we cannot control the inevitable, but we can have a say in how it manifests itself.

Seventeen

What is the Meaning of Illness?

Every human has four endowments- self-awareness, conscience, independent will, and creative imagination.
These give the ultimate human freedom...the power to choose, to respond, to change.

Stephen R. Covey

We are what we think. All that we are arises with our thoughts. With our thoughts we make the world.

Buddha

Character cannot be developed in ease and quiet. Only through experience of trial and suffering can the soul be strengthened, ambition inspired and success achieved.

Helen Keller

For I am convinced that neither death, nor life, nor angels, nor rulers, nor things present, nor things to come, nor powers, nor height, nor depth, nor anything in all creation, will be able to separate us from the love of God in Christ Jesus our Lord.

Romans 8: 38, 39.

Attitude, suffering, and faith as depicted in the above quotations can dictate how we view illness. There are those for whom the scripture, as in *Romans* (Bible), defines and explains illness in their lives. Regardless of the severity of the illness, their deep faith remains solid and the illness does not separate them from God.

Some people believe that we have to suffer in order to achieve inner strength and growth. If we are never challenged, there is no impetus for growth. They think, as did Helen Keller, that significant growth can occur when we effectively manage adversity.

For others, how they understand illness can affect the outcome of the illness or crisis situation as suggested in the Buddha quote.

Our attitudes toward illness develop through our life experiences, our belief structures, culture and societal norms. Family attitudes and interpretations of illness tend to define for us what illness means.

The Canadian Oxford Dictionary (2000) defines illness: a disease, ailment or malady; the state of being ill (p. 490). Being ill can refer to being unwell in body, mind and/or spirit; so if one area is unwell, the rest of our whole being may be affected. A young boy who started high school and vomited every morning before school illustrated an example of body-mind-spirit imbalance. His parents were frantic, had him seen by numerous doctors, and tried to have the boy tell them what was really going on. Interestingly, the day he received his first report card the vomiting stopped and has not recurred. We may not make the mind-body connection when we are physically ill, but we need to examine the balance (or imbalance) in our lives.

A parish nurse will learn how different people respond to illness. There are countless possible reactions and fears associated with illness.

Personal Reactions To Illness; Feelings And Fears About Illness May Include:

- being bedridden and physically isolated from others.

- feeling different from other people, even *less valued* than others.

- finding ourselves emotionally separated from others who can't understand how it is for us.

- feeling abandoned by God and others whom we believed would protect us.

- fearing outcomes and being anxious about treatments.

- becoming angry with God or the doctor.

- wearing down because of pain, suffering, and abandonment.

- feeling resentful that we have an illness while others appear healthy.

- asking questions (e.g. Why me? or What did I do to deserve this?)

- thinking that God is punishing us for our transgressions.

I have identified some possible reactions, feelings, and beliefs about illness. There can be a combination of any of these; so the parish nurse should find ways to be sensitive to a person's beliefs and work with that person to develop healthy ways to manage the illness.

To be effective, parish nurses should examine their own interpretation of illness. By working through the process and developing some clarity for themselves, nurses will be better able to help people discover their own way of understanding illness.

Some Possible Questions To Ask:

- When I am sick, I feel_____.

- How do I view illness in others? Do I blame them?

- Is it my fault that I am ill? Am I being punished?

- Is there anything good that can come out of illness?

- Where is God in all of this? Did He cause my illness?

- Is my illness a convenience so that I don't have to do something I don't want to do?

While many family doctors look at illness as a physical problem, increasingly family physicians, psychotherapists, nurses, and theologians are examining the emotional, spiritual and psychological origins of physical illness. Conversely, there is an increasing awareness that a physical illness can cause emotional and spiritual distress (McKee, 2000).

Illness can sometimes provide an escape, a way out of a difficult situation. An example might be the caregiver of an elderly person who has reached a point of not being able to care for a loved one at home. The caregiver arranges for the person to be admitted to a care facility, but continues to visit, often on a daily basis. When illness strikes, the caregiver cannot maintain that visiting schedule and so is freed from the regime she has set for herself. Illness in this case can be viewed as an escape, and/or the result of cumulative stress.

Western medicine has its own belief system about illness, based upon the theory that viruses, bacteria, and other parasitic organisms invade the body (Smucker, 1998). Treatment protocols involve giving people drugs to counteract these *invaders*. The treatments provide limited help for people with chronic illnesses such as cancer, arthritis, and Parkinson's disease. Recognition of these limitations has motivated people to look for help in other areas.

Alternative approaches to health care are gaining increased recognition. Oriental medicine is based on the premise that illness is caused by an imbalance of energies in the body. Unblocking these pathways can promote healing in areas where traditional Western medicine cannot. Naturopathic medicine views disease as being the result of toxins and stress accumulating in the body, causing a breakdown of the systems. Nutritional supplements, fasting, and clearing out the toxins are the recommended treatments. I mention these differing views to broaden our thinking. Each has had some proven success over the years. Each has some measure of truth (Quigley, 2000).

For parish nurses, the objective should be to *walk alongside* people as they try to find meaning in their illness. Imposing one's own view is not appropriate, but gently outlining some other possible interpretations might be useful. In seeking to understand other people's belief systems, parish nurses may help people to clarify their beliefs. Their attitudes, faith, and interpretation of suffering will have an impact on the outcome of their illness. It is critical for parish nurses to be aware of their own limitations, and be willing to refer people to someone with the expertise to assist in meaningful ways.

Eighteen
Chronic Health Challenges

The human spirit will endure sickness, but a broken spirit – who can bear?

Proverbs 18:14

Chronic illnesses are ambiguous. Their symptoms are changing all the time, and there is not enough known about these conditions. As nurses, most of us were taught in the *medical model* and were trained to relieve suffering. Some new curricula are focused on caring for the whole person rather than on the disease process.

Acute illnesses are *preferred* as they have a distinct beginning, course of treatment, and an end, cure or death. Chronic illnesses do not follow that path. How do you deal with someone with a chronic illness when you cannot support him or her in the process of resolution of the problem? Chronic illness, in the early stages of onset, is often attributed to emotional or mental problems because initial symptoms can be sensory, and invisible.

People do not get sick in a vacuum (Fennel, 2001). Any illness, acute or chronic, has an impact on family, friends, doctors, and the community. People in our society are socialized to work towards and strive for perfection, or as close to it as possible. When people develop chronic illnesses, society perceives them differently. At the onset they perceive themselves differently, too. They may become invisible. There may be intolerance, as people cannot explain chronic illness scientifically. Those living with chronic illness may be seen as lazy and unproductive. They may be stigmatized, and categorized differently. They have become outsiders to the *healthy people's* group.

Individuals living with chronic illness must deal not only with the symptoms and unpredictability of most chronic illness, but also the inevitable emotional and spiritual pain. Their perception of themselves may be altered, and what used to be normal for them is no longer normal. People living with chronic illness and their families have to let go, grieve what was normal, and establish a *new normal* that may be constantly shifting (Topf, 1995). Uncertainty may be the only constant!

The parish nurse needs to show sensitivity when dealing with people living with chronic illness. Quietly supporting and being available to listen may be the most valuable gifts the nurse can offer, particularly after a recent diagnosis when someone is trying to assimilate the new information. People are seeking validation that they are still valuable human beings. They begin to come to terms with this new, and usually frightening, reality when they tell their stories many times. Some listeners may react by rolling their eyes and thinking, "Oh, she's telling that story again", but over time that is how he/she comes to terms with it.

The challenge for parish nurses is to use good listening skills and ask questions for clarification, as sometimes those carefully selected questions can help the person with a chronic illness express the deep fears that he or she is avoiding. Depending on the relationship with the person, the nurse might inquire as to what is the greatest fear. The response can lead to a new and useful discussion.

Please see Chapter 12 on Listening.

Implications of Chronic Health Challenges for Individuals and Their Families

- The most thoughtful response when people disclose their feelings about a diagnosis is to listen. Judging their reactions is not productive.

- Anger and fear, disappointment, uncertainty, and probably many other emotions will come and go for those with a new diagnosis. Shattered dreams may be expressed, as well as feelings of uselessness. Telling people that they are still useful, at this early stage will not make them feel better. Right now, that is how that person feels and debating that only denies the feelings. *Walking alongside* lets people know that you are there to be a support, while they struggle to make sense of it all.

- When blindsided by a frightening diagnosis, individuals may fail to mobilize the skills and strategies that they have utilized to solve problems in other areas of their lives. Proficiency developed through education, employment, and in relationships can be applied to dealing with a chronic health challenge. The parish nurse can assist people to *marshal their resources* and remind them of previous success in managing challenges.

- Showing pity for a person with a chronic illness changes the relationship. The person on the receiving end can be made to feel worthless and not the equal of the person doing the pitying. Empathy, trying to understand what it is like for the person with the illness, can be empowering.

- Avoid speaking of someone else with a similar condition. It has nothing to do with this situation. Each person's pain is his or her own. I have observed people who, upon hearing about a person's new diagnosis, expound on the worst case they have ever seen. I have observed nurses doing it, and I am at a loss to explain the behaviour!

- *But you look so good*! A comment like that challenges the person's reality. It may be heard as *you look good, so I don't believe you are sick.* If the person were in a cast or bandages, the problem would be more visible. Perhaps an individual makes an effort to look good in order to feel better, to avoid discussion about the illness, or to hide true feelings.

- People with a new diagnosis generally want to know more and understand what it all means. The nurse can ask if that person would like to read some information about the condition.

- If people feel angry with God and are struggling with their faith, the nurse might suggest that speaking with the clergy could, conceivably, be helpful. Reassuring people that they are not bad because they cannot pray right now, and reminding them that others can pray for them when they are not able, can help to alleviate some guilt and ease some of the emotional turmoil.

- Healing prayer may be appropriate with the understanding that healing of emotions and spirit can help cope with the new reality. The objective of healing prayer is increased peace of mind and a greater awareness of the power of the Holy Spirit in one's life, rather than seeking cure.

- People's attitudes govern how they view an illness and can have a major impact on how they plan for, and live out their lives. People may choose to explore alternative therapies such as meditation, massage therapy, reiki, and healing touch. There can be significant benefit in utilizing different modalities.

There is more often acknowledgement that the individual with a chronic illness has a problem but it is important to recognize that the family needs support too. As the family members adjust to changes in the person with the illness, they also go through a grieving process. In her book, *The Chronic Illness Workbook,* Patricia A. Fennell speaks of the "vicarious trauma" suffered by family members who are intensely sympathetic to the ill person and who may have to make changes in their own lives to accommodate the disruptions caused by the illness (Fennell, 2001). These caregivers and family members are often overlooked.

Please see Chapter 49 on Caring for the Caregiver.

I see how family members go through a great deal of pain watching what is happening to their loved ones and having no power to change or halt the process. Ask them directly how this chronic illness is affecting them. Acknowledge that it must be difficult for them, too. The family members' pain may be invisible. The parish nurse has an opportunity to encourage dialogue about that pain. Without an outlet for their feelings, family members may become ill themselves. When people are encouraged to speak early on about their feelings, they can learn to come together as a team. It is within the power of the client and family members to manage the illness rather than let it take over their lives.

Taking control of a difficult situation takes time, and the process will involve numerous struggles. The ultimate objective, as stated in the quotation from Proverbs at the beginning of this chapter, is to avoid *the breaking of the spirit*, while learning to live with the chronic illness.

Nineteen

Preparing for a Doctor's Appointment

It is more important to know what sort of person has a disease than to know what sort of disease a person has.

Hippocrates

Being clear about the purpose of a visit to the doctor and planning for the desired outcome makes infinite sense, but it is a task that many people find difficult. Suggesting a meeting prior to a doctor's appointment, one where you might be accompanying the person or where the individual can manage alone, encourages the person to think ahead and plan for the greatest benefit. The approach to health care today differs from when the current seniors were young. Then, partnering with the physician to manage one's own health care was not considered. Doctors were seldom challenged, and people generally complied with what the doctor recommended.

Doctor's visits can be unsatisfactory because people are afraid to ask questions and may downplay the severity of the problem or omit some details. Helping the person to develop a list of issues and questions to be addressed improves physician-client communication. Physicians need to know what medication a person is taking so listing the medications and identifying those needing to be refilled streamlines the process. People may not think about their medications, particularly if the doctor's visit is for a new or different issue. Reminding the client about medications and providing a form to keep track of them promotes client responsibility. Check at a local pharmacy for these medication cards or obtain them from pharmaceutical companies.

The family doctor should be thought of as the *hub of the wheel* in the health care system. Each person should strive to have a family physician that can be an advocate when a person is ill. In many areas there is a shortage of family doctors, but often hospitals, nurses, and the College of Physicians and Surgeons are aware of doctors still taking new patients. The family doctor looks at the whole picture, refers patients to specialists as needed, and receives reports back from the specialists. This provides some continuity in care.

Being responsible for looking at the bigger picture means that knowledge about medications prescribed by other doctors, perhaps specialists, is imperative. Non-prescription and over the counter drugs and herbs should be included. The parish nurse should stress the importance of using one pharmacy for all medications. If questions arise, the doctor has one person to contact regarding potential drug incompatibilities. The pharmacist and physician work together to reduce drug reactions. A substance that is strong enough to elicit a positive response in the body has the potential to produce a negative response as well.

When I meet with someone to plan for a visit to the doctor, I ask if people are clear about the purpose of the visit. I inquire as to what the person hopes will happen as a result of the visit. If the expected outcome seems unrealistic, I suggest that we may need to modify the expectations. Unreasonable expectations can lead to disappointment. Like Freedman (1990), I ask what the person plans to tell the doctor about the problem and help organize the information. I list the questions and leave space for the answers. I ask how much the condition is affecting the person's lifestyle, sleeping, eating, et cetera.

I enquire about the person's anxieties and the specific questions that need to be answered. I record the issues, feelings, and the negative effects the condition is having on the person and read them back to ensure that I have not misinterpreted the statements. With permission, I make copies for the physician and myself (if I am attending the visit.) Providing a copy for the doctor facilitates communication between doctor and patient.

If the client wants me to attend the appointment with the doctor, my role is to listen, record answers to the questions, and prompt if the client forgets a major detail. If the doctor has missed a question, I draw attention to that point. I also check that the person understands the doctor's explanations.

Follow-up after the visit includes a conversation to encourage feedback from the client about the doctor's answers to the questions. Were the doctor's responses clear? Did the client understand the diagnosis and its implications? If medications have been prescribed, we make note of possible side effects that should be reported. When tests have been ordered, we look at what preparation may be required.

An important part of the follow-up debriefing is a conversation from a holistic perspective, looking at body, mind, and spirit. There may be disharmony or imbalance in the person, causing physical manifestations (Fontaine, 2000). A discussion about those possibilities encourages the individual to look beyond the physical symptoms and perhaps identify areas of imbalance. Many times people are surprised that their lifestyle has such an impact on their wellness. Conventional medical practice has tended to focus on physical illness and treatment. Looking at illness from a holistic perspective may be a new way of thinking for the individual.

> *The relationship between the body and the mind is so intimate that, if either of them get out of order, the whole system would suffer.*
>
> Mohandas Gandhi

I create a written summary of the doctor's visit, outlining any recommendations made, along with the answers given to the questions. It is difficult to remember all that is said so the summary provides a reference, and a guide to follow in carrying out the recommendations.

Attending a doctor's visit with a client is a privilege and should be treated as such. The nurse's role is one of support and encouragement. It can be beneficial for both the client and the doctor. From the client's perspective, having someone else present can inspire confidence in discussion with the doctor. The parish nurse assists the physician by helping the client understand the issues, and by encouraging compliance with the doctor's recommendations. When the individual is well prepared for the visit, there is a greater likelihood of satisfaction as the person moves toward a partnership with the doctor in managing personal health care.

Overview of Key Points

- Details and questions are discussed prior to the visit.

- The nurse's role is a supportive one.

- The nurse helps the person determine what medications need reordering, if he/she needs assistance. (This is a good time to see how well the person is managing the medications.)

- The parish nurse ensures that all the questions are answered to the client's satisfaction.

- The parish nurse writes a summary of the visit to promote understanding and encourage compliance.

Twenty

Advocacy

Action is the catalyst that creates
accomplishments.
It is the path that takes us from
uncrafted hopes to realized dreams.

Thomas Huxley (1825-1895)

Opportunities arise in health care for the intervention of a third party to advocate on behalf of an individual or family. The parish nurse should be familiar with normal entitlements in the system. In an overloaded health care system, individuals might be rushed through the system and feel they have little choice in their level of care. They may not be aware of their rights.

A parish nurse may well advocate for and support a client's wishes. The nurse can offer to lend a hand to the client in making his/her wishes known. By helping people understand how the health care system works, while identifying the key players, the nurse assists clients in taking more control of their health care. When the nurse's objectives for the client differ from the client's own objectives, the nurse should support the client. If the nurse finds that impossible, an alternative advocate must be enlisted.

Please see Chapter 8 on Ethics.

When a physician has deemed a client to be mentally incompetent, the parish nurse's role changes. The client may make demands that are not logical, reasonable, or appropriate, so the nurse should strive to protect the client until the substitute decision maker becomes involved. The substitute decision maker might seek the support of the parish nurse, and the nurse can work with that person for the client's benefit.

I have been involved in several cases where

knowledge of the system, willingness to challenge the status quo, and advocacy for a different strategy have greatly influenced the outcome. I have included three positive examples of advocacy from my own practice.

Situation # 1

Mr. D's wife was in hospital with a fractured hip. The hip had been pinned, and it had been noted in the course of her hospital stay that Mrs. D. was showing signs of early dementia. There were no children or close relatives in the country. A few days before there was to be a team conference at the hospital regarding future plans for his wife, Mr. D. came in to talk to the minister who had visited him when he was in hospital some time previously. Mr. D. was quite anxious about the upcoming meeting and told the minister about it. After listening to Mr. D., the minister said that the parish nurse might be the one to assist him and brought Mr. D. to meet me.

My Activities Included:

- listening to Mr. D's story as he described his fears that his wife would be sent to a nursing home, and he wanted to care for her at home.

- discussing what would need to be in place if he did have her at home.

- offering to attend the team conference with him.

- making notes about the issues that we felt needed to be addressed.

- supporting Mr. D at the team conference when he was adamant that he could care for his wife at home. I encouraged the others to give him a chance to try.

- assisting Mr. D. to obtain the appropriate services and safety equipment for his home when he was given the go ahead to take his wife home.

It was a challenge, but Mr. D. (nearly 80 years old) managed very well in caring for his wife. As Mrs. D's dementia and cancer (diagnosed several months after discharge) progressed, my role became one of helping Mr. D. to see what he needed to do for himself, as he was becoming exhausted and needed some respite.

Working closely with the Case Manager at the Community Care Access Centre (the government health care organization) and with an agency from which he hired overnight help so he could get some sleep, we were able to keep Mr. D. healthy so that he could care for his wife. I believe that people should not be denied the opportunity to fill a caregiving role if they want to do it. Mr. D. would have so many regrets now if he had not cared for his wife at home. Mrs. D. died (at home) with Mr. D. holding her hand, a nurse present to support him. The nurse called the minister, who had been visiting on a regular basis, to have prayers with Mr. D. at the bedside.

Situation # 2

A woman in her early 70's was becoming more and more confused and was rapidly losing her ability to function at any level. She had been to her doctor, and he thought she had had a stroke. He ordered an MRI but not on an urgent basis and, with the health care system constraints, it was booked for weeks ahead. When I visited the woman, she was unable to sign a cheque she was attempting to write and was struggling to find words. I was very concerned, as I had seen the deterioration in just two days. I asked her permission to call her doctor and one of her daughters. Things moved very quickly from there. The MRI was done two days later and surgery for a massive brain tumour was done two days after that. While recovery was a long, slow process, the woman has continued to live on her own with help from personal support workers and her family. Without the early intervention, the outcome may not have been as favourable.

Situation # 3

Mrs. M., who had been in our local hospital, was transferred to a specialist at a larger hospital for treatment of acute pancreatitis. It was a long, hard fight, and she was close to death several times but came through it. Mrs. M. had improved to the point that she was going to be moved to a nursing home. Prior to her illness, Mrs. M. was the *ultimate* volunteer. It appeared that the social worker at the hospital, not knowing how well this woman had been before admission, decided that Mrs. M. would be discharged to a nursing home.

Mrs. M's husband was very upset and came to see if I could have any influence on this decision. I was unable to get the social worker to return my calls, so I called the doctor and requested that he transfer Mrs. M. to our local hospital where she could have rehabilitation. He agreed and told me what I needed to do there to get things set up for her. She spent several weeks in our local hospital, as she fractured a hip and got an infection. She did return home and lived there with help for several more years.

My point in giving these examples is to encourage you to question those things that you instinctively, as a nurse, know are not right. We cannot always have the outcomes we would like, but if we don't try, we will never know. It is very rewarding for both client and nurse, when we are able to dramatically affect an outcome that impacts so significantly on someone's life.

> *Most of the important things in the world have been accomplished by people who have kept on trying when there seemed to be no hope at all.*
>
> Dale Carnegie

Twenty-one

One Model of Intervention

Blessed is the influence of one true loving human soul on another.

George Eliot

How do you offer support and assistance without diminishing a person's power and control over his or her own life? Respecting the limits set by the individual, no matter what potential outcomes you have identified, requires that you not lose sight of your role as parish nurse. The parish nurse cannot operate in *rescue mode*, as people want to be in charge of their own lives. That sounds like basic knowledge but it is very easy, when a person is so needy, to move into the area of *taking over*, rather than *walking alongside*. A question to ask yourself is, "whose need is it?" The mandate of the parish nurse is to assist in developing the *menu* of options available, while helping the person to envision the potential implications of each choice. I am very careful to ensure that the decisions are informed and made by the individual and the family, *not by me.*

Mr. J. was a gentleman with a large tumour surrounding his heart. He had completed the maximum radiation and chemotherapy and still the tumour was causing problems. Mr. J. had been on Morphine for several years when I became involved in his situation. He felt that he was receiving minimal support from his physician and requested my assistance in acquiring another family doctor. Although his wife was a nurse, she, too, had cancer and was going through chemotherapy and radiation. The family was in crisis! The son's reaction to the stress was to become involved in drugs and theft. The young daughter was trying to be caregiver, cook and housekeeper as well as going to school. She was unable to cope with the tremendous responsibility and was caving in under the pressure. She was only 12 years old and could not respond to all the needs of her parents. As a result, the opportunities for intervention were plentiful.

Keeping in mind that parish nursing is a ministry of the whole parish; I developed a plan to involve the parish while maintaining the confidentiality of the family. The daughter was doing her best to make the meals; so, after offering assistance with meals and checking out dietary restrictions, I invited the parishioners to provide meals to be frozen and sent in disposable containers. They were left in the freezer at the church and delivered to the family by the lay visitor, the clergy, or myself. I requested disposable containers as the burden of having to return dishes would take away from the benefit of having the meals provided. Volunteer drivers were recruited to assist with transporting the wife to chemotherapy and radiation appointments and the husband to other tests and treatments. Volunteer teachers from the parish worked with the daughter to help her catch up with her studies. The teachers were stable, caring adults who provided consistent and dependable support for the daughter when her own parents were too ill. Mother Theresa was quoted as saying, "It's not how much you give, but how much love you put into the giving". The parish family responded with a great deal of love and felt good about what it was able to offer to a family in need. The concept of parish nursing as a ministry of the whole parish was exemplified in this instance.

In a situation such as this, the role of the parish nurse is significant, providing the link between the family and the volunteers. When Mr. J. expressed his lack of faith in his family doctor, I was able to have him seen by another physician who provided excellent care and support to the whole family. At Mr. J.'s request, I accompanied him during his visits to the doctor. Firstly, because of his pain and the high doses of analgesics, it was not safe for him to drive. Secondly, he could easily forget what the doctor said, and I was there to help him remember the issues he needed to mention. Before a scheduled appointment, Mr. J. and I met and identified issues needing to be addressed. I always let Mr. J. take the lead in conversation with his doctor. I documented the doctor's recommendations and left a copy with Mr. J. as a reminder. The visiting nurses found it helpful to maintain contact with me as I had been present at the doctor's visit and could support their efforts by helping to fill in gaps with volunteer support.

Mr. J. was a man of deep faith and reading scripture and discussing his faith was important to him. The clergy visited when they were able, but Mr. J. really needed more spiritual support than the clergy and I could provide. A retired man in the parish was asked if he would be able to go in once a week for a period of time to read and discuss scripture with Mr. J. Those visits were rewarding for both Mr. J. and the parishioner.

This family's situation provided a broad range of opportunities for parish nurse and congregational involvement (health teaching, spiritual and emotional support, meal provision, tutoring, and transportation). Throughout this process I worked with the family members to help them meet their goals. People in the congregation lovingly supported this family through practical assistance and prayer.

Core Concepts

- Assess each situation for the potential areas of need, including

- physical, emotional, and spiritual needs.

- Discuss with the family before implementing any new strategies.

- Maintain the confidentiality of the family in the congregation.

- Select volunteers who will be an asset and not be needy themselves.

- Monitor the situation with the family and the volunteers.

In small congregations with limited resources, use your imagination and inventiveness to do your best, but accept the fact that you may not be able to accomplish everything you would like. Focus on what you <u>can</u> do, rather than feeling guilty about what you cannot achieve.

Twenty-two

Teddy Bears (as tools for ministry)

The teddy bear plays a great part in the psychological development of people of all ages over the world. This is because he is a truly international figure that is non-religious and yet is universally recognized as a symbol of love and affection. He represents friendship. He functions as a leavening influence amid the trials and tribulations of life.

Colonel Bob (Robert) Henderson from *Bear Tracks*

I guess I have always loved teddy bears. My mother made bears for each of my children, and they became part of the family and went wherever the children went.

When I set up my office as parish nurse, I placed several of my own teddies around, and people seemed to enjoy seeing them. When I took a teddy to an elderly lady who lived alone, she said it was *silly* but she felt like she had a companion now. I was delighted that the teddy brought her such pleasure. A big bear named Ed sits in a chair in my office. People coming in have a choice of moving Ed out of the chair and putting him on the floor or holding him in their lap as we talk. It is easier sometimes to talk when you have a bear to hug.

My mother loved stuffed animals and when she was ill in hospital, I could always find a little friend for her. Her pleasure from such a simple gesture on my part taught me how comforting a little buddy could be. In her last days, a small monkey hung on her IV pole, keeping watch.

I took a small teddy bear to a man who was in intensive care. He tucked the little creature in his hand under the blanket and seemed very comfortable with it. He kept it by his side and when he was well at home, the little bear was sitting on a table. People don't usually take teddy bears to men!

To another critically ill man, I gave a cuddly blonde dog. He said it was just like one he had owned as a child, and he immediately named it after that dog. Until he was no longer aware of his surroundings, the dog was snuggled in the bed with him. When the man died, his wife took the dog home and sat him in the man's chair so that it wasn't empty. A few years later when I visited the lady in a nursing home, there was the same dog on her bed. He was a comfortable link to her late husband.

I took a wonderful little black and white puppy to one of my favourite ladies who was to undergo major, life-threatening surgery later that day. The puppy was similar to a childhood pet, and she immediately identified with it. We had laughter, tears, and prayers, as we were aware of the risks. When I left the room, the puppy was snuggled in beside her as she remembered the real one of her childhood. It was the last time I saw that lady alive. I took comfort in the fact that we had shared some special time together that day.

When a person is no longer able to live at home and moves to a care facility, a stuffed animal waiting in the room, with a note introducing himself as a friend, can be a true comfort in a time of great emotional upheaval. It is gratifying to contribute in a small way to the solace of another human being.

Some teddies have been returned to me after the people have died. Others I have seen among the flowers at funeral homes. A few have been passed on to grandchildren who have played with Grandpa's teddy after Grandpa was well and teddy's job was finished.

One time I gave a teddy to a man who was very ill with cancer. Since I was going away and didn't expect him be alive when I returned, I wanted him to be reminded that I was thinking of him and praying for him. When he died, his young daughter took over the love and care of Daddy's teddy.

The gift of a teddy bear is not just a simple act of giving a gift. For a teddy to have real meaning there needs to be a connection between the people. The teddy is a visible symbol of love and caring that can be accepted at whatever level the individual needs. It is not about teddy bears. It is about the love and respect of one human being for another.

Part Three:

The Parish Nurse
As Educator

Twenty-three
Educating Self and Others

Nothing in life is to be feared;
It is only to be understood.

Marie Curie

I believe that possessing a natural curiosity and desire for knowledge is vital to being a successful parish nurse. Reading medical newsletters, monitoring societal changes, keeping up to date on spiritual issues, and attending workshops and seminars prepares a parish nurse for providing relevant educational programs. Getting to know the congregation and the community by listening to the people, watching the news, and reading the local papers helps the parish nurse identify common issues and concerns.

Education occurs at many levels. If a parishioner comes in to talk about a personal health issue and doesn't know the implications of a diagnosis or treatment, the parish nurse has an opportunity to alleviate some of the anxieties by determining what level of knowledge the person has and offering resources to further the individual's understanding. I have learned that most people want to understand, as they can face the reality better than worrying about the unknown. It is wise to test that out through general conversation, rather than telling all the truths that an individual is not yet ready to hear. A zealous approach may do more harm than good. I believe that it is a good practice to ask if the person would like more information and then find some appropriate resources.

Increasingly, the internet is a useful tool as long as you gather information from a reliable source. Some of the most useful sites are the ones specific to a disease or condition sponsored by an association for that particular disorder. Some examples are the Multiple Sclerosis Society, Canadian Mental Health Association, and The Parkinson's Foundation. There are often international links that provide a broader background of knowledge for your own education as you search for specific material for your client. It is time-consuming but worthwhile, especially if you *bookmark* the useful sites to shorten your search time when you next need that specific information.

Sometimes a group of people are interested in an educational program consisting of a few sessions. There may be a small number of individuals having specific problems such as parenting issues, aging parents, job loss, retirement, chronic illness, or grief that could benefit from small, supportive, educational programs. A parish nurse with proficiency in the specific area can lead the program or find someone with that expertise if his/her own is lacking. Other members of the staff team may be able to help with a program that is being offered.

When leading a program for adults, I always remind the participants that we all have knowledge that can be helpful to others. While I may be the group facilitator, I do not presume to know it all. Even though I have done reading and research, have organized a program and my thoughts, and have had many years of experience, we all have experiences from which others can learn. The nurse should be open to that learning.

Facilitating a Small Group Effectively Includes:

- identifying the objectives of the program as you see them.

- asking the group whether the objectives are consistent with their expectations and negotiate, if they are not.

- outlining the process you plan to use, and check it out with the group.

- establishing group guidelines (acceptable behaviour, listening to others, mutual respect, confidentiality).

- encouraging the involvement of all members in discussion.

- using different methods and materials to keep the program interesting (videos, quizzes, role-plays and stories).

- evaluating each session and making notes (what worked, what didn't, ideas for another time). You may think that you will remember, but I find it useful to have notes reflecting my thoughts at the time.

- having the group do an evaluation at the end of the program. I usually develop an evaluation form asking what was helpful, what would have been more useful, and so forth.

Successful small group topics I have organized over the years have included Parenting Skills, Networking for Those Who Have Lost Jobs, Growing

Through Our Losses (offered each year), You and Your Aging Relatives, Using Medications Wisely, and Funeral Preplanning.

The Health and Wellness Committee with which I work is part of the healing ministry of the parish, as is the Healing Committee. Each offers an important program, open to the community, once a year. We work together on these programs, one in the spring and the other in the fall.

We developed a joint mission statement to describe our mandate:

To promote wholeness of spirit, mind, and body within the parish and community by providing sacramental, educational, and prayer support, following Christ's example of love and compassion

When the Health and Wellness Committee and the Parish Nurse plan a program, we identify topics that people may not readily discuss: subjects that relate to a large number of people, issues identified on evaluations from previous workshops, or those frequently mentioned in the media.

Successful Topics from My Practice

- Osteoporosis - with a physician, physiotherapist, and nutritionist

- Living Wills - a three-evening series with a lawyer, physician, and clergy.

- Urinary Incontinence - co-sponsored by The Continence Foundation Of Canada with a

Chief Of Urology from a teaching hospital, and an RN specializing in urology– presented by a urologist, pharmacist, and family physician.

- Stress Reduction Interactive Workshop with Eli Bay

- Breast Self-Examination - registered nurses from the Ontario Breast Screening Program were sponsored by The Canadian Breast Cancer Foundation.

- Get Real: Some Honest Talk about Depression - co-sponsored by the Canadian Mental Health Association of York Region with a speaker from the Mood Disorders Association of Ontario, and a person living with a mood disorder

- Herbal Medicines: Do They Harm or Help? - Presenters included a family physician, and two pharmacists

Some Things I Have Learned

- Be clear about your objectives.

- Make sure that your speakers understand those objectives.

- Be specific about the content and allotted time for speaking, and manage it.

- Target specific groups who might be interested in the topic, as well as the general public, for publicity.

- Encourage those target groups to promote your program.

- As part of your evaluation, ask people to leave their name and address, or preferably email address if they would like to be notified of your next event.

- If a group is co-sponsoring a program, tap into their publicity resources.

- Attempt to obtain coverage by your local cable station.

- Try to find connections with your local newspaper. (If you are not paying for advertising, it is difficult to get more than a public service announcement.)

- Approach the health writers in the larger newspapers (e.g. The Toronto Star).

- Advertise in your church newsletter and weekly bulletins as well as at events in the church.

- If you can find a radio announcer willing to publicize your program, take advantage of that.

- Link with other churches in your community to promote your program and do the same for their programs.

- Have people pre-register so that you have

some idea of how many are coming. Some of those people will not come but others who have not registered will.

- Charge a small entrance fee. It gives the program credibility.

- Rather than paying speakers, we make a donation in their name so that they get a tax receipt, or we make a donation to the organization they represent.

- Connect with the local family physicians and make them aware of the program so they can inform their patients.

- We provide attendees with a folder containing resource material. The folders have labels with the church name and phone number so people remember where they acquired the information.

Please see Chapter 26 on Planning a Major Educational Event.

I believe that if people take the time to learn about their own or their loved one's illness, they can overcome their fear. Using the *ignorance is bliss* method of coping does not alleviate fear and only delays the pain. Facing life's challenges and learning as much as we can helps us to gain understanding, and ultimately, to cope with the realities in a much healthier way.

Twenty-four
Promoting Health

Health is equilibrium;
It is harmony among physical,
mental, spiritual, and community
aspects within every being.
Miriam Dobell Healing Centre

Being healthy is more than being without a physical ailment. The root causes of disease have been identified most frequently as social, economic, and spiritual, as well as biomedical. Worldwide, health is most often an issue of justice, peace, spirituality, and integrity of creation (Caiger, 1997). It is well documented that socio-economic status is an important determinant of health outcomes in Canada; low-income groups are more likely to die of falls, accidents, pneumonia, cirrhosis of the liver, and chronic respiratory illness (Health Canada, 1986). Mental illness, tuberculosis, and high blood pressure occur more often in the low-income groups (Health Canada, 1986).

When we think of illness, we often refer to the physical aspects of illness. Increasingly, medical science is acknowledging that stress and social supports do have an impact on wellness and risk of disease (WHO Bulletin, 2004). Unresolved grief, anger, resentment, and guilt have been found to be suppressants to the body's immune system, while being in harmony with God and your neighbour promotes overall health, even when physical healing is not a possibility (Clinebell, 1991).

Promoting health is a more complex task than just educating people about healthy eating and regular exercise, and involves more than providing print and other resource materials.

The World Health Organization's definition of health promotion is:

> *the process of enabling people to increase control over, and to improve, their health. It represents a mediating strategy between people and their environments, synthesizing personal choice and social responsibility in health to create a healthier future. (WHO, 1986)*

The impetus for personal and societal change should be combined with social policy change, public involvement, and personal commitment. Many successful campaigns have come from the community. One example is *Mothers Against Drunk Driving (MADD)*. This well-established group evolved from families whose children died as a result of drunk drivers. Out of tragedy and loss, parents were motivated to promote a healthier lifestyle where alcohol consumption is concerned. Police have introduced initiatives supporting the aforementioned cause through education, spot checks, and penalties for those convicted of violation of the laws.

The state of wholeness is a dynamic process involving several interdependent aspects of a person's life.

Clinebell Suggests The Following Are Important Areas For Growth Toward Wholeness (1991, p 31)

- Enlivening one's mind

- Revitalizing one's body

- Renewing and enriching one's intimate relationships

- Deepening one's relationship with nature and the biosphere

- Growth in relation to the significant institutions in one's life

- Deepening and vitalizing one's relationship with God

Growth in any one dimension can have an impact on other dimensions. For example, if we focus on revitalizing our bodies, more time will be utilized in that pursuit and thus taken away from other aspects of our lives. For optimum results it is be important to strike a reasonable balance.

Howard Clinebell (1992) believes that love is central to well-being and by developing our unique gifts of body, mind, and spirit throughout our lives, we are better equipped to share that love with others. The late Henri Nouwen (1990) in his writings spoke eloquently about the value of community. He firmly believed that if we could live our lives in communion with God and others, a greater sense of wholeness would be ours. Taking his view another step further means we have to take care of our environment as well, if we truly seek wholeness.

Living as we do in communities and societies, we both contribute to, and are affected by, the social and physical environments we inhabit.

The presence of violence and discrimination in our society is an indicator of a different type of illness that permeates our world. We are beginning to see the impact of environmental pollutants such as nuclear waste, buried landmines, gas emissions, and non-recyclable wastes. A prominent and tragic example is the meltdown of a nuclear reactor in Chernobyl, causing the release of large quantities of radioactive materials. Many people died or became ill as a result of that catastrophe.

Parish Nursing Involves Promoting Health And Well-Being In Numerous Ways:

• One way is by helping congregations to identify areas where they can make a difference in the lives of others.

• A second way is by working with an individual to unearth areas of imbalance and assisting the person to take steps toward restoring equilibrium.

• Another is by gaining support for parishioners' worthy causes that promote the well-being of others.

• Faith communities should address and support the spiritual component of wellness. Individuals frequently crave this element but may not recognize the need, or may see it but may not know how to become spiritually healthy.

• The parish nurse should be able to identify

resources that can potentially assist in achieving spiritual wellness.

Potential ways to assist individuals include:

- discussions with clergy and/or parish nurse.

- joining Bible study groups.

- counselling.

- healing rituals and prayer.

- support groups.

Regular monitoring and checking in with the individual demonstrates that someone does care and is willing to walk alongside, as the person takes charge of re-establishing or developing equilibrium in his or her life.

The congregation in which I have had the privilege of working has been involved in helping single mothers in the community; providing meals for families living in poverty; sponsoring refugee families; assisting with annual Homeless Shelter programs; volunteering with UNICEF; donating money and time to Christmas Assistance programs; and providing food and money to food banks, to give a few examples. A philosophy of caring for self, the earth, and other human beings evolves over time and the parish nurse, in partnership with others, is a catalyst in the process.

Life-changing behaviours take time to develop. I believe that the parish nurse role includes identifying opportunities for people to be exposed to resources that can give them new insights and knowledge, empowering them to be proactive and assertive about expressing their own health care needs.

Successful Health Promotion Programs

- Breast self-examination workshops where women were taught individually how to do these examinations

- Organizing discussions with experts on osteoporosis, urinary incontinence, and prostate health

- Creating awareness about the potential dangers of herbal medicines

- Linking people with support services in the community that help them to stay in their homes

- Sponsoring an audience participation workshop on meditation

- Opening the door to talking about depression by linking with mental health organizations to put on a workshop, and providing opportunities for getting help

These programs were educational, but also gave people a sense of not being alone in their difficulties. Participants seemed most appreciative of learning about where to get help. A parish nurse has the privilege of meeting people wherever they are in their struggles, being a supportive presence, and identifying with them areas of imbalance, as well as prospective lifestyle changes to help improve their health.

An Example From My Practice

A man was caring for an elderly parent living with dementia. When the parent could no longer live at home because of aggressive behaviours and wandering, the son felt so guilty that he visited the parent every day, even though the parent's care had now been assigned to a care facility. The son was having difficulty sleeping and was experiencing headaches and back pain. It was important to help him come to terms with the fact that someone else was responsible for his parent's care, and that he now needed to focus on taking better care of himself. That is not to say that he should abandon his parent but, having been burdened with the parent's care for a long time, it was now important to have a more balanced life. The son needed ongoing support and reassurance to help him work through his guilt, until he came to the realization that his behaviour had to change if he was to remain healthy himself.

A significant role for churches and other faith communities in health promotion today is addressing poverty, promoting justice, and working towards a more healed and healthy world by sharing ideas and resources to encourage self-reliance. The parish nurse can be a leader by creating awareness about these issues and outlining definite ways for people to become involved. I have learned that people are more willing to volunteer when there are clearly defined needs and objectives.

Core Concepts

- Increase your knowledge of the determinants of health, and health promotion.

- Educate your faith community about the multiple factors in well-being.

- Provide opportunities for individuals to adopt behaviours for personal growth.

- Identify specific ways for the congregation to become involved in promoting wellness for themselves and others.

- Encourage people to become leaders in advocacy for improvement in the global issues of poverty, justice, peace, and care of the environment.

Twenty-five

Working With a Health and Wellness Committee

Never doubt that a small group of thoughtful, committed people can change the world. Indeed, it is the only thing that ever has.

Margaret Mead

Currently in most churches a health and wellness committee is formed prior to the hiring of a parish nurse. The committee may operate under a somewhat different name, but the usual protocol is that an interested group of parishioners researches the potential need for a parish nurse.

Once the decision has been made to hire a parish nurse, the committee usually continues to provide support for the nurse on an ongoing basis. Since parish nursing was unknown here when I started, and the church hired me on a three-year contract after I submitted a proposal for a ministry position for a nurse, there was no health and wellness committee in existence then. Over time, as the news of parish nursing in the United States spread into Canada, the concept of a *health cabinet* came to my attention. As the parish had already determined that it was beneficial to have a nurse on staff, the health committee would focus on the support role from the outset.

When advertising for members, I asked for people who understand the importance of caring for the whole person and who would work with me toward bridging the gaps between the segments of our lives. As I was an anomaly in the community, I was pleased when some nurses were interested, and were willing to be available to act as a support for me. In total we had six people on the committee. In the beginning we worked at defining our role and communicating that to the parish.

Our Mandate Includes:

- sponsoring health-related activities through existing structures, such as worship service, church school, and seniors' groups.

- working with the parish nurse to initiate new educational programs, such as blood pressure clinics and nutrition education.

- providing a bulletin board with current, relevant educational information.

- looking at the overall health and *unwellness* of the congregation

- asking people through a survey what they need from us.

- linking with the Healing Committee, coordinating our educational events and supporting each other in them.

- contacting community groups with expertise on requested topics, and inviting them to put on a workshop that would promote healthy practices for the community. An example was linking with a local pharmacy to sponsor a *Using Your Medications Wisely* program.

The Health and Wellness Committee meets about eight times a year and plans a major educational event for each October.

The Healing Committee's focus is anointing, healing services, the prayer chain, and education programs to help people develop a clear understanding of the role of the healing ministry in the church.

Please see Chapter 26 on Planning a Major Educational Event.

Examples of Health and Wellness Committee Activities

- We were concerned about the cleanliness of the nursery used on Sunday mornings, and developed a protocol for maintaining it. Members of the committee keep an eye on it.

- We set up a display center with *Care Notes*, small booklets with information on issues throughout the life span. One member monitors which ones are used most often, and keeps the supply up to date.

- When I began working in partnership with Public Health to help struggling single mothers, the committee assisted and supported me. While maintaining the mothers' confidentiality, the committee members brought in others from the parish to assist with the mothers' needs. Parishioners help with driving to doctor's appointments, as transit costs are high. Clothing, toys, furniture and even housing have been offered. For some of the mothers, this assistance has led to greater independence. Others have not been as successful.

- We learned that people had questions about

appropriate visiting in the hospital. Another concern was how to help a family when someone is critically ill. The committee developed information sheets on these topics, with input from a palliative care nurse.

Please see Appendix Items:
Tips for Visiting a Friend or Family Member in Hospital
Tips for Making Life Easier for Families With Someone Critically Ill at Home or in Hospital

- We were successful in identifying health issues that concerned parishioners, and sponsored small educational events to respond to the needs. One session was with a funeral director where all those awkward, unanswered questions could be asked. At another, mentioned previously, a local pharmacist encouraged people to go through their medications and take the out-of-date ones to him for disposal. Blood pressure clinics on a Sunday morning gave people the opportunity to talk with a nurse about their health issues.

The support role of this committee is an important one. The committee's collective wisdom has helped me clarify next steps in dealing with some difficult situations. We discuss problems and potential options, but I maintain the confidentiality of the people involved.

Twenty-six

Planning Major Educational Events

The wisest mind has something left to learn.

George Santayana

Our major educational events are planned for October each year and over time people have come to anticipate them. The workshops are open to the community, and we encourage parishioners to bring friends and neighbours. Each time we hold an event, we offer the opportunity to be on our mail or email lists and be notified of the topic, time, and date of the next event. We have built up a database that facilitates promoting the events. Choosing the topic for the next educational event is usually started soon after a seminar, as people can make suggestions on the evaluation forms that we use.

Please see Appendix for Program Evaluation Form.

Part of the process for selecting the focus for the next workshop is to see what other organizations are offering, or are *not* offering. In many instances, we have selected topics that are not being talked about in our community, but that we know are issues for people.

Seminars with topics such as: *Dispelling the Myths of Prostate, Who Decides? (Power of Attorney/Living Wills)* and *Urinary Incontinence* have been well attended in spite of the sensitivity of the subject matter. The secret to success is to attract high profile speakers, and our experience has been that if you do not ask them, you don't know what the answer will be. For each of the above topics we invited specialists in our community, and they were pleased to be involved.

We strive for a first-class event and people have come to expect that. We ask people to register in advance so that we have sufficient seating. There are always people who do not come even though they have registered, but the ones who come without registering usually make up for them. We charge a small entrance fee and donate it to the organization represented, in the name of the presenter, so that he/she receives a tax receipt.

We believe that looking professional gives our events credibility. We provide participants with a folder, containing information, paper, and pencils so that they can take notes. We apply a label on the front of the folder, giving the name and phone number of the church in case people want to contact us in the future. The event is a good outreach program for the church to the community.

It is important to begin planning early for where and when you will promote your event. We usually start putting up posters about one month in advance of the workshop. Our posters are on the same paper each year so people recognize them. There are some locations such as other churches, local businesses, shopping malls, hospitals, community centres, and doctors' offices that we usually target.

Depending on the topic, we develop a list of specific areas where there might be some interest. One of our most recent, and certainly our largest, turnouts (200 people) was an interactive relaxation techniques workshop with a recognized presenter. I met a parent who was dealing with an autistic child and was interested in any techniques she could learn to help her manage stress. Following our discussion, she sent an email letter to all the members of her association, and many of those parents came to the workshop. We learned from that experience that if we target groups that could benefit from a particular topic, they might do some publicity for us by informing their members.

We have had some luck with the local cable television channel but planning well ahead of the event is essential, as they may require two weeks notice before they will run an item.

Promoting the event on the church's website can be done even two months in advance, particularly if the event is in the fall. In early September people often plan for commitments ahead of time, as this is when new programs and activities begin. If the organization putting on the workshop has a website, request that they promote your event there. Most are willing to advertise the program, as it looks good for them too.

We contact our personal connections about advertising our event. It's *whom you know* that works sometimes. Church bulletins and newsletters are used, and in surveys we have found that many parishioners have learned about workshops through those venues. We have used short dramas in church to draw an upcoming event to people's attention. For several years we enlisted a couple of characters, *Ned Goodpastor* and *Gertie Whitewig* who, through the use of humour, could promote just about anything. People loved to see what these two characters would dare to say and do.

Ned was one of the ministers and *Gertie* was the parish nurse.

Getting local newspapers to promote an event has been a frustrating experience. Because a church does not have great amounts of money for advertising, we can usually only get a public service announcement (PSA). The PSA's are usually just two or three lines in a narrow column. We have been successful on some occasions in having a health writer for one of the larger papers do an article, if there is a catch-phrase they can pick up on. Urinary incontinence fascinated them and they printed a story.

Organizations employing nurses and personal support workers may be interested in certain topics that could increase their knowledge. One example was the prostate awareness event. A workshop on depression and mood disorders attracted a diverse group of people for whom this was a significant area of concern. With each topic there are interest groups, and it is important to identify those groups. Some topics will count for professional credits, so it is good to be aware of that and be prepared to sign for those who can use them.

One workshop, *Herbal Medicines: Do They Harm or Help?* was fairly controversial, but people were interested in hearing the debates. We invited a family physician and two pharmacists to be presenters. A few people from health food stores challenged some of the statements made by the presenters. Our purpose for having this workshop was to create awareness that there are risks in using herbal medicines. If they are effective, they can also have side effects.

There are more parish nurses now, so there are opportunities to partner with others for joint events. A recent workshop on depression was so successful that two other groups held similar events in different locations. A group of nurses sharing the parish nursing position in another church in our community was one of those groups. One of our objectives was to get people talking about mood disorders to attempt to reduce the stigma. Having other groups run similar programs was more success than we anticipated.

It is rewarding to attract significant numbers of people who increase their knowledge and develop more skills for managing their own health care. Being in tune with the issues with which people grapple is the key to attendance.

Core Concepts

- Be aware of the current *hot* issues for people.

- *Wh*en promoting an event, have particular interest groups in mind and inform them.

- Notify the general population, as you will not know who might have an interest in the topic.

- Book your speakers early, and check in with them from time to time to confirm their commitment.

- Create your advertising materials in advance, with the locations for their placement pre-determined.

- Ask parish members who work in locations you want to target to place posters there for you.

- Use whatever connections you have to get the word out.

- Pre-registration gives you an idea of how many people will attend.

We have learned that people feel that they are taking charge of their lives when they attend workshops and gain knowledge. Making it easy for people to learn is a great service to the church and the community. Offering rides for those who cannot come on their own is an even greater service and encourages people to help others attend.

Part Four:

Cultivating Solutions For Human Challenges

Twenty-seven

Families:
An Overview

It appears that the family unit continues to be important in Canadian society.

Reginald Bibby

The Vanier Institute of the Family Defines Family As:

Any combination of two or more persons who are bound together over time by ties of mutual consent, birth and/or adoption or placement and who, together, assume responsibilities for variant combinations of some of the following:

- Physical maintenance and care of group members

- Addition of new members through procreation or adoption

- Socialization of children

- Social control of members

- Production, consumption, distribution of goods and services

- Affective nurturance – love (Vanier Institute, 2005).

> *What cannot be achieved in one lifetime will happen when one lifetime is joined to another.*

Rabbi Harold Kushner

A study commissioned by the Vanier Institute of the Family outlines the findings from *The Future Families Project: A Survey of Canadian Hopes and Dreams in 2003,* conducted by Dr. Reginald Bibby (Bibby, 2004).

Four Key Findings of This Survey

1. Family continues to be highly valued by Canadians. Family is experienced in many ways, but almost everyone sees it as essential. If we look at the majority of Canadians, we see that our partners, children, parents, siblings, grandparents, and other relatives really do matter to us.

2. Our hopes and dreams are fairly traditional. According to the study, which may seem to contradict what we believe we are seeing, the vast majority of Canadians do want to marry and have children, to be good parents and to have lasting relationships, to care for aging parents and be cared for in later years, if that proves to be needed. Ninety percent of teenagers have these same traditional aspirations.

3. In spite of the traditional ideal, the reality is that things do not always work out as planned. Unexpected events occur; people change or disappear from our lives; money, and the time required to earn it create circumstances that may be problematic. What seemed to be a reasonable goal may become elusive. Nineteen percent of all participants in the *Future Families* survey have been either separated or divorced at some point. That number rises to 25% when considering those aged 35 to 55 years. Even with those statistics, people go on remarrying, thus creating families with new sib-

lings, mothers or fathers, stepchildren, numerous in-laws, and grandparents.

4. Some people choose to experience family life in non-traditional ways. Some make a conscious decision to live together, but not marry. Children may or may not be part of that choice. Some people may choose to raise a child alone without marriage or a relationship. Sizeable numbers of people are opting for same-sex partnerships. A relatively small number of Canadians distance themselves from families and choose to have no contact with them.

There can be no vulnerability without risk; There can be no community without vulnerability; There can be no peace, and ultimately no life, without community.

M. Scott Peck

Implications for Churches and Parish Nurses

This is an important study for churches and parish nurses, as the general consensus is that people desire, and cherish relationships that for many are unattainable. That means many people are hurting because of broken dreams, shattered partnerships, societal ostracism, and estranged family members. Traditionally, churches have provided a sense of community that many people have been seeking. When parish nurses assess their congregations, they should be mindful of the opportunities to initiate support groups and information sessions to enhance the lives of members who are living with emotional and spiritual pain. It may well be beneficial to work with the clergy to offer worship services and/or Bible studies in response to identified needs.

Social support offered by friends and/or family groups has been shown to have a positive effect on people's perception of illness and their ability to cope with it (Justice, 1987). Justice suggests that the quality of our relationships may have more to do with how often we get sick and how soon we get well than our diet, environment, genes, or chemistry. A famous nine-year study by Berkman & Syme (as cited in Justice, 1987) showed that people in California with close ties, (e.g. those being with marriage partners, close friends, or membership in church or other groups) had lower mortality rates than those with poor social ties.

Parish nurses have a significant role to play in promoting family health by offering education and support to families of all types. While there are common factors associated with family strife, it is important to remember that each situation is unique. Nurses who have had many years in the profession may begin to feel that situations are the same as others they have seen. While there may be similarities, it is more likely that nurses have learned numerous strategies through experience that enable them to be competent in a variety of situations.

Please see Chapter 14 on Assisting with Decision Making.

Twenty-eight
Families
With Children

The need to find meaning...is as real as the need for trust and for love, for relations with other human beings.

Margaret Mead

Families with children have numerous challenges in today's world. In many instances, both parents are working outside the home. If either parent's job requires travelling, coordination of before and after-school childcare can seem overwhelming. Families with sufficient resources to hire a nanny must then deal with employment issues. Families with limited resources have to examine the economics of having one parent stay at home to care for the children, rather than paying for daycare. Driving children to hockey, dance, soccer, music lessons, and other activities intensifies the job of organization. Is it any wonder that stress levels are so high in families today?

There is no shortage of resources available to assist parish nurses in their ministry with families. While each province in Canada will have its own programs, I expect that there are consistent themes. In Ontario, the *Healthy Babies, Healthy Children Program* is a network of prevention and intervention services for families (Government of Ontario, 2001). There is recognition that early childhood experiences have a critical and long-term effect on healthy development. The program offers screening, information, and referral to all families. Municipal public health units work with community based resources in partnership with Ministry of Community and Social Services, and Ministry of Health and Long-Term Care. Families with children from prenatal to six years are linked to the most appropriate resources. It is important for parish nurses to increase their knowledge of local services and have that information readily available. When families approach the church for assistance, their needs are usually immediate.

The Health Behaviour In School Aged Children Survey (HBSC)

This survey is carried out every four years in Canada by the Social Program Evaluation Group at Queen's University, in conjunction with Health Canada (Public Health Assoc. of Canada [PHAC], Division of Childhood and Adolescence). It is sponsored by the World Health Organization and includes research from 35 countries in Europe and North America. The 2001-2002 survey uses Health Canada's population health framework and examines the broad sets of determinants of health, and health behaviours in children and youth. More than 7000 students aged 11, 13, and 15 (considered to be representative of the critical ages for early adolescent development) were selected from across Canada. The main purpose of the study is to look at patterns of health behaviours and trends. Some areas examined are socio-economic inequalities, the home, the peer group, the school experience, youth health risk behaviours, emotional health, bullying and fighting, and injuries. The information gathered every four years is valuable for parish nurses as it identifies issues of importance for education, support, and guidance. A parish nurse who keeps up to date on current issues and challenges can focus articles, newsletter reports, and education programs for families based on the most recent concerns. Getting parents and children together to hear each other's feelings can provide a tremendous service to families in the parish and the community. Parents may not take the time, or are not comfortable expressing their love for their children. Asking the children what love means and how love can be expressed opens avenues for discussion. Outside speakers with expertise in specific areas will enhance the nurse's efforts.

Family Meetings

Some families are willing to work at learning better ways to talk to their children. In raising my own children, we held regular family meetings where all members had a turn at chairing the meeting, and all members had input to the agenda. It may not have been perfect but it was an attempt to listen to our children.

The Canadian Mental Health Association Guidelines For Family Meetings (Tammet, 2001)

- Schedule regular meetings

- Keep meeting short

- Have and follow an agenda

- Eliminate distractions (e.g., phone)

- Make sure the focus is positive

- Be clear, especially when setting timelines

- Be consistent

- Treat everyone with respect and make sure each person has an equal say (but parents have veto power for harmful / unhealthy decisions)

- Ensure that nobody becomes a scapegoat.

- Evaluate decisions at the next meeting

- Remember to plan for fun!

Parish nurses can organize workshops to help parents get started with family meetings. There may be members in the parish that can assist in developing and running the program. Role-playing can help parents see how children might feel intimidated in certain situations. It is helpful to have input from parents prior to the workshop, so that the nurse has an opportunity to develop role-plays that relate to expressed issues and concerns. Working in pairs or small groups and then presenting to the whole group is sometimes an effective way to have all involved without too much discomfort.

Suggested Topics Are:

- Bullying – either dealing with a child who is bullying a sibling or another child, or strategies for helping a child who is being bullied

- Household responsibilities, and debates about who should do what

- Homework schedules and play time – how to negotiate those

- Fears –ways to provide a safe environment where fears can be expressed and not ridiculed

- Communication strategies – asking children what works for them

- Finding appropriate ways for younger children to articulate their concerns

- Curfews, and appropriate parameters (e.g. how far can they go on their bikes?)

- Computer guidelines, electronic games, television time etc. (I used TV tickets for my children. They were issued in 15 and 30-minute denominations. We negotiated a suitable number of hours per week and the children paid as they watched. They learned to plan, budget, and negotiate for more time on special occasions).

In a group, the leader sets the tone for the workshop and should involve everyone in setting the guidelines for acceptable behaviours in the group. I attempt to create a non-threatening environment. It is helpful to have prepared an outline for the workshop and be willing to stray a little from that outline if *burning issues* arise. I suggest alternative ways to address the burning issues and then resume the approved agenda. I use scenarios or case studies to help people see how it feels for others in similar situations. This allows for a variety of suggested solutions, while giving people the opportunity to form and evaluate their own views.

One issue that is mentioned frequently is the inability to be consistent. A healthy discussion around this topic can be fruitful. The parish nurse, or any other leader, is not expected to have all the answers. Collectively, the group can usually come up with some healthy strategies for becoming more consistent. Children need to know that rules and boundaries are important and dependable, and not created on the spur of the moment. Children should trust their parents and their decision-making. Loving parents that spend time with their children and show unfailing parental love through the child's lifetime will instil a sense of self-worth and value in their children. A child's fear of abandonment is lessened by regular participation of parents in the child's life (Peck, 1978). Children need to feel a sense of security. It is important to create awareness of children's fear of abandonment.

> *We are what we repeatedly do. Excellence, then, is not an act, but a habit.*
>
> Aristotle

Children, truly, are gifts from God, and the church has a responsibility to be involved in supporting the parents, as they strive to build strong, healthy families. Some parents may struggle to encourage values and beliefs consistent with the teachings of the Bible because the more immediate issues of providing food and shelter are overriding. In any case, the faith community and the parish nurse should uphold all families. The nurse can be a role model, capitalizing on opportunities to interact with the children in the parish and to reinforce healthy ways of living.

Twenty-nine
Families
With Teens

The world is passing through troublesome times.
The young people of today think of nothing but themselves.
They have no reverence for parents or old age.
They are impatient of all restraint: they talk as if they alone know everything.

Matthew Paris, 13th century

While parents and teens face tremendous pressures today, the quotation from Matthew Paris in the 13th century indicates that there were challenges even then. Yes, some issues are similar today, but there are additional ones to be addressed as well.

Some of Today's Significant Challenges

- Single parent families
- Blended families
- Newcomers from another culture
- Children with special needs
- Influence of peer group
- Drugs and alcohol
- Gangs, runaways
- Greater pressures to succeed
- Poverty
- Teen depression and suicide
- Questions and struggles about sexual orientation
- School dropouts
- Eating disorders

What Are the Biggest Risks Facing Teens Today?

The biggest risk facing teens today is drinking and driving (Ferguson, 2000). Along with substance abuse, a major risk is suicide (Ferguson, 2000). The media contributes to *sensationalizing* violence, tragedies, and suicides, and broadcasts them worldwide, which has been known to produce a "clustering phenomenon" (Korenblum, 2000, p.9). These events can affect adults in similar ways, but young people are still establishing friendship patterns. Teens are more likely to become depressed and/or suicidal; as it seems that "the whole web feels fragile" (Korenblum, 2000, p.9). Teens are more vulnerable than adults to identification and imitation when faced with these tragedies.

According to Korenblum (2000), adolescents are old enough to understand the media manipulation, but fragile enough to buy into their advertisements. The pencil thin, attractive female models and the muscular, handsome males (often airbrushed to create those images) are very high and unhealthy objectives that some teens attempt to emulate. When these goals are unachievable, teens become ill, develop eating disorders, and feel that they are worthless. When these struggles become the focus of their lives, school grades drop, and teens look for other ways to *feel good*. Drugs, alcohol, and aggressive behaviours can begin to enter teens' lives as their self-esteem tumbles.

What Do Teens Need to be Healthy and Well Adjusted?

Recent research shows that we need to focus on building the strengths that promote healthy living and success in learning (McCreary Centre Society, 2004). We should help adolescents develop healthy relationships (starting at home) and learn coping skills and responsible behaviours. The importance of education should be stressed, but parents, extended family, teachers, and the community ought to be part of creating the healthy environments in which learning can take place. Environments where families are living in poverty, where there is anger and discord, crowding and chaos are not conducive to learning. A recent school-based study in British Columbia revealed that adolescents with strong family connections are more likely to rate their health as good to excellent, are less likely to smoke cigarettes or marijuana, drink alcohol, and get into fights. Those teens experience less emotional stress and are less likely to consider suicide (McCreary Centre Society, 2004).

A 1996 study of 2600 Saskatchewan youths dealt with attitudes and behaviours toward issues of well-being and high-risk behaviours. This study found that there was a negative correlation between high-risk sexual behaviours and satisfactory attachments to family, school, and friends (Health Canada, 1999).

Gabor Maté (2004), a Vancouver physician and author of *Hold On To Your Kids: Why Parents Matter,* strongly suggests that the increasing violence and frustration being demonstrated by youth is the result of something that is missing in their lives. A Vancouver developmental psychologist, Gordon Neufeld, agrees that teens are turning to their peers, not adults, for satisfaction of their emotional needs. He calls this *peer-orientation*. Dr. Neufeld states "peer orientation is the result of unprecedented social breakdown: the erosion of the attachment nexus in which child development ought to take place" (Neufeld, Globe and Mail, 2004, as cited in Maté). He suggests that the extended family is often separated, geographically or emotionally, and that the nuclear family is under economic pressures, as shown by the high divorce rates. Into this void steps the peer group, with devastating results. Dr. Neufeld asserts, "kids were never meant to nurture one another or to be role models to one another. They are not up to the task"(Neufeld, Globe and Mail, 2004 as cited in Maté). Children relying on one another are frustrated and in order to be accepted, they have to be "cool" (Maté, Globe and Mail, 2004). To be cool is to shut down emotions, or at least pretend to shut down. Maté believes that the façade of being cool disguises fear and dissatisfaction, and frightened children are masquerading as self-sufficient adults. Those young people, because of high levels of frustration and feelings of vulnerability, are more likely to strike out in rage at others. They may harm themselves because they are "so emotionally benumbed" that they want to feel something (Maté, Globe and Mail, 2004). It appears that unless adults reconnect with young people, these youth will continue to rely on their peer group, and the anger and pain will continue.

What Do Parents Need?

Information, Support, and Guidance

Parents may need to learn about normal development of adolescents and about some of the risks facing teens today. Clear and concise information about drug and alcohol use, tobacco, depression, suicide, and sexuality gives parents some insight into the teens' struggles (Health Canada, 1999). Other topics may include self-esteem, eating disorders, and bullying.

To help parents understand the causes of the risky behaviours exhibited by some young people, the importance of spending time guiding and supporting children throughout their lifetime should be reinforced with parents of young children.

For new Canadians, the conflicts faced by their young people in trying to fit into a new country, while struggling to maintain their cultural heritage, ought to be addressed in ways that facilitate the parents and young people hearing one another. The parents and grandparents frequently find it difficult to understand and accept the young people's cultural values shifting from traditional to those of the dominant culture. Parish nurses can link with families, schools, and community agencies to share knowledge of the available resources for teens and their families.

Positive Interventions by Parish Nurses Can Include:

- offering space at a church for community groups to run educational and/or support programs for youth.

- connecting with respected leaders representing the cultural mix of the community to begin to determine ways to help the young people *straddle* the cultures.

- identifying strategies and programs to help parents and grandparents understand and accommodate the young people's changing values.

- getting to know the children in church school and spending time with them.

- working with the youth and taking part in some of their activities.

- inviting students to drop in for a chat.

- working with youth groups on self-image; helping them see that God loves them all, no matter how they look.

- showing the love of God to troubled youth by building a trusting relationship.

- listening to young people and encouraging them to follow their dreams.

- working with other staff to start a *coffee house* drop-in at the church, with responsible adults in attendance.

Positive Experiences From My Practice

Example # 1

A physical education teacher from a local high school invited me to work with some students who were interested in learning more about older people. It gave me an opportunity to get to know the students as a group, and as individuals. We talked about how they could make a positive contribution to the community by visiting an isolated person. Each student met with an older adult four times. I accompanied each one on the first visit. The feedback from the students, the teacher, and the older people confirmed the value of the experience. The seniors enjoyed the interaction and felt that they were adding something to the youths' development. The students had the undivided attention of an adult other than family members. Several long-lasting relationships developed beyond the required assignments.

Example # 2

I was asked to meet with several groups of Girl Guides, Cubs, and public school classes to talk about ways that students could help older people, and the benefits of spending time with seniors, family members, friends, or neighbours. We had good discussions and I listened to their ideas, questions, and concerns. I helped them understand the value of older people by using a 100-year-old book as a starting point, and demonstrating that even though the book showed signs of its age, it still contained all the information. We talked about the cover being a bit ragged and some of the pages being well used, but the worth was still there. We compared the merits of the book to the value of older people. The young people were excited about how they could learn from the seniors and in the process enhance the lives of older people. Some learned to knit. Others learned about the history of our community. One young lad who had escaped from a war-torn country learned how to play cards. I believe that in a small way I contributed to the self-esteem of those children as they developed a new appreciation for older people.

Strategies For Helping Families

Parents need to learn appropriate strategies and skills to enable them to deal with the issues of schoolwork, peer relationships, family relationships, and responsibilities (Health Canada, 1999). It is important to help families learn new ways to talk with their teens, and ways to create an environment where teens feel safe and accepted. Helping families set up mutually agreeable systems of actions and appropriate consequences can alter families' ways of being.

A 1993 survey sponsored by the Canadian Psychiatric Association (*Youth Mental Health and Illness Survey*) revealed that youth identified the following stressors as being important:

- Parents (80 %)
- Drugs and alcohol (65.8 %)
- Poverty (64.2%)
- Peer issues (61.7 %).

When asked to whom they would turn for help in coping with such stressors, the number one source of support identified by youth was a friend (86 %) with family coming a distant second at (50 %).

Parish nurses can work with agencies and organizations to offer programs in effective communication, problem solving, appropriate behaviours and dress, anger management, and self-esteem. In order to encourage teens to attend programs like these, they may have to be offered at a coffee house or a youth centre. Adults have to meet the teens where they are, rather than counting on them to come. Nurses can work with youth and youth leaders in the church to reach young people. It takes time for mutual respect to be earned and developed.

In order for changes to be made, families require ongoing support and encouragement, not just a single educational event. Factors other than those discussed above can surface and have an impact on strategies that seemed to be working. Parents may become discouraged and have their confidence shaken when their teens become uncooperative and argumentative. When parents feel inadequate, their authority can be undermined, and they will be less effective (Health Canada, 1999).

Parents struggling with difficult issues may approach parish nurses for assistance. It may be appropriate to suggest a meeting with other parents having similar worries. The nurse should become familiar with community resources so that parents can be made aware of them as well. The role of the parish nurse may be as a referral source in some situations. Learning about effective support groups, videos, books, and reputable web sites may be a more comfortable option for some parents and teens. The parish nurse must set limits on what he/she attempts, as the role will have more demands than can be filled by one individual. Health Committees can assist the nurse by investigating community resources.

What Must Parents, Family, Church, School, And Community Do To Develop Better Relationships With Their Teens?

- Listen and be interested

- Be available

- Create positive family communication

- Work at developing balance at home

- Spend time with teens

- Discover ways to help teens succeed at school

- Involve young people in decision-making

- Have clear rules and consequences, and follow them consistently

- Expect students to do well

- Provide responsible role models

- Promote cooperation over competition

- Value their opinions

- Find opportunities to model the acceptance of differences

- Learn how to strike a balance between freedom and responsibility

- Hold nurturing of children as the highest value.

Adults may feel that they do not have a place in a teenager's life, but positive adult-youth relationships in family, school, church, and the community will help young people learn the skills needed to be healthy. Parents should remember to pray for strength and guidance when choosing approaches for enhancing the lives of teens. Ongoing respect and encouragement help young people to develop a sense of hope, belonging, and optimism.

Trust in the Lord, with all your heart.
Never rely on what you think you know.
Remember the Lord in everything you do,
And He will show you the way.

Proverbs 3: 5, 6

Thirty

Adults – Singles and Couples

To mature is in part to realize that while complete intimacy and omniscience and power cannot be had, self-transcendence, growth and closeness to others are nevertheless within one's reach.

Sissela Bok

Congregations are usually made up of people of all ages. I have discussed families with children, and families with teens, but there are many people who do not fit into those categories. Adults can be young, single, and growing in their faith. They can be young couples without children. Adults may be living in same sex relationships. They may be *empty nesters* whose children have grown and moved away. Adults can be older, single, and happy, or may be older, single, and lonely. They may be middle-aged couples who seem to have no purpose in life. They may have joined a church to build friendships. Others may have lots of friends but feel a need to give something back to society. Some adults are so needy that the church is a refuge where they feel accepted. There are as many reasons why people join churches, as there are types of adults.

The observation skills of a parish nurse are useful in detecting what people are seeking from a church, and also what they are able to contribute. The offering of skills and talents should never be ignored as individuals may have mustered up their courage to offer. It is a real tragedy to have the offer of a gift declined or, even worse, ignored.

It is important to determine which people want to be involved but may be too shy to offer, versus those who just want to attend on a Sunday and choose to have no further involvement. These people do not want to be asked repeatedly to become involved in other areas of the church. Having said that, part of being members of the church is living out their faith in some way. They may do this in the community rather than in the church, for example serving as a hospice volunteer or giving time to *Habitat for Humanity* programs. As the parish nurse becomes more familiar with the congregation, opportunities to inquire about a person's well-being will be more honestly addressed, once people sense that they will be heard.

Human beings are generally seeking to be cared for and appreciated, respected and welcomed, recognized for their abilities, and accepted by their peers. Once the basic needs of food, shelter, and safety are satisfied, people's growth and development depends on those other factors (Maslow, 1962). Enlisting the help of the pastoral team and the health committee, the nurse can find meaningful ways for people to use their talents.

In our congregation, when two or three with similar needs or skills are identified, we look for significant ways for those people to be connected and encouraged to use their skills and talents. An example is the formation of a gardening committee by people with gardening knowledge, some of whom live in apartments and love to garden. The church property has been beautified, and the gardening committee has become a cohesive group who enjoy planning for further enhancements to the property. New members and ideas are welcomed. People can also contribute funds to buy a tree or shrub to celebrate an event, or in memory of a loved one, even if they choose not to garden. Singles and couples can all be involved.

If there are newly retired people who are a

bit uncertain about how they might help, inviting them to come together for coffee and a chat may uncover ideas to benefit the group and the church. We have a group of men who enjoy getting together to do some painting inside our church building. They take coffee breaks, with cookies provided, and lots of laughter is evident.

Clubs and groups with a specific focus can be offered if there are some adults who have shown an interest. Many adults today are seeking to have short term commitments (Putnam, 2000), so being a member of a prayer chain, or assisting at a coffee hour three or four times a year may be just the right amount of commitment.

A perceptive parish nurse can thoughtfully probe, if there is a sense that an adult is struggling. When asked, "How are you doing?" most people will answer "Fine." I have found that people, when asked again, "How are you, really?" will more often tell you what is actually troubling them. If the concern is beyond the realm of the parish nurse, that person can be referred to clergy or another appropriate resource.

Lay pastoral visiting has proven to be an excellent way to connect people. I have frequently heard from the visitors that they have gained so much more than they have given. Two lonely or isolated people can be connected in this way, but the parish nurse must ensure a good match for maximum benefit. Developing a telephone link when neither is able to leave home can bring joy back into a lonely person's life.

For More on Lay Pastoral Visiting Please See Chapter 35.

The parish nurse is an integral part of ministry to and with adults, but should not be expected to be the sole person responsible. Larger congregations may have a volunteer coordinator with whom the clergy and parish nurse interface. In smaller congregations the nurse and pastor may be the initial contacts, but others need to be involved in working with new volunteers.

The Parish Nursing Ministry With Adults Involves:

- revealing opportunities for individuals to grow and deepen their faith.

- helping adults find ways to demonstrate the love of God to others.

- developing opportunities for adults to help carry the burden of others.

- showing adults how a deeper meaning of life can be made known to them through commitment and service.

> *Life is a succession of lessons,*
> *which must be lived to be understood.*
>
> Helen Keller

Thirty-one
Older Adults

Age is opportunity no less
Than youth itself, though in
another dress,
And as the evening twilight
fades away
The sky is filled with stars
invisible by day.

Henry Wadsworth Longfellow

Older adults have much untapped wisdom and knowledge that can enhance their own lives and the lives of others. In many cases people do not recognize the significance of their experience because society generally focuses on youth. As we age, we look back on times when our bodies were more attractive, our physical abilities were better, fulfilment of dreams was ahead of us, and we had the ideals of those lacking much life experience.

Many people fear being old, facing the physical decline that is a normal part of aging. In spite of the increasing numbers of older people in our population and more active older folks, it is the frail, lonely, and infirm image of the elderly that is often in the forefront of people's minds. That is what most people fear. It is true that there are people for whom the aging process is difficult and unpleasant, but there are many more where that is not the case. Our attitude toward life throughout our existence influences how we handle the adversities that can occur at any age.

Researching Aging And Health

Increasingly, research is confirming the connection between the physical, emotional, and spiritual health of individuals. At the Centre for Mindfulness in Medicine, Health Care, and Society (University of Massachusetts Medical School), Saki Santorelli and Jon Kabat-Zinn have incorporated *mindfulness meditation* into medicine and health care for the past twenty-five years (Santorelli,

2000). Referring physicians in the specialties of cardiovascular medicine, orthopaedics, and internal medicine give credit to the practice of mindfulness as a significant factor in the improvement of pain, stress, and hypertension in their patients (Kabat-Zinn, 1991). Ayurvedic medicine, one of the oldest medical systems in the world, has been practiced in India for 4,000 years. This sophisticated, holistic system integrates the balance of spirit, body, and mind (Fontaine, 2000). Anger, sorrow, joy, fear, and rumination have been identified as key influences in health status in Chinese Medicine for centuries (Beinfield & Korngold, 1991). Modern medicine has been slower to recognize the significance of the person as a whole being and not just a body with an affliction.

Healing of past emotional wounds can result in improved spiritual and physical health. People *can* choose to confront those painful events and leave that ache behind. When a parish nurse meets someone who is ready to tackle those issues, recommending an appropriate professional may encourage that person to take the first difficult steps. It is important to remember that for today's elderly, talking about their problems, *airing their dirty laundry,* was not proper. Burdens were to be borne in silence. The nurse can encourage these individuals to accept that there is no shame in sharing their stories with a trusted professional. It is appropriate to offer prayer support and to leave the door open for further discussion if the person desires.

> *Even though our outer nature is wasting*
> *away, our inner nature is being renewed*
> *day by day*
>
> 2 Corinthians 4:16

We have heard the myth that *you can't teach an old dog new tricks.* I don't know about the old dog, but certainly older people can learn. An 88-year-old lady to whom I was teaching flower arranging, said, excited with her newfound skills, "I guess I can still learn new things at my age!" Motivation and opportunities for learning are key components for persuading older adults to embark on developing new skills. Churches can sponsor activities and provide access for older people who have no transportation, encouraging them to become involved. Younger seniors can assist older ones by driving, assisting with shopping, or ordinary tasks like replacing burnt-out light bulbs, and through these activities, new friendships may develop. Everyone benefits! The older person's self-esteem improves, as there are opportunities to participate in activities, albeit with assistance. The younger senior feels good about making a difference in someone's life, and the concept of parish nursing is surreptitiously spreading through the parish. Through these processes, the parish nurse involves more people in caring for others. It is vital for the helper to be mindful of the feelings of the person being helped. The helper should focus on the capabilities of the other person, not the frailties.

The church has a significant role to play in supporting the health and wellness of older adults, particularly with the increasing demands and diminishing resources available to sustain the growing numbers of elderly. Friendships develop through church involvement, and friendships are different from family relationships as they are voluntary. Friendships are usually based on common interests and mutual affection and, because they involve giving as well as receiving, they boost our self-esteem. These relationships remind us that we are useful and worthwhile.

Parish nurses assisting older people are helping people of all ages. Older people benefit when opportunities for ministry, volunteering, gaining access to needed services, and connecting with others to reduce isolation are available. Families and friends can enjoy their lives when these folks are taking charge of their own lives, assisted and supported by a parish nurse and the church family. Empowered older persons begin to recognize their own value and, with increased self-worth, contribute to the well-being of others around them. The challenge for the parish nurse is to identify isolated people and encourage them to discover ways to improve their lives. I recently heard of a program that utilizes the knitting skills of many older people. Wool and a pattern are provided and people can knit as much of a *prayer shawl* as they wish, and then pass it on to another knitter. The idea is that the knitter prays while knitting. Upon completion, the shawls are given to children at their confirmation or to people who will benefit from receiving them.

Myths Of Aging

Myth: Older people today have less contact
            with their families than older people in
            the past.

Reality: In past generations it was common to
            have two or three generations living
            together. While that is less apparent
            today, older people do have consider-
            able contact with their family members
            (Novak, 1997a). Generally older people
            do not choose to live with their adult
            children, but those family members are
            involved in their lives. There is often
            reciprocal visiting and helping out in
            times of need (Atchley, 1980).

Myth: Most old people live in institutions.

Reality: Only a small percentage of older peo-
            ple live in institutions. According to
            the 1996 census, looking at people 65
            years and older, less than 10% require
            institutional care. It is important to re-
            member that there can be 30 or more
            years' difference in age in the cohort
            we call seniors. People at 95 are usual-
            ly very different than those at 65, and
            their needs are more diverse (Novak,
            1997a).

Myth: In general, most old people are alike.

Reality: Nothing could be further from the
            truth. A group of five year olds are

much more alike than a group of eighty year olds. The vast number of experiences accumulated over a lifetime has a dramatic influence on the personality, behaviours, and attitudes of people as they age (McPherson, 1983). At five, children's experiences are limited and thus their opportunities to develop in different ways are limited. Historically, older people have been viewed as a group, and often treated the same. That trend is changing as the numbers of older people increase in relation to the population (McPherson, 1983.

A challenge for congregations wanting to involve older people is to create opportunities to become acquainted and listen to their ideas.

Encouraging The Participation Of Older Persons

- Invite small groups to have tea with the minister and the nurse, providing drives for those needing them.

- Sponsor a coffee hour or luncheon on a regular basis after a mid-week worship service and encourage people to bring their friends.

- Host *daytime* educational programs of interest to older people, as many prefer to stay in at night.

- Organize an every-member visitation with a well-planned questionnaire to gain some understanding of the needs of older people (and the whole congregation).

- Send out questionnaires in the church news-letter requesting input from all ages and outline specific areas for each age group.

- Encourage families and friends of older people to accompany them to events at the church and to introduce them to the minister and the nurse.

When the needs and desires of the older members have been identified, the parish nurse, along with the ministry team and the governing body, should set realistic priorities about how the church can meet some of the needs. Other organizations in the community may already have some of the areas covered, and the nurse's role may be to connect people to the existing services. It is important to remember that the needs of older people are not distinctly different from those of other age groups. An ongoing growth in spiritual life, with opportunities for worship and prayer, discipleship and mission are relevant at all ages.

> *He who is of a calm and happy nature*
> *will hardly feel the pressure of age,*
> *but to him who is of opposite disposition*
> *youth and age are equally a burden.*
>
> Plato (c 427-347 BC).

Rapid changes in the way health care is delivered and the different expectations of patients, compared to the time when people relinquished decision making to their doctors, can be confusing and overwhelming for older people. The parish nurse can help guide people through the maze of the health care system.

The grief and losses accumulated over a long lifetime can become overpowering with the death of a spouse or close friend, a health crisis, or other significant change in a person's life. The feelings of powerlessness and lack of control in a rapidly changing world can be precipitating factors in the isolation of frail elderly people. The parish nurse can assist in these situations by encouraging others to become involved. Younger seniors can reach out to the older ones; young people can visit and help with odd jobs; families can *adopt* an older person and include that person in family events. Events at the church often need greeters or people to take tickets and older people can be invited to fill these roles.

Human connection is vital for all people; without it we become detached and lonely, making us less able to relate to other people. Our own problems become our whole focus, and life ceases to have meaning. This is not how God intended that we live. Older people can be part of a prayer team. Praying for others is something that people can participate in at any age. Being part of a team offering prayer for others includes isolated people in the ministry of the church. Older people can be invited to participate in a telephone ministry, where contacting another person to check on the well-being of that person usually benefits both people.

Sharing Wisdom Between Generations By:

- telling their stories of another era to children and youth.

- teaching a church school class with another person.

- becoming a member of the prayer chain.

- joining church committees.

- reading lessons in church.

- participating in the *shoebox program*, an international program that fills shoeboxes for Christmas with gifts for children in underprivileged countries.

- taking part in Remembrance Day programs with young people.

Developing Activities To Encourage Involvement

- Run social programs like the *Tuesday Group.*

  Please see Chapter 54 for more on the Tuesday Group

- Offer educational programs during the day, on subjects such as safety, using medications wisely, and meeting with a funeral director to ask questions.

- Link older people with others of similar age and interests.

- Make connections with community youth groups wanting to volunteer with older people. Girl Guides and Scouts without grandparents in their lives are carefully screened, as are the adults, to promote safe and healthy experiences for all.

As we age and our physical bodies slow us down, we can use our accumulated knowledge for the benefit of others. The parish nurse can tap into this pool of wisdom and increase support for ministry. Understanding of the needs of older people is gained by speaking with those people. When we call upon older people and seek their advice or counsel, we are acknowledging their worth. Each person, no matter what age, is a child of God. Each person has something to offer that will be of benefit to another human being. Our task, as parish nurses is to get past the *outer shell that is wasting away* and draw out the *inner nature that is being renewed day by day.*

Thirty-two

Family
Conferences

To observe without distortion is only possible if there is complete attention with your body, your nerves, your mind, your heart, your ears. Then you will see, if you so attend, that there is no entity or being called the observer. Then there is only attention.

J. Krishnamurti

When the parish nurse is working with families with considerable challenges and several family members with differing views, bringing everyone together can be a useful strategy. Some situations become so complicated that it makes sense to get all the players together in order to insure that all are on the same page and that each person hears the other. If everything is on the table and all are part of the process, the anxiety level is greatly reduced. Using an appropriate model (e.g. McGill Model of Nursing) as cited by Clark and Olson (2002), the parish nurse should work collaboratively with the client and family while raising awareness of the issues and coaching them in the resolution of the problems. The nurse provides resources, helps the family focus on the issues and supports them in the negotiations of compromise and solution.

The need for a family conference usually becomes apparent when there is one member, often a parent, whose health status has changed or is declining. Family members become concerned about the parent's safety and believe that moving the parent to a care facility is the way to reduce risk. In most cases the parent resists moving and does not want to leave home. If the parish nurse calls the meeting or is invited to participate in it, there must be clarity about the objectives for the meeting. If the desired outcome is *to get Mom to agree to go to a nursing home*, the parish nurse has a responsibility to assist the parent and family members to set an agenda that is focused more on looking at all options, rather than coercing the parent into complying with the family's wishes. I have learned that family members often have different agendas, so the parish nurse should speak to each member prior to the meeting and determine where the conflicts exist. The nurse can develop a plan to allow each person to be heard and can, in knowing where the conflicts are, be prepared to defuse them. I find it constructive to propose guidelines for behaviour at the beginning of a meeting and gain agreement from all.

Suggested Meeting Guidelines

- Each person will have an opportunity to speak.

- Each person's view will be heard without interruption or debate.

- Each person will be treated with respect and dignity.

- The parish nurse's role should be clarified and supported.

- The parish nurse can take the leadership role, as it is advantageous to have a skilled facilitator who is once removed from the family. The parish nurse has to remain neutral in the discussion, while identifying potential positive and negative outcomes.

Some Points To Consider When Planning A Family Conference

- Who should be in attendance?

- Based on the objectives, should there be any other professionals present (e.g. physician, case manager)?

- If there are family members who have an interest but cannot be present, how can their voices be heard?

How Can The Parish Nurse Contribute To The Family Conference?

- The parish nurse should be prepared with information about potential options and the possible implications of each one.

- The nurse should listen and feed back what she believes she is hearing. This helps everyone determine if the family is moving forward.

- The nurse should inquire if there is any way she can be of assistance when the family comes to a decision. One example is *would it be helpful if I made that contact or referral for you?*

As an advocate for the client

- The nurse should inquire as to how the older person feels about the discussion and the decisions being considered. It is critical to know the client's objectives for the meeting, before the meeting.

- The nurse ought to ensure that the older person's voice is heard as a parent can feel powerless seeing that the adult children want something different from what he/she would choose.

A Family Conference Example From My Practice

The family of Mr. and Mrs. J. was concerned about the elderly parents' ability to remain in their own home any longer. At the time of the meeting, Mr. J. was in hospital and was not well enough to return home. He was quite elderly and was clear mentally, but his diabetes was out of control. He had had several automobile accidents in a short period of time, and the doctor had requested that the Ministry of Transport suspend his license to drive. Mrs. J. was having some memory problems, so there were concerns about her safety at home alone if Mr. J. was not able to return.

The family consisted of two married sons, both living in the community and a daughter living elsewhere. The sons were having difficulty accepting the fact that their father might not be able to come home and wanted to try to keep their mother at home. The sons were quite attentive to the parents, but most often the daughters-in-law were the ones who responded to the requests for help. The daughter wanted her mother to stay at home, but she was unable to be of much help, as she did not live in the community and had many problems of her own.

The sons and daughter were adamant that they wanted to keep their mother at home. The daughters-in-law, both nurses, were concerned that, even though they could provide support, they both had full-time jobs and would not be available all the time. They were able to predict more easily the challenges ahead of them. The elderly parent clearly wanted to stay in her home.

I have learned that in most situations, changes have to be made in stages. At the beginning the discussion was centred on the premise that the father would come home from the hospital. The parents would not have transportation, as the father could no longer drive. The family members decided that they would explore the possibilities for driving and focused on that as being a big issue. It was of course an immediate concern, but the bigger one was the mother's safety, particularly if the father did not return home.

I believed that the family needed to address the longer-term issues, so suggested that they work together to develop a plan for the future. None of the blood relatives was prepared to entertain the idea of placement in a care facility at that point. With my input on available community support resources, the family decided that a personal alarm system would make sense and the mother agreed to that. I gave the family information on other available services for help in the home, volunteer driving, and social opportunities. I asked the mother if she would like to have a lay pastoral visitor from the church. She decided that she would like that as she wanted to have more connection with the church. The lay pastoral visitor could take her to church for services and social events but more importantly, could be an attentive listener.

I helped the family make connections with the appropriate services. For about a year, the mother was able to manage and the family provided support to fill the gaps. The father did not return home but was admitted to a care facility and died within a few months. The mother's health declined. When there was a vacancy in the nursing home, family members were exhausted and were able to see that their mother would benefit from being in a long-term care facility. While the parent wanted to stay at home, she realized that the family and community resources could no longer meet her needs.

The positive outcomes indicated in this situation are not always the norm. This family had no ulterior motives. Their concerns were for their parents, and they were respectful and inclusive in their dealings with them. The family needed to try some options to keep the mother at home but, having done that, were prepared to move to a different level of care when the existing one was no longer appropriate. I recognize that sometimes families need to attempt to care for the parent at home as long as possible. I *walk alongside* and support them when they request assistance. I also check on the older person to see how he/she is coping. If I have concerns, I discuss them with the individual and, with the client's permission, confer with the family. It is important to remember that the parish nurse's role is one of support to the individual and the family. Keep all interactions transparent and do not be put in the position of taking on some of the decision-making.

There are situations where an adult child, living near the elderly parent is judged and chastised by one or more siblings living a long distance away. Resolution under these conditions can be much more difficult, and the parent may be caught in the middle. I have found that families with considerable conflict are not interested in participating in a family conference. In situations such as this, the role of the parish nurse is one of support to the older person and to the adult child who is involved in the care giving. If mediation is required, a person trained in that area should be contacted.

There are times when the parish nurse can anticipate some of the problems that the family will face and may be able to help them avoid common pitfalls. The nurse needs to listen carefully and try to assess the emotional status of all the family members. Giving family members an opportunity to state their feelings and concerns about the decisions they have made prevents *behind the scene rumblings* that can cause people, already under stress, to crumble. Attending to the older person's wishes and assisting the family to carry out those wishes empowers the older person and enhances self-esteem.

Please See Chapter 14 on Assisting With Making Decisions.

Thirty-three
Support For Extended Families

No great thing is created suddenly.
Epictetus

When a relative (often an adult child) of a parishioner with whom you have been working comes in from out of town, the parish nurse may be seen as a threat, an angel, or anything in between. I have experienced a broad range of reactions from family members. It is understandable that a person living far away from an ailing relative may feel threatened when a parish nurse is assisting in areas where the relative feels he/she should be involved. Some relatives are anxious and fearful. Others are suspicious. A greater number (especially adult children) are grateful that someone is helping his or her parents.

A parish nurse should look beyond the relative's sometimes bewildering behaviours while trying to identify what is behind them. We don't know what relationship existed between the relative and the client. The association may have been tenuous at the best of times, so there may be resentment because of the need to be involved at all. As part of the assessment process, it is important to identify the health issue from the family member's perspective, and place it in the context of the whole family. Interviewing skills are required to discover the physical, emotional, social, and spiritual components of the situation (Clark & Olson, 2000).

Transparency is essential so that the relative understands the parish nurse is not making decisions but is merely supporting the person who is making decisions. I meet with the adult child or relative in the presence of the person needing assistance, so that *all the cards are on the table*.

In some instances, the behaviour of the relative is the result of the stress of care-giving responsibilities. I try to focus on the recent concerns while acknowledging the historical issues.

Examples From My Practice

Situation # 1

An elderly, unmarried woman was living alone, with no family except a sister living a long distance away, and a niece in fairly close proximity. Friends of Ms. A. approached me with concern about this woman's well-being and asked me to become involved. I had had previous contact with Ms. A. and had visited in her home, so my asking to visit was not an unusual occurrence. I noted that the woman's health status had deteriorated significantly since my previous visit. I learned that the woman's doctor had referred her to a neurologist. A friend was taking her to see the specialist, so I asked permission to call following the appointment. A few days later Ms. A. had a dreadful seizure while in her home. When a friend found her, she called the ambulance to take Ms. A. to hospital. The woman's friend contacted me, and I went to visit Ms. A. in hospital. Tests indicated a brain tumour, and, needless to say, Ms. A. was frightened.

Ms. A.'s niece, a young married woman with two small children and a full-time job, called me in a panic about her aunt. She cared deeply about her aunt, but was overwhelmed with the prospects facing her. She interrogated me about what she should do, what was I going to do, and where was she going *to put* her aunt. She fought with the doctors and criticized the nursing staff. This young woman was overwhelmed and fearful; she lashed out at everyone. She was suspicious of me until she realized that my role was one of support. I explained to her that I did have knowledge of how the health care system works and was available to speak with her as needed. The niece visited as often as she could, and tried to get her aunt moved to a hospital closer to her. The *red tape* involved proved to be more than she could handle. We talked about the possibility of having her aunt moved to a nearby hospice when the palliative care placement in hospital did not come to fruition.

Ms. A's condition deteriorated quite rapidly, as the brain tumour was malignant and inoperable. By this time, the niece was appreciative of my knowledge of the health care field and of my assistance in trying to have her aunt moved. Finally all systems were in place for Ms. A. to be transferred to a hospice near the niece. Ms. A. died the night before her transfer. Ms. A's niece had done all she could to make her aunt's last days the best they could be, but felt that she had failed. Some follow up discussions with the niece helped her to realize that she had done all that could be done for her aunt.

It is important to *stay the course* in the early stages of a relationship with a family member, as the initial reactions of a person are often not representative of how that person usually behaves. This young woman put forth an incredible effort on behalf of her aunt, and I was privileged to have gained her trust.

Situation # 2

Ms. B. was a woman in her 70's who seemed much older than her years. She resided in a seniors' complex, on her own, after her partner died. Her only sibling, a sister, had died, and she was alone except for a nephew who visited occasionally. Ms. B.'s sister had adopted a daughter who had been estranged from the family for many years. When Ms. B.'s partner died, the adopted niece reappeared. She claimed that she was interested in supporting her aunt and did visit occasionally. Ms. B. had a lay pastoral visitor who helped her with shopping and general organization of her life. The visitor took her to church, and made me aware of her diminishing capabilities. Ms. B. was suffering tremendous guilt because she had been unable to care for her partner at home. Ms. B's partner was placed in a care facility, where she died. Ms. B's grief and self-blame could have explained some of her decline, and we worked with that. She seemed to be coming to terms with her pain and guilt about her partner's last days, but, increasingly, Ms. B. was appearing more confused and disoriented. She was not paying her bills and neither was her niece even though she had appointed the niece as her substitute decision maker.

The manager of the seniors' complex could not get Ms. B.'s niece to return her calls. She did not return calls from the family doctor either. Here was a woman whose condition was deteriorating, and the person with power of attorney would not respond! The family doctor called me to see if I could accompany Ms. B. to an appointment with a neurologist. She wanted to ensure that Ms. B. got there. The niece was furious when she heard that I was taking Ms. B. to the doctor. She and her brother, who had not been adopted by Ms. B.'s sister, and so was not a relative, insisted on taking Ms. B. to the appointments for the diagnostic tests. Ms. B. asked me to go with her to the follow-up appointment with the doctor, as she would be getting the test results and wanted my help in interpreting them.

It was obvious that Ms. B. was not capable of making good decisions. Her niece had power of attorney, but was inconsistent and unreliable in dealing with her aunt. The niece's brother took over and did his best to alienate the lay pastoral visitor, the visiting nurse, the administrator at the residence, and me. We did not know what was motivating this man, but we could only do our best to protect Ms. B., as she was unable to protect herself.

Ms. B. was diagnosed with hydrocephalus and had a shunt put in; it blocked and was redone twice. When the shunt was working, Ms. B. was more alert and aware of her surroundings. When the shunt became blocked, Ms. B. became very confused. The niece and her brother decided to move Ms. B. to a nursing home near them, but too far for the church to maintain contact with her. This saddened all who were supporting her but, in the end, we had no power or authority to change anything. We kept Ms. B. in our prayers and hoped that she was receiving appropriate care.

The majority of parishioners' family members welcome the support and knowledge I can offer. It takes time to gain the respect and trust of family members, and listening to their stories is a good beginning for developing that relationship. I believe that relatives of parishioners often need as much support as the parishioner, and parish nurses have a true opportunity for outreach to the relatives, while exemplifying the ministry of the church. It may take time to build that trust but, once achieved, all benefit. Sometimes though, as depicted in Example 2, the outcome is not what the nurse would have wished. Even then, the nurse can feel satisfied that all that could be done was done.

Thirty-four

Offering Support in the Wider Community

We stand in life at midnight;
We are always at the threshold of
a new dawn.

Martin Luther King Jr.

Participating in the wider community beyond the nurse's own church demonstrates to the world the special role that a parish nurse can have. Sharing the resources ecumenically strengthens the whole community. Over the years, numerous opportunities have presented themselves, with positive outcomes.

In the very early stages of my ministry, as people were just beginning to see and understand the potential of the role, the Ministerial Association, consisting of the local clergy, benefited by the contacts and expertise I was developing. In discussion at our ministerial meetings, I became aware that clergy were ill equipped to deal effectively with people with significant mental illness. All had stories of situations where they felt uncomfortable, as they lacked the knowledge or training to deal effectively with, for example, a person living with schizophrenia. As I had been working with a family struggling with the illness, I identified some potentially useful resources. I invited a person from the *Friends of Schizophrenics* to speak at our meeting. Questions were answered and strategies were developed on how to be effective in different situations.

Another speaker came from a local agency dealing with women who had been harmed by their partners. Her visit provided the clergy with some new resources to use when faced with a woman in an abusive situation. Sharing your knowledge of neighbourhood resources with other religious communities expands the benefits of your ministry.

Outreach by the parish nurse can take many different forms. A secondary school teacher who had some students interested in learning about older people approached me. The students were to visit with these people and provide assistance as deemed necessary by the older person. The tasks ranged from just visiting to playing cards and listening to stories. My role was to speak to the group at the school to suggest ways to work with older people, prepare them for some of the situations they might encounter, and then to help them establish learning goals.

I interviewed the students and matched them with an older person with whom there were common links. I attended the first meeting and introduced the older person to the student. Three more visits were to follow. The older people shared stories and the younger people learned that increasing age did not mean that people could not have fulfilling lives. Interestingly, the majority of students participating in the project were male. The feedback was upbeat, and in some cases new friendships were formed and maintained. The seniors felt that they were still useful and could contribute something to the development of young people.

The influence of each human being on others in this life is a kind of immortality.

John Quincy Adams (1767-1848)

Girl Guides and Brownies participated in other activities with older people from our parish. The girls made cookies and cards to take to the people they visited. This activity resulted in first-rate experiences for all involved. An ancient Chinese proverb states "it is only good when the old and young respect each other", and these tasks, though time consuming, did contribute to developing that respect.

Any time a parish nurse is involved in setting up one-on-one encounters, it is critical that the nurse know the parties well, and/or has a good reference from a reliable source. The new guidelines for screening volunteers in the church provide some protection, but when students are coming from outside the church, the nurse must feel confident that vulnerable people are not being put at risk. I always have a responsible, trusted adult attend the initial meeting to assess the situation. It is also important to ensure safety for the students by carefully selecting appropriate people for them to visit.

Increasing awareness of barriers encountered by people with disabilities is essential, in my opinion. A government program entitled *Through Other Eyes* (OCSA, 1974-2004) was designed to help able-bodied people gain insight into what it is like to live with some of these disabilities. Donning goggles, rubber gloves, weights on ankles, earplugs, and using a cane, participants (clergy, staff, lay pastoral visitors) were given a list of tasks to accomplish in different businesses in our community. A local bank opened in the evening and provided staff to work in their specific roles to provide *real life* conditions. The managers of a grocery store and a drug store participated by attempting to complete the tasks in their own stores in order to experience the challenges for people with disabilities. Other customers in the shop took an interest in the project and offered assistance to participants who were having difficulty completing some tasks. The media covered the event and unquestionably the outcome resulted in increased awareness. Following the debriefing, each establishment received a list of barriers encountered and some changes were made.

I am always pleased to speak to another church that is considering initiating a Parish Nursing ministry. An anonymous quote states that "footprints on the sands of time are never made by sitting down" and this is so true. I love creating scenarios identifying the endless possibilities and configurations that might work for another church's setting. It gives me great pleasure when I feel that I may be witnessing a burgeoning new ministry. Sometimes people just need to hear various things than can, and do work, and they are then inspired to envision the possibilities for themselves.

In the current climate with increasing pressures on the health care system, the presence of a parish nurse becomes an even greater asset in a community. By helping ministers with health related issues, increasing the awareness of barriers to accessibility, providing educational workshops open to the community, and sowing *the parish nursing seeds* in other churches, the parish nurse can have influence in empowering people to take charge of their own health care.

Part Five:

Lay Pastoral Visiting

Thirty-five

The Visiting Program

I was sick and you visited me.
Truly, I say to you, as you did it to
one of the least of these who are
members of my family, you did
it to me.

Matthew 25: 36, 40

Lay pastoral visiting is a ministry by lay people showing the love of God to the ill, grieving, lonely, and homebound members of the parish family. A lay pastoral visitor must understand that the purpose of a visit to a parishioner is to listen with empathy, love, and acceptance. Carl Jung, the German psychiatrist, once stated that everyone wants to tell his or her story and have it accepted. Lay pastoral visitors are in a position to offer that gift of listening and acceptance. Listening is not always easy, as one has to set aside one's own needs and attend to the person being visited. The visitor may experience a profound sense of helplessness when hearing the pain and suffering of another person. It is a natural human instinct to want to fix whatever is amiss, but that is beyond the mandate of the lay visitor role.

When an individual feels called to the ministry of visiting, that person is agreeing to be a companion to a fellow pilgrim on the journey to wholeness. Lay pastoral visiting can be thought of as a ministry of mutuality, as each person has the potential for being transformed by the encounter. Thomas Hart suggests that the purpose for visiting others is to listen, to love, to be a companion, and to be oneself (Hart, 1980). Being oneself means being authentic and true to one's own values. Because of their own *woundedness*, as described by Henri Nouwen (1990) in his book *The Wounded Healer,* lay pastoral visitors fulfil an important role in the ministry of the church.

Visits may be made in a person's home, in hospital, a nursing home, or even the local coffee shop, if that works. The guidelines for visiting may differ slightly according to the venue, but the guiding principles are the same.

Goals and Objectives of Lay Pastoral Visiting Include:

- showing the love of God to another person.

- developing a friendship with an isolated, ill, or lonely person.

- emphasizing the intrinsic worth of the individual, as a child of God.

- reconnecting the person with the church and the outside world.

- sharing thoughts and feelings.

- promoting emotional and spiritual health.

- encouraging people to share their stories.

- listening to a person's stories with empathy.

- bringing some joy into a person's life.

- assisting people in accepting life's challenges.

- finding ways to boost a person's self esteem by focusing on his/her strengths.

- being with people in their pain instead of avoiding it.

People of all ages can be trained to be effective lay pastoral visitors. There are various ways that lay pastoral visiting can be carried out. In my practice there have been times where lay pastoral visitors have become unwell, but not so ill that they are unable to contribute. When I have assigned a visitor for that person, the visitor and the person being visited (the former visitor) minister to one another. The more experienced visitor, even though he/she is unwell, has the opportunity to mentor the less experienced one. In one particular situation, the visitor became too ill to visit in person, so they visited over the phone. Having had the face-to-face experience, they could picture one another as they enjoyed their phone calls. Genuine friendship and concern for one another was evident, when I spoke with each person.

In some situations, it may not appear as if ministry is taking place. For example, a male visitor regularly played cribbage with Ed, an avid player. How does playing cribbage fit in with the lay pastoral visitor mandate? The activity demonstrated that someone did care about Ed as an individual, and it brought joy into this isolated man's life. Ed was becoming more disabled with Parkinson's disease and was experiencing extreme side effects of the medication. Imagine having someone come to visit and play a game with you when you are used to aversion or pity caused by your distorted, uncontrolled body movements. The visitor was able to show the love of God by being there, and the two men enjoyed some good times together. There were conversations about what was going on at the church, so Ed was still being connected to the congregation. A genuine caring relationship developed because of the skills of the lay pastoral visitor, who attempted to make each encounter a positive experience and helped to make God's presence a reality for Ed.

I was sick and you visited me...

Essential Skills And Qualities Of Lay Pastoral Visitors

- Having a genuine interest in, and love for, other people

- Being able to maintain confidentiality

- Possessing good listening skills

- Being accepting of people and their situations

- Having some life experience from which there has been learning

- Respecting someone's home or personal space

- Being able to resist the desire *to rescue*

- Recognizing that people compromised by illness, grief, and isolation still have a need for friendship, empathy, and assurance of God's love

- Maintaining a cheerful and positive attitude

- Demonstrating the ability to show patience

- Having a sense of humour

- Being willing to learn and grow

Lay pastoral visiting is of benefit to those visited and also to those who visit. Visitors help by keeping people connected to the church and the outside world and, in the process, they become more caring and understanding, and sensitive to people's needs (Peel, 2000).

Thirty-six

The Role of the Parish Nurse

Before you speak, it is necessary to listen,
For God speaks in the silence of your heart.

Mother Theresa

Lay visiting programs may have been in existence in a church long before a parish nurse is hired. The team of visitors may feel threatened when a new parish nurse has been assigned to oversee this area of ministry. I have known of numerous conflicts in many churches because members believed that the parish nurse was going to *take over* their ministry. The best approach is to be open and direct with the visitors, affirming their ministry as valid and worthy, while demonstrating that you are open to learning from them. A prudent parish nurse will seek to understand how the lay pastoral visitor team functions and, over time, when the confidence and respect of the team has been gained, suggest alternatives to the existing program, as needed.

Lay pastoral visiting is not for everyone. Careful screening and training are essential, as the people being visited are usually vulnerable. Sometimes people want to be visitors but their reasons for wanting to visit sick, elderly, or isolated individuals may not be appropriate. It is the responsibility of the pastoral team to ensure that its screening process is focused on identifying suitable people for this role. Currently, in most churches, an official screening process is undertaken for all staff and volunteers. This may include a police check and contacting references supplied by the individual. This screening does not determine whether a person would be an effective lay pastoral visitor, only whether that person is considered *safe* to be a volunteer in any capacity in the church.

In my practice, on occasion I encourage people to explore other areas of ministry, when it becomes apparent that their attitudes or intentions are incompatible with lay pastoral visiting. I am sensitive to their feelings and propose ministry areas that would make better use of their particular gifts and skills. All prospective visitors are invited to attend the monthly educational and support meetings. This provides me with an opportunity to observe them and gives the individual a chance to listen to the experiences of other visitors. In keeping with nursing ethics, we protect the privacy of people being visited by discussing only the issues, not the people (CNO, 2004).

I encourage parish nurses who are responsible for recruiting and training lay pastoral visitors to be careful when selecting people for visiting.

Be Vigilant When Individuals Are People Who:

- exhibit an excessive need to be needed.

- believe that they are *good at cheering people up.*

- Think that if a person is ill, he or she must have *sinned* or is *weak in faith.*

- demonstrate an inability to be a reflective, empathetic listener.

- assume that they have the answers to people's problems.

- show signs of emotional or mental instabil-
  ity.

- are new parishioners who want to get involved in everything at once.

- show an unwillingness to reflect upon, and
  grow in their spiritual life.

An Example From My Practice

A young mother with two small children and no access to a car expressed an interest in being a lay pastoral visitor. I did not know this woman but suggested that she attend our next education/support meeting. When she did attend, she took issue with much of the content that I was discussing with the visitors. She claimed that her professional background gave her the knowledge to challenge what I had carefully researched for that meeting. I thanked her for her input and carried on, in spite of her attempts to discredit me.

At the end of a frustrating meeting, I explained that all new visitors are required to participate in a training program. Following that, I select appropriate people for new visitors to meet. After the meeting I suggested that until the next training session, she could benefit from attending our meetings and that her input at our meetings could be helpful. She felt that she did not need training and should be given a person to visit immediately. As she did not have access to a car, she would have to walk to whomever she would visit. When I inquired about her children, she said that one was in nursery school and the other one she would take with her, as older people enjoyed children. I discussed the situation with the clergy and we decided to see what happened at the next lay visitor meeting and one of the clergy would be in attendance. At the next meeting she was very quiet. She did not attend any other meetings so I did not have to express my concerns about her ability to be a good visitor.

My Immediate Concerns Were:

- the degree of anger she displayed.

- her belief that she did not require training.

- her lack of judgement in thinking it would be beneficial to take a toddler to visit an older person, without considering the needs of the person she might visit.

- her own need to have a *grandmother*, as hers had died recently.

I did make a follow up phone call, but she had decided that she really didn't think that visiting was for her. (I mentioned that we offered a grief education and support group that might help her to work through her grief). In many cases people come to the decision themselves, and I can then recommend other areas of ministry that they might enjoy.

When a person exhibits an approach such as this, it is important to listen and try to determine what is really going on behind the smokescreen.

In this instance, her grief over her grandmother's death had clouded her judgement. Her aggressive behaviour was, in fact, a cry for help. Upon further discussion with this young woman, I learned that there were several issues in her life. I recommended that she talk to one of the ministers and helped set that up. This example is only one of many similar cries for help. Some needy people have very low self-esteem and just require some validation. In pastoral meetings I express my concerns, and as a team we develop strategies to locate the help they require.

The recruitment, screening, and training of lay pastoral visitors require good evaluation and teaching skills. The pastoral team and other experienced visitors can offer many insights, and should be involved in the education of new visitors. Recruiting volunteers for long-term visiting and requiring their attendance at training and support sessions is becoming very difficult. People's lives are too busy and few want to be committed for extended periods. This problem is occurring in many areas of North American society, as discussed by Robert Putnam (2000) in his book *Bowling Alone.* Putnam concludes that television, urban sprawl (resulting in longer commuting times), and pressures of time and money account for only one half of the reasons for "civic disengagement." (Putnam, 2000, p.247) The biggest reason is "generational change – the slow, steady, and ineluctable replacement of the long civic generation by their less involved children and grandchildren" (Putnam, 2000, p. 283). To accommodate for the declining interest in volunteering, I have modified the visiting program by requesting help for shorter periods, and contacting the visitors for feedback on their visits. People are more comfortable having a shorter commitment with a foreseeable conclusion.

Lay pastoral visiting is a valuable ministry in the church, and parish nurses must be willing to adapt and modify programs in order to respond to the changes occurring around them. Paying attention to the feedback from lay pastoral visitors will help to ensure that this ministry carries on, even if it happens in different but equally significant ways.

Thirty-seven

Challenges and Pitfalls

I am not afraid of storms for I am learning how to sail my ship.

Louisa May Alcott

Little Women (1868)

Visiting sick, homebound, or isolated people appears, on the surface, to be a simple, straightforward activity, but it is amazing how many complexities can occur. My purposes in writing this chapter are to create awareness of those complexities and, hopefully, to assist parish nurses in preventing similar situations from occurring.

In the beginning, I was naïve in thinking that I didn't need to find the right match of personalities to create meaningful relationships. It was surprising too, as I had been a lay pastoral visitor and had been exposed to a system where I was advised by telephone to contact a lady who was in the end stage of cancer. I was intimidated, nervous, and probably quite ineffective as a telephone visitor.

To have a successful lay visiting program, the parish nurse should meet with the client to be visited, to ensure that he or she does want to have a visitor. Sometimes other parishioners say that a certain person wants to have a visitor. I always arrange a visit to check it out. While getting to know the person, I explain how the lay visiting program works. I use an intake sheet so that I can remember details when I am considering an appropriate visitor. It is worthwhile making a connection with that person, as there may be opportunity to assist at a later time. I try to choose a visitor who shares common interests with the client, and who can be an effective liaison with the church. If I follow my instinct, the match usually works very well; if I have any doubts, frequently there are problems. The visitor may well lose interest, or the client makes excuses in order to avoid having a visitor. It is crucial that neither the visitor nor the client feel like a failure when this happens. I meet with each separately and talk about the fact that there are times when relationships do not work out.

Please See Appendix for Lay Pastoral Visitor Intake Forms.

Please See Appendix for Client Intake Forms for Lay Pastoral Visiting.

Examples From My Practice

Situation # 1

In one situation, the client and the visitor enjoyed each other's company so much that the visitor became over-involved in the client's life, to the detriment of her own health. The client was in need, and the visitor wanted to be a helper. The two elderly women became very close friends. I expressed concern to the visitor that she needed to set limits on her time and energy, but she seemed unable to do it. The client's increasing needs were far beyond the scope of a lay pastoral visitor. I sought advice from the pastoral team, and we worked with the visitor and the client's family to resolve an unhealthy arrangement. The visitor understood what needed to happen; she just didn't know how to let go. From the above example I learned that careful monitoring, particularly in the beginning, is essential. Both client and visitor are aware that I check in with the other party. Misunderstanding is reduced through honesty and transparency.

Situation # 2

I have worked with lay pastoral visitors who have difficulty showing empathy toward a client. In one instance, the visitor was having difficulty being non-judgemental. The visitor was not privy to confidential information that would have helped him understand certain behaviours. He learned to accept things as they were and a healthy relationship developed. The visitor demonstrated considerable personal growth through this experience.

Situation # 3

There was one relationship where a client with an alcohol addiction requested repeatedly that the visitor drive him to a liquor store. The visitor was uncomfortable with this request and came to talk to me. I spoke to the client about his request being inappropriate and suggested that it would be better if he made alternate arrangements. We spoke about his difficulty with the addiction, and whether he was prepared to seek help. He was not, but that was his choice. Once we dealt with that issue, the relationship worked well.

Situation # 4

A woman agreed to visit another woman who was in long term care. The visitor was keen to meet the client, but when I accompanied her on her first visit, she seemed very uncomfortable. We kept the visit short and I suggested to the visitor that we go out for a coffee. During our chat, the visitor said that she would be unable to visit that woman because it was a painful reminder of her own mother and what she had endured. The visitor thought she had dealt with her grief over her mother, but found that when she was in a similar environment, the memories came flooding back. We agreed that visiting someone living in her own home would be more comfortable.

In most churches today, people are screened for being *safe* to work (paid or volunteer) in the church. They are not being screened for abilities or interests. It is important to interview a prospective visitor, as a person may not have the proper attitude or aptitude for the role of lay pastoral visitor.

Please See Chapter 35 on The Visiting Program.

Suggestions For Improving Lay Visiting Programs Include:

- interviewing the potential visitor.

- getting to know the client.

- explaining the guidelines for the program to the visitor and the client.

- ensuring that visitors are well trained.

- choosing appropriate matches for visitor and client.

- accompanying the visitor to the first meeting with the client.

- monitoring newly matched situations closely.

- keeping an eye on all visitor/client relationships.

- intervening in unhealthy situations.

- providing ongoing education and support for visitors.

Lay pastoral care is a valuable ministry in the church. Caring for one another is inherent in the concept of parish nursing. There will be times when things do not work out the way they were planned; there are many opportunities for learning, and personal growth. Coordinating a lay pastoral visiting program can be challenging, but with experience a parish nurse begins to recognize the pitfalls and can avoid them.

Thirty-eight
Training the Visitors

One of the best ways to educate our hearts is to look at our interaction with other people, because our relationships with others are fundamentally a reflection of our relationship with ourselves.

Stephen R. Covey

When I work with adults in any educational capacity, I assume that each individual has knowledge and experience, and that the purpose of the encounter is to *pool our resources*. As parish nurse, I may have information that is useful to others, but I never presume to have all the answers. I follow the generally accepted principles of adult learning (outlined by Mezirow, as cited in Redman, 1984).

Principles Of Adult Learning

- Make use of each person's experiences
- Seek the participation of all members in setting goals for the group
- Engage all in the learning process, through interaction
- Incorporate participant's goals in the routines
- Use a variety of learning activities (e.g. discussion, group activities)
- Demonstrate practical application of the knowledge through role playing
- Provide opportunities for self-appraisal
- Afford chances for feedback to the instructor

I ask each prospective visitor to fill out a form that provides me with some information on previous education and experience that might be useful in lay pastoral visiting. I enquire as to why each person believes that he or she would be an effective lay pastoral visitor. I request that he/she identify any situations that would be uncomfortable, preferred times for visiting (day, evening, weekend), and what level of commitment is desired.

Please See Appendix For Lay Pastoral Visitor Intake Form.

The training program consists of four, two-hour sessions during either the day or evening, depending on the availability of people. While there are specific topics that I will include in the training, I ask the participants to tell me what topics they feel should be incorporated in the program. I adapt each program according to the interests and skills of the participants. At the beginning I discuss the overall rationale for pastoral care. I use the Gospel of Matthew, chapter 25, starting at verse 35 as a discussion starter for justifying the ministry of visiting:

> *For I was hungry and you gave me food, I was thirsty and you gave me something to drink, I was a stranger and you welcomed me, I was naked and you gave me clothing, I was sick and you took care of me, I was in prison and you visited me. And the king will answer them, 'Truly I tell you, just as you did it to one of the least of these who are members of my family, you did it to me'* (NRSV, p. 29).

Pastoral care should be seen as a mission of the whole congregation. Clinebell (1991) cites a study done by Niebuhr, Williams and Gustafson that concluded the church's unifying goal is its charge to increase the love of God and neighbour among people. In a congregation that has adopted the parish nursing concept, the main objective is to transform the faith community into a source of health and healing (Solari-Twadell, McDermott, Ryan and Djupe, 1994). Another passage from Matthew supports the concept of spirit-centred wholeness:

> You shall love the Lord your God with all your heart, and with all your soul, and with all your mind. This is the greatest and first commandment. And a second is like it: You shall love your neighbour as yourself. On these two commandments hang all the law and the prophets. (Matthew 22:37-40 NRSV, p.25)

Early in the program, I encourage people to reflect upon the skills they already have and to claim those skills as being useful tools for lay pastoral visiting. We acknowledge our strengths and identify areas where we could benefit from more education. Through this process, we develop a course outline.

Communication Skills

Developing excellent listening skills is an important part of lay visitor education. I ask the group to identify the characteristics of a good listener. I record the positive attributes on a flip chart and we discuss the listening skills and *appropriate response* skills. I invite members to partner with another person in the group and try role-playing, using scenarios from my own experience. At first, each pair works together and then communicates the example to the group. We discuss each situation and explore other possible responses. This method of teaching listening skills has been very successful, based on participant feedback.

Communication Questions For Participants To Ask Themselves

- Was I looking at the person who was speaking?

- Was I thinking of something else?

- Was I observing the person's body language?

- Did I interrupt the person to say what I was thinking?

- Did I give advice?

- Was I offering false reassurance?

- Was I making judgements as the person was speaking?

- Did I deny, or argue with what the person was saying?

- Did I check to see if I understood what was being said?

- Did I ask open-ended questions to encourage dialogue?

Please See Chapter 12 on Listening.

Confidentiality

Lay pastoral visitors can only be effective if they gain the trust of the people they visit. To gain that trust, the visitor must respect the privacy and confidentiality of the person. But lay visitors have needs too, and may need to share concerns, fears, anger, and frustrations about their visits. Sharing these emotions helps to put them in perspective. An appropriate place to share is with the members of the visiting team. The person being discussed should remain confidential with just the issue revealed. If a person is uncomfortable discussing his or her emotions with the group, the parish nurse can offer individual support.

How to Visit

An important discussion that should be part of a lay visitor education is one that establishes the guidelines and parameters of the visiting program (what is OK and what is not OK).

Topics To Include

- How often should a person visit?

- How long should a visit last?

- Is it proper to take someone else along on a visit?

- What should topics of conversation include?

- Is it appropriate to accept a gift? *Please See Chapter Eight on Ethics.*

- Is it necessary and/or appropriate to pray with the person being visited?

- How do you gracefully end a visit when it is clear that the person wants you to stay?

- Should you share any of your own problems with the person you are visiting?

Understanding the Aging Process

A large proportion of the people being visited are elderly. They may be living in their own homes or in a care facility, and, while their situations may be different, they may be striving to find meaning in their lives. I usually include a *Facts and Myths of Aging* quiz to start conversation on the topic. It is helpful to have the visitors understand that older people are not all the same; the more life experiences they have, the more different they become.

As people age there can be gradual physical, mental, emotional, and spiritual decline. When the lay pastoral visitor develops a relationship with a person, opportunities for promoting positive approaches to life challenges may arise. Preparing visitors with useful tips and strategies for visiting persons with dementia, depression, grief, and a loss of sense of purpose, increases the visitors' confidence and benefits the persons being visited.

Spiritual Support and Prayer

As lay pastoral visitors are representatives of the church, they must have some comfort in speaking about spiritual issues. Many people are not comfortable in this area, so preparing them and providing some tools to use makes everyone feel better, and can avoid those *uneasy* moments. The clergy can be a great resource. Our minister spends time teaching the components of prayer and we develop prayers together. The advantage is that all contribute their ideas in a non-threatening environment. Having been part of creating prayers for specific purposes, the visitors have a small repertoire upon which to build. A handout with the guidelines serves as a good reminder. It is necessary to discuss with the visitors what to do when they find themselves in situations beyond their scope.

It should be emphasized that lay pastoral visitors must ask if people wish to have prayer. If it is not helpful or comfortable, the visitor may pray for the person after leaving. This is about the client's needs, not the visitor's wishes.

Visiting Difficult Parishioners

It is unrealistic to think that all visits are going to go well, and that all people are going to be a joy to visit. I have found it useful to develop some role-plays with *difficult* parishioner scenarios. While most people are very pleasant, it is wise to be prepared with strategies for tricky situations.

Awareness of Available Services in the Community

While it is not an expectation that a lay pastoral visitor have a solution to every problem, a general knowledge of community resources is beneficial.

Abuse

Abuse of any kind is not pleasant to contemplate, but a lay pastoral visitor should learn to recognize signs of abuse. As a trusted friend from the church, a person might confide in the visitor about something that is happening to him or her. The lay pastoral visitor needs to know what steps are appropriate, depending on the age and mental competence of the person allegedly being abused.

Death and Dying

It is important to have discussions about visiting people with life- threatening illness. Many people are uncomfortable talking about death and dying. A lay pastoral visitor must develop some skills for responding to an individual who wants to talk about his/her impending death.

Rescuing

When a person is having a difficult period in his/her life, most visitors instinctively want to fix the situation. Most people welcome support, but want to solve their own problems. Rescuers may see themselves as saviours, but may make the clients feel diminished; when rescuers are rebuked, they feel hurt. Making use of other options such as listening, supporting, and just being there, create more equality between visitor and client. Enthusiastic visitors may need to have this concept brought to their attention.

A training program cannot provide all the answers for lay pastoral visitors. What it *can* do is teach problem-solving skills that may be applied to many different situations. I make every effort to help visitors increase their self-awareness, while learning new skills, and developing new relationships in the group. I offer challenges to encourage personal growth.

Notes
Barbara Caiger R.N. in her role as parish nurse at Holy Trinity Church in Thornhill, ON developed the outline for this program. It was revised and enhanced by Marg Stanford when training lay pastoral visitors in Holland Deanery. Used with permission.

Part Six:

Family Violence and Emotional Trauma

Thirty-nine

Abuse and Trauma: An Overview

There is a light in this world, a healing spirit more powerful than any darkness we may encounter. We sometimes lose sight of this force when there is suffering, and too much pain. Then suddenly, the spirit will emerge through the lives of ordinary people who hear a call and answer in extraordinary ways.

Mother Theresa

How do we listen to and *really* hear stories of the violent behavior endured by others? The child who was physically and/or sexually abused? The spouse who was beaten? The older person who has been slapped and pushed around? The women who were sexually assaulted? Some violations of our social fabric are too terrible to be spoken aloud. "This is the meaning of the word *unspeakable*" (Herman, 1997, p 1). But these violent crimes do not disappear. Denial does not work! The "lava pit of anger" (Virtue, 1994, ¶ 11) bubbles beneath the surface until erupting in a physical, emotional, or spiritual symptom later in life. And that is not all! Traumatized individuals frequently have feelings of abandonment, grief, guilt, betrayal, and defeat (Valent, 1998). Other symptoms may fall into the category of *moral judgments* including feelings of shame, outrage, low self-esteem, embarrassment, and shattered values and principles (Valent, 1998). People who have been abused are more likely to experience anxiety, depression, suicidal thoughts, and post-traumatic stress disorders (Doherty, 2002). The physical ramifications of abuse can heal with time, but the emotional damage, including feelings of inadequacy and worthlessness along with repressed anger or open hostility may not end. "Unless these problems are treated they can last forever" (Ateah & Mirwaldt, 2004, p.5).

Predisposing Factors For Domestic Violence

When such abhorrent behaviour exists in a society, people are looking for causes and explanations. A study by the British Medical Association (as cited in Shipway, 2004) established that perpetrators in certain situations may be under the influence of alcohol or drugs. Mullender, (as cited in Shipway, 2004) notes limitations in this explanation though, as many men misuse alcohol or drugs and do not abuse their partners. Other research reveals that some abusers feel the need to dominate their partners because of low self-esteem, jealousy, and inability to control anger and other strong emotions (Goldsmith & Vera, 2000).

Researchers have looked for behavioural, biological, and societal origins of abuse. Hague & Malos (as cited in Shipway, 2004) have noted that some adult abusers were former victims of child abuse. That link is comforting to those who believe abuse happens only in deviant families, but it fails to explain non-abusive adults who were previous victims and abusive adults with no previous history. If abuse is strictly a family phenomenon, then it needs to be treated only within the family context in which it occurs. On the other hand, if societal factors predispose and contribute to domestic violence, then societal changes are needed in addition to family treatment.

Domination and violent behaviour is usually caused by a combination of individual and situational influences (Goldsmith & Vera, 2000). Henwood, (as cited in Shipway, 2004, p 15) asserts "that given the pattern of domestic violence is one of escalation, there is no level of abuse which should be viewed, as acceptable or insignificant.

Indeed intervening at an early stage has the potential to prevent the abuse escalating".

Types of Neglect and Abuse

- Physical abuse can occur in any age group with either sex being perpetrators (violence against people, property, pets)

- Sexual abuse may take place in any age group or sex (violation of children and infants; incest, date rape, spousal or same sex partners; random attacks)

- Neglect of infants, children, elderly adults, and adults unable to care for themselves crosses all economic, social, and cultural lines (withholding food, water, infant feedings; no assistance with bathing, toileting, laundry)

- Psychological and/or emotional abuse may be hidden but can be destructive (intimidation, bullying, harassment, name-calling, threats, humiliation, blaming, controlling, playing *mind games*)

- Medication abuse can be subtle but may cause discomfort, illness or even death (withholding essential medications, giving too much medication)

- Financial abuse most often affects the elderly, but can occur in other age groups when a person is powerless: the perpetrator is usually a family member (Wahl, 1996)

Statistical Evidence of Abuse in Canada and the World

In order to comprehend the prevalence of family violence, we should examine the statistics. "It is important to recognize that violence against women is an international reality, only recently acknowledged as a major public health issue" (Shipway, 2004, p.7).

Europe

In Germany, approximately 40,000 women per year seek refuge in shelters, but these data are not included in crime data collections. There are no official data collections in Italy, Russia, and Thailand (Shipway, 2004).

Jamaica

Summers & Hoffman, (as cited in Shipway, 2004) have revealed that in Jamaica, domestic violence is recognized as a factor in 34 % of the 900 annual murders in Kingston alone.

United States and United Kingdom

In the 1980's in the United States, sociologist Diana Russell conducted a sophisticated study (as cited in Herman, 1997). Using random sampling techniques, 900 women were interviewed in depth relating to experiences of domestic violence or sexual exploitation. The results were shocking! One in four women had been raped and one in three had been sexually abused as a child! (Herman, 1997).

The United States Department of Justice documented that family violence accounted for 11% of all reported and unreported violent occurrences between 1998 and 2002, and that 22% of all murders in 2002 were family murders (U.S. Dept. of Justice, 2003).

In the United Kingdom in 1997-98, it was estimated that 19,910 women and 28,520 children stayed in shelters in England. Likely costs were over £1 billion per year. Meyer, (as cited in Shipway, 2004) conducted a study at the Rush Medical Centre in Chicago in 1992. This study demonstrated that the average cost for medical services provided to abused elders, women, and children was $1,633 per person per year. As an annual national cost that amount translated to $857.3 million. And that was just the cost of medical services!

Canadian Statistics

A report released by Statistics Canada and posted at globeandmail.com on Wednesday June 15, 2005, indicated that 95,326 people (58,486 women and 36,940 children) were admitted to shelters in Canada on an annual basis. On April 14, 2002 in Canada, 6,000 women and children sought refuge in abuse shelters (Weber, 2005). For about one third of the women, this was not their first visit. Most of the women were in the 25 –34 years age bracket. On the day of the "snapshot" not all of the women in shelters were there because of domestic violence; however, the majority were. Other reasons included drug and alcohol abuse, mental health issues, and housing problems (Weber, 2005). Clearly these statistics are predominately dealing with abuse of women and children by men. As mentioned earlier, women can be perpetrators as well, and I will elaborate on that in Chapter 41 (on spousal abuse).

People who have witnessed family violence are regarded as being in the same category as those who have experienced it. The problem with the term *violence* is that it refers only to the physical manifestations of abuse. *Abuse* covers a broader range of mistreatment including neglect; psychological, social, and financial abuse; and manipulation (Shipway, 2004).

Health Outcomes of Family Violence

Physical trauma

Sexual abuse can result in unplanned pregnancy, bladder and urinary tract infection, and sexually transmitted disease. Physical abuse may result in considerable damage to limbs and skin, requiring surgery to deal with fractures, suturing of lacerations, or skin grafts for burns. Babies born to women living with physical and/or sexual abuse will more often have low birth weight. Lower birth weight can be linked to disabilities, childhood illness, and even death (Doherty, 2002).

Injury to self and infants

People living with domestic violence, in attempting to dull the pain, may develop addictions to smoking, alcohol, and/or drugs. If a pregnant woman consumes large amounts of alcohol, her infant is at risk of developing fetal alcohol syndrome and other fetal alcohol effects in childhood (Doherty, 2002). Smoking, as we know, can contribute to heart disease, cancer, and high blood pressure.

Psychological harm

Severe psychological harm can develop as a result of chronic abuse. In the past, women have been accused of having psychological problems as an *explanation* for being abused. While some abused women do have predisposing psychological problems, research does not support this theory (Herman, 2004). Dr. Herman is dismayed at the lengths to which people have gone to explain male behaviour by looking at the traits of women (Herman, 2004).

Greater likelihood of illness and disorders

The ongoing stress of living with chronic abuse, regardless of the age or sex of the perpetrator, increases the likelihood of developing physical conditions and diseases including sleep disorders, high blood pressure, migraines, digestive problems, back pain, and colds (Kirsta, 1986).

How Does One Recover From These Horrific Events?

Some people choose to think *matter-of-fact-*

ly, "It has happened, it's over," but their stories should be told. Judith Herman, M.D. suggests that one needs to remember and tell the truth about the terrible things that have happened. She believes that these are "prerequisites both for the restoration of the social order and for the healing of the individual victims" (Herman, 1997, p.1). Shipway (2004) believes that healthcare departments are important members of the team (including law enforcement agencies, social services departments, and community support agencies) as there is often need for assessment to determine the magnitude of health care issues resulting from domestic violence.

One should emphasize that exposure to family violence does not mean that a person is destined to a life of emotional trauma and ill health (Doherty, 2002). Many people can develop positive coping strategies and healthy relationships and live rewarding lives. Others may alternate between reliving the trauma and detachment from it (Nijenhuis, van der Hart, & Steele, 2004).

Recovery from domestic abuse and trauma is dependent on several factors. As disempowerment and disconnection from others are the core experiences of psychological trauma, recovery is based on "the empowerment of the survivor within the context of relationships; it cannot occur in isolation" (Herman, 1997, p.133). The basic stages of recovery include determining safety, learning to tell the story, and finding ways to restore a link between survivors and their community (Herman, 1997).

Potential Opportunities for Faith Communities and Parish Nurses

- Advocating for more health care dollars to be spent on prevention as well as intervention (presumably eventually, if prevention strategies are successful, the need for intervention funding will be reduced)

- Challenging society on the attitudes and behaviours around the use of physical force with children

- Offering support and resources to community agencies

- Partnering with community groups to offer awareness programs to educate the public (normal child development, dealing with teenagers, mental health promotion, healthy communication, and community resources)

- Making connections with other faith communities and cultural groups to find common ground on values and beliefs about personal autonomy

- Researching the available printed resource material in order to have it available for people to pick up

- Providing brochures and pamphlets as alternative means of communication

- Offering primary interventions for youth violence prevention that are directed to an entire population (Ateah & Mirwaldt, 2004) Examples could include an awareness presentation done at a community event or programs targeted to health care professionals or educators.

- Identifying particular groups that may be at risk for abuse; designing programs and strategies for reaching them

- Offering training for families grappling with youth violence against parents (may be hidden as parents are embarrassed that their children act in these ways)

- Developing support groups or *support resources* (prayer, temporary shelter, interim financial assistance, peer support) within a faith community

- Listening one-on-one to individuals in the midst of a crisis

- Referring to clergy for counselling (or to appropriate community resources)

- Facilitating trust building with the parish nurse

- Developing a program and recruiting peer groups to work with those at risk (respected peers can be a positive influence)

- Assisting women and children who are choosing to leave the family home to find a safe haven

- Recognizing that perpetrators can be male or female

Please See Chapter 41 on Spousal Abuse

- Offering support in the way of respite for care-givers (young mothers, and families caring for the elderly or persons with disabilities)

- Recruiting and screening volunteers for this very important respite ministry

The topics of emotional abuse, violence, sexual assault, child abuse, and neglect are ones that are often ignored. Legislation is somewhat behind in dealing with some areas of abuse. By advocating and lobbying for change rather than remaining silent, the parish nurse can help promote changes over time. Education is essential in changing society's attitudes toward any kind of abuse. Ultimately each person needs to do his or her part in redefining acceptable behaviour and what can be done to prevent undesirable acts. For individuals who have survived, their self-worth and humanity depends on their feelings of connection with others.

> *Repeatedly in the testimony of survivors there comes a moment when a sense of connection is restored by another person's unaffected display of generosity. Something in herself that the victim believes to be irretrievably destroyed – faith, decency, courage – is reawakened by an example of common altruism. Mirrored in the actions of others, the survivor recognizes and reclaims a lost part of herself. At that moment, the survivor begins to rejoin the human commonality.*

> (Herman, 1997, p.214)

Forty
Family Violence and Children

Let the little children come to me;
do not stop them;
for it is to such as these
that the kingdom of God belongs.

Mark 10: 14

Young children who experience emotional and physical pain blame themselves. They may not understand why violence is happening in the home, so they often believe that it must be their fault. Children rarely point the finger at Mom, Dad or other adult (Virtue, 1994). When the violence continues, their thinking moves from it being their fault to "I must be a horrible person." (Virtue, 1994, ¶ 2). Repeated abuse in childhood "forms and deforms the personality" (Herman, 1997, p. 96). Children learn in three ways. The first is by modeling the adults in their lives. The second is by being told the rules by their parents, and the third is by trial and error (Doherty, 1994).

Children ensnared in an abusive environment have to learn ways to adapt to volatile and changing situations. They look for ways to maintain trust when trust is so often broken, seek safety when there is none, and try to maintain control in terrifying and unpredictable situations (Herman, 1997). For little people, these are huge tasks! These situations foster altered states of consciousness, which both reveal and conceal the hidden language of secrets too horrible for words (Herman, 1997). Freud, (as cited in Herman, 1997, p 96) described this state of consciousness as "hysteria", whereas George Orwell, (as cited in Herman, 1997, p1), a truth-teller of the twentieth century spoke of this dichotomy of being numb and reliving an event as "doublethink". It is important for nurses to recognize behaviours that may be indicative of a child who is experiencing abuse or family violence. Holden & Ritchie, (as cited in Shipway, 2004) state that children who are living in a home where another person (usually their mother) is being abused can be as negatively impacted as if they themselves are beaten.

Children Who Possibly Are Experiencing Abuse or Violence May:

- have to side with the abuser to protect themselves (they might also abuse the mother, feel guilty and powerless, but lack the maturity to understand what is happening).

- display signs of fear, anxiety, mistrust, and hyper-vigilance.

- have been threatened with being taken out of the home if they tell of the atrocities; often appear nervous and insecure.

- experience nightmares, bedwetting, upset digestive systems and loss of appetite, or may *eat their pain* and gain weight.

- blame themselves for the violence and appear as if they are carrying *the weight of the world* on their shoulders.

- appear silent and withdrawn; are afraid that if they say anything they might reveal *the secret* and be punished for it.

- regress in their development or show delayed development.

- mimic the behaviours they have experienced when playing with siblings and other children.

- appear very sad for long periods and may become depressed.

- if under the age of five, shrink from physical contact and appear extremely fearful or might demonstrate excessive clinging (Psychologist 4therapy, 2005).

Children are negatively affected by family violence and may have immediate visible reactions, or symptoms of stress may become apparent days or weeks later. Children can be quite resilient and may not have adverse effects later in life. According to Mullender & Morley some children remain well adjusted despite living in an abusive environment (as cited in Shipway, 2004).

Abuse of Children

Child abuse can be manifested in numerous horrendous ways. Physical abuse includes hitting, biting, burning, choking, kicking, and shaking. Sexual abuse refers to the use of a child for sexual gratification of an adult or older adolescent (Public Health Agency of Canada, 1998). This includes sexual touching, intercourse, and other kinds of sexual exploitation.

Neglect is more difficult to pinpoint, as the signs are often not detected. As a result, neglect can be more devastating than other forms of abuse. Examples of neglect consist of failing to provide appropriate food, clothing, or shelter. Emotional abuse is similar to neglect in that there are not specific acts or events, but there is suffering recurring over time, with devastating outcomes. Imagine how terrible it is for children who are repeatedly degraded, ignored, and rejected by the people who should be the nurturers!

It has been suggested that the length of the abuse, the severity of the abuse, and the relationship of the abuser to the victim are factors that influence the consequences of the abuse (PHAC, 1998). It is important to determine the impact in order to implement appropriate interventions. However, if a child is being abused I agree with the authors of the Canada Public Health Agency's reference guide: "Child maltreatment, regardless of the severity, can pose serious risks to the immediate and long-term physical, psychological and spiritual health of children. Indeed, in some instances, it can be life-threatening" (PHAC, 1998 ¶ 87).

Adolescents

Adolescents learn to "take the role of the other" (Virtue, 1994, ¶ 5). That means they are able to see that their parents are not perfect and are capable of making mistakes. In many instances, youth who have suffered childhood abuse, become perpetrators and/or victims of youth violence. Boys who have witnessed their mothers being abused may in turn abuse peers and/or family members. Girls abused in childhood may go on to suffer abuse at the hand of boyfriends (PHAC, 2005). Data about the relationship between survivors of child abuse and those who become adult perpetrators or abuse victims are inconclusive.

Teens repeatedly experience guilt at not being able to control the aggressive behaviour of their parents. This stress can manifest itself in the form of withdrawal and isolation, substance abuse, suicidal thoughts, depression, self- mutilation, antisocial behaviour, risk-taking, flashbacks, and sleep problems. Resulting feelings frequently include self-hatred, frustration, sadness, hopelessness, guilt, and emotional exhaustion (Williams & Catalano, no date).

Adolescents exposed to continuing abuse may become involved in abusive behaviours with siblings, peers, and in dating relationships. Teens may believe that abuse is just physical violence and not consider that verbal assaults including yelling, criticizing, intimidation, threatening, and name-calling constitute emotional abuse. This type of abuse may be less visible but can be as devastating as physical violence.

An Interesting Study Undertaken By Mullender (As Cited In Shipway, 2004) Revealed That:

- more than 75% of boys aged 11-12 believe that women get hit when they make men angry.

- more boys than girls of any age think that some women deserve to be hit.

- boys, particularly teenage boys, do not seem to recognize that men should take responsibility for their violence.

Possible Predisposing Factors For Youth Violence (P.H.A.C., 2005)

Familial factors

- Violence experienced or witnessed as a child

- Family history of violent behaviour

- Harsh and severe physical punishment

Socio-demographic factors

- Gender (male youth are more often violent but can also be victimized: street youth, homosexual relationships, visible minority gangs)

- Ethnic origin (may feel compelled to join gangs because of racial slurs, language barriers, diminished educational or employment opportunities)

- Poverty (more likely to experience mental health problems, school drop-out resulting in reduced financial success)

School factors

- Low grades

- School drop-outs (linked to serious effects on self-esteem)

Risk factors particular to males

- Patriarchal values: belief that males are more important than females and have the right to control females

Bullying and Conflict Resolution

People develop numerous dysfunctional methods to express hostility throughout the lifespan, but some that most often affect adolescents consist of bullying, intimidation, sexual harassment, dating violence, assault (both physical and sexual), and gang attacks.

While there can be multiple manifestations of bullying in adolescence, we do not expect brutal murders such as we have seen in the case of Reena Virk, a British Columbia teen. Most situations of bullying and intimidation do not progress to those extremes but, as we have seen more than once, it can happen! Some behaviour that may be a precursor to severe physical injury or death can begin insidiously, and escalate over time. Repeated taunting, name-calling, racist remarks, and threatening lead to increasing distress in the targeted individual until the bully wears down the youth's self-esteem, further contributing to the bully's sense of power.

Adolescents of either sex can be subjected to emotional trauma in dating relationships through verbal degradation and extreme jealous behaviour. Self-esteem and personal growth may be diminished. Physical violence and sexual coercion and/or assault can occur in dating relationships as well.

RESPONSIBILITIES OF PARISH NURSES AND FAITH COMMUNITIES

If a person has reasonable grounds to suspect that a child is or may be in need of protection, the person must promptly report the suspicion and the information upon which it is based to a children's aid society. Definition of "child" means a person under the age of eighteen. (Ontario) Child and Family Services Act s.3 (1)

Responsibility to Report a Child in Need of Protection (Ontario) Child and Family Services Act CFSA s. 72 (1)

SPECIAL RESPONSIBILITIES OF PROFESSIONALS AND OFFICIALS, AND PENALTY FOR FAILURE TO REPORT

Professional persons and officials have the same duty as any member of the public to report a suspicion that a child is in need of protection. The Act recognizes, however, that persons working closely with children have a special awareness of the signs of child abuse and neglect, and a particular responsibility to report their suspicions, and so makes it an offence to fail to report.

Any professional or official who fails to report a suspicion that a child is or may be in need of protection, where the information on which that suspicion is based was obtained in the course of his or her professional or official duties, is liable on conviction to a fine of up to $1,000.

Special Responsibilities of Professionals and Officials, and Penalty for Failure to Report CFSA s.72 (4), (6.2)

While the above legislation reflects Ontario laws, parish nurses must adhere to the laws in their own jurisdiction. The provinces and territories are responsible for providing the services necessary to protect children's safety and welfare. The federal government is responsible for ensuring that the Criminal Code provides protection for children from extreme forms of abuse and neglect. People who abuse children can be charged under the Criminal Code (Dept. of Justice Canada, 2005).

How Faith Communities and Parish Nurses Can Promote the Safety of Children

- Make protecting children a priority

- Work with community groups to educate parents on ways to discipline children without using violence

- Meet with parents and ask how the faith community can help them

- Research community resources available for caregivers and young parents

- Provide support for caregivers in stressful situations

- Link with community youth programs to learn their concerns, and explore opportunities to collaborate on education programs

- Have educational presentations on abuse prevention done by community groups such as community services officers of local police department, and mental health units

- Encourage and support youth workers in the community

- Become familiar with predisposing factors for abusive behaviours

- Educate self and others on signs of abuse

- Gather resource materials from child welfare agencies

- Make it known that staff is available to talk about abuse

- Encourage those who may be abusers to get help; provide information on sources of assistance

Family violence will not disappear, never to be seen again. Part of the human condition is the ability to make personal decisions. Those decisions will not always be in the best interest of others or ourselves. We must not lose hope. Our objective must be to focus on what we can manage to do to make *our world*, however small it may be a healthier and safer place for our children and adolescents.

> *It is to those who have the most need of us that we ought to show our love more especially.*
>
> Saint Francis de Sales

Forty-one

Spousal Abuse

The way out is to tell:
Speak of the acts perpetrated upon
us, speak the atrocities, speak
the injustices, speak the personal
violations of the soul. someone will
listen, someone will believe our
stories, someone will join us.

Charlotte Pierce-Baker (author of
Surviving the Silence)

On Thursday, July 14, 2005 globeandmail. com reported the latest Statistics Canada numbers relating to spousal violence. Terry Weber's article stated that more than one million women and men in Canada have been victims of spousal violence over the past five years. When we think of domestic abuse we often focus on men's violence against women. We should remember that violence does occur in same-sex relationships, and that women do abuse men, both physically and emotionally in heterosexual relationships (Shipway, 2004).

What is Spousal Abuse?

The Department of Justice Canada refers to "the violence or mistreatment that a woman or man may experience at the hands of a marital, common-law or same-sex partner" (Tutty, 1999, ¶ 1). Spousal abuse can occur at any stage of the relationship, including when it is breaking down or has ended.

Abuse in Heterosexual Relationships

- Physical abuse may occur only once or repeatedly over time. It includes using physical force to injure someone, or at least to put a partner at risk of being injured. Kicking, biting, choking, slapping, beating, burning, or assaulting with a weapon are some ways physical force may be used.

- Emotional abuse includes verbal attacks such as screaming, yelling, criticizing, ridiculing, and name-calling. Stalking, harassing, and threatening are other ways to torment an individual and cause emotional stress.

- Sexual abuse may include forcing a partner into "unwanted, unsafe or degrading sexual activity" (Tutty, 1999, ¶ 3). Any unwelcome sexual tactics that are used to exploit, denigrate, or control a partner can be classified as sexual abuse. Sexual abuse is rarely about sexual gratification but is more about coercion and control (Shipway, 2004).

- Financial abuse is another way of exerting power over a partner. Financial abuse can range from stealing, defrauding, and withholding financial resources, to preventing working, or controlling choice of a job (Shipway, 2004).

- Spiritual abuse includes prohibiting a person from participating in religious practices and activities. This type of abuse has a greater impact than just being barred from religious customs. People may cry out to God, and when they believe that cry is not answered, their basic trust is shattered, and they feel deserted. "Traumatized people feel utterly abandoned, utterly alone, cast out of the human and divine systems of care that sustain life". (Herman, 2004, p 52) When that sense of trust is lost and a sense of alienation and disconnection prevails, individuals have difficulty with close and/or distant relationships. Damage is very deeply rooted!

Domestic violence can occur in any intimate relationship. Issues can be diverse in the various relationship configurations. Female violence occurs in some heterosexual relationships. Women can, and do, bully, intimidate, and brutally attack, and sometimes kill their male partners. The vast majority of incidents involve male violence against women, but the reverse also occurs Statistics related to domestic aggression towards men remain open to doubt, (mostly by men) but the reality is that men who are being abused by their female partners are using the healthcare system (Shipway, 2004).

Violence in Gay and Lesbian Relationships

Domestic violence does exist in some gay and lesbian relationships. Letellier estimates (as cited in Shipway, 2004) that between 25 and 30 per cent of all people in intimate same-sex relationships suffer abuse at some point in their relationship. There are limited data on the contributing factors and the patterns or dynamics of abuse in same-sex partnerships (Shipway, 2004). A significant aspect particular to these relationships is that the abuser may threaten to *out* the partner as part of the control. If families are not aware of the liaison, exposure is a real threat. Expectations of societal hostility, prejudice, and homophobia are deterrents to seeking help.

Vandalism - the threat of or the act of - is common in same-sex relationships. Articles of sentimental value are the usual targets for destruction. Abuse to pets is another way of exerting power and control. According to Smith (as cited in Shipway, 2004), with the prevalence of AIDS/HIV in homosexuals, infected abused partners may be reluctant to leave, as they fear dying alone. Similarly, the abused man may feel that he cannot leave if his partner has HIV.

Girshwick, (as cited in Shipway, 2004), alleges that the lesbian community perpetuates the myth that women are not violent and that lesbian relationships are ideal. It can be difficult for an abused lesbian partner to get support if lesbian friends will not acknowledge that sexual or physical abuse occurs in lesbian relationships. Finding a safe refuge for abused lesbians is difficult due to the lack of such specialized places. Lesbians can be faced with homophobic hostility in a *traditional* woman's shelter. Leaving abusive same-sex partnerships means facing some harsh and complex realities not visible to someone on the outside. People naively suggest, *if it's that bad, why don't you just leave?* We cannot predict what those who leave will encounter. There is a lack of research on leaving abusive same-sex relationships because, until fairly recently, these relationships have been concealed.

The general public lacks understanding of the challenges faced by *anyone* leaving an abusive relationship. The same simplistic questions are asked regarding abused women in heterosexual relationships, *why don't they leave?*

Why Don't They Leave? (Shipway, 2004)

- Strong emotional attachment to the perpetrator

- Cultural or religious beliefs about *keeping the family together*

- Fear of retaliation

- Economic dependence on the perpetrator

- Social isolation – feeling like there is no place to go

- Language or communication barriers

- Fear of stigmatization

- Low self esteem

- Perpetrator shows repentance following abusive assault

- Escalation of abuse following previously reported violence

There are many challenges to face when a woman decides to leave an abusive situation. "Women are taught to think of the needs of others" (NiCarthy & Davidson, 1997, p 25). It becomes a habit to put the needs of others ahead of one's own needs, particularly when a woman has been *beaten down* and has low self worth. When a woman arrives at the point where she truly decides to leave, she has to have a safe place to go with her children and may not know where that will be. She may be so traumatized from the most recent assault that she is psychologically damaged and not able to think clearly. Her fears about financially supporting herself and her children are looming, coupled with figuring out the logistics of actually leaving the home safely. And then there are the questions: "What if he comes after us?" "What if he kills himself?" "What if I can't make it on my own?" "What if the children want to go back to live with him?" These are very real issues for which there are no answers at the point of departure. It is a long and painful journey to make the decision and then, in fact, carry it out. The Metropolitan Police Service records show (as cited in Shipway, 2004) that a woman is most at risk of severe injury or death at the point of leaving, or after leaving the abusive relationship.

The Road to Recovery

The core experiences of psychological suffering are disempowerment and disconnection from others (Herman, 1997). For recovery to begin, survivors need to be provided with the means necessary for increasing independence and developing new relationships. Parish nurses can offer support and help connect the traumatized person with appropriate community resources, as well as tapping into the resources of the faith community.

Key Points For Parish Nurses

- Be aware that domestic violence is happening around you

- Educate yourself on the signs of domestic violence

- Work with the pastoral team to develop strategies for assisting survivors

- Consider the perpetrators. (Their actions are unacceptable but they should not be abandoned)

- Become familiar with community resources

- Display brochures on available community resources

- Initiate dialogue with a woman who may be abused

- Post the ethical guidelines for your practice (highlighting confidentiality)

- Capitalize on opportunities for conversation when initiated by a woman who is developing trust in you

- Listen carefully for clues of domestic stress *(Please See Chapter 12)*

- Recognize that the road to recovery is a long one and will involve various professionals and resources

- Remember that the survivor is *at the helm* on this journey

- Keep in mind that the nurse's role is to *walk alongside*

It takes courage to leave any relationship, abusive or not. There is a certain comfort in the familiar, even when it is not pleasant. Prior to the mid 1970's when the American women's movement raised public awareness of sexual assault and rape, women often endured terrible atrocities *behind closed doors*. Feminists defined rape as a tactic employed by men to terrify and control women (Herman, 1997).

In 2005 there is still hesitation in women to confront the issues without putting the blame on themselves. Each person must take responsibility for his or her own behaviour. There will always be actions and activities that will anger, irritate, and annoy us. We decide how we respond. If our responses are inappropriate, we need to learn new ways of responding. The challenge for parish nurses and faith communities is to *walk alongside* the perpetrator as well as the survivor.

> *Peace is not the absence of conflict but the presence of creative alternatives for responding to conflict – alternatives to passive or aggressive responses, alternatives to violence.*
>
> Dorothy Thompson

> *Peace I leave with you; my peace I give to you. I do not give to you as the world gives. Do not let your hearts be troubled and do not let them be afraid.*
>
> John 14:27

Forty-two
Elder Abuse

There is in every heart a spark of heavenly fire which lies dormant in the broad daylight of prosperity, but which kindles up and beams and blazes in the dark hour of adversity.

Washington Irving

I first met Ethel at her daughter's house. Eighty-six year old Ethel came from England to stay with her only child, Anne, who had two daughters of her own. Ethel was nearly blind as a result of diabetes. In England she had been living on her own but was not managing well, so Anne brought her to Canada to live with her family. Ethel and Anne did not have a close relationship when Anne was at home, but Anne felt it was her *duty* to look after her mother. Ethel had difficulty being tidy when she ate, as she could not see her food. Rather than teaching the children how to help their grandmother with meals, Anne decided that Ethel should eat upstairs in her room so that her children would not be *exposed* to Grandma's *poor manners.*

Anne's husband travelled frequently so Anne was responsible for the children most of the time. A few months after Ethel arrived, Anne's eldest daughter was diagnosed with juvenile diabetes at the age of 8. Jessie had been quite ill prior to diagnosis and then struggled with learning how to give herself insulin injections, and eat healthy meals and snacks on a regular schedule.

Anne did not cope well with the stresses and seemed unable to find ways to help herself. She was clearly overwhelmed. She was also feeling extremely resentful! Her mother was an added burden that she could do without, so she forced her mother to stay in her room. Ethel did not know anyone in Canada and had no contacts other than her daughter, as the grandchildren were discouraged from visiting her. She felt abandoned and wished that she had stayed in England. Not surprisingly, Ethel's health declined, and she was admitted to hospital after being found unconscious in her room.

After several weeks, Ethel was well enough to leave hospital, but she was adamant that she was not going back to her daughter's home. Ethel was admitted to a long-term care facility and had a much happier time for the remainder of her life. A lay pastoral visitor saw her regularly and read to her, took her outside in her wheelchair, and encouraged interaction with other residents. Ethel's daughter visited her at the residence, and the relationship improved once Anne did not have to care for her mother.

I use this example of psychological abuse, neglect, and abandonment of an older person because many believe that abuse stems from caregiver stress. The evidence is limited, and countless researchers have noted that many caregivers who undergo stress do not resort to abusive behaviours (Gov't. of Canada, 2005a). In this particular situation, the daughter had no love for her mother and just took her in because she felt it was her duty. With the added stress of her daughter's illness and her husband's travelling schedule, this woman was not coping well at all. Her mother became the scapegoat. Most families that I have worked with have shown love and respect for the frail elderly person entrusted to their care. It does not mean that they do not experience stress, but they do not abuse the older people as an outlet for their stress.

What Factors Play a Role in Abuse of Older Persons?

One perspective suggests that as the older person develops more physical and/or cognitive impairments, the caregiver feels an increasing burden. Another perspective intimates that the abuse is not caused by the dependency of the older person, but the dependency of the abuser on the older person. The abuser may be financially dependent on the older person and continues to provide care to keep the person from being admitted to a care facility so that the abuser avoids losing the person's pension cheque (Hawranik & McKean, 2004).

Other theories include the *cycle of violence* theory that violence is a learned behaviour, and that when abused children grow up, they adopt the same patterns as coping strategies to "get back" at the parents (Swanson, 1999, p 2). Situational stress can be a factor when there is an imbalance of power (e.g. ageism, sexism) in individuals' families (Swanson, 1999). Another theory to explain elder abuse may be the lack of mental stability, history of anti-social behaviour, or drug and/or alcohol problems of the abuser (Wahl & Purdy, 2002).

Who Are the Abused and the Abusers?

The abused older adult is:

- more likely to be living with someone rather than alone.

- more likely to be living with grown children rather than a spouse.

- most often isolated from friends, neighbours and other family members.

- most often female (when physical harm is involved).

- usually mentally competent and capable of taking care of his/her own needs.

- more vulnerable if there are mental or physical disabilities.

The abuser is:

- most often a family member.

- frequently financially dependent on the older person.

- one who may have personal or psychological problems.

- likely to have limited social supports.

- one who may well have poor employment history.

- possibly a person with previous police arrests.

- sometimes an inadequately trained caregiver in the community or in a long term care facility.

Types of Elder Abuse

There are forms of abuse than can happen in any age group. I have discussed those in the previous chapters. In this section I will address the ones that are more specific to older adults.

Financial Abuse (Wahl & Purdy, 2002)

- Forcing an older person to sell a residence or personal property

- Stealing pension cheques or forging signatures.

- Wrongfully using the Power of Attorney for property

- Fraud and extortion

Neglect (Wahl & Purdy, 2002).

- Failing to provide food and water

- Abandoning

- Failing to provide safe, clean environment

- Ignoring health needs (too much or too little medication)

Physical Abuse

- Assaulting by slapping, beating, or pushing

- Tying to furniture

- Confining by locking the older person in a room
- Burning or scalding
- Inflicting unnecessary or traumatic treatments
- Sexually assaulting an older person

Psychological Abuse

- Humiliating, insulting, or criticizing
- Threatening to harm
- Threatening abandonment
- Intentionally frightening
- Lying
- Ignoring
- Treating like a child
- Withholding relevant information
- Being disrespectful

Physical and financial abuses are criminal offences and are punishable by law. Psychological abuse and neglect are also criminal offences but can be more difficult to prove.

Signs of Elder Abuse

- Anxiety, fear, passivity, increasing depression
- Lack of food, dehydration

- Unexplained physical injuries, bruises, cuts
- Poor hygiene, pressure sores, dried urine or feces
- Over-sedation
- Aggressive behaviour, hostility, mounting resentment
- Conflicting stories
- Confusion, unresponsiveness
- Wanting to die

Why is Elder Abuse Infrequently Reported? (Wahl & Purdy, 2002)

- Fears that abuser might harm the victim more if he/she tells
- Worries that abuser will not provide food, clothing, and shelter
- Fears of being institutionalized
- Ashamed that a family member is hurting him/her
- Suspicion that agencies and/or police cannot really help them

Why Are Visiting Caregivers Not Reporting Suspected Incidents of Abuse?

- The older person requests that incidents not be reported

- They may not know whom to speak to or what can be done

- People may not want to get involved

- Some may feel that giving out information to police is violating confidentiality

- Others may not be aware that theft, assault, and severe neglect are criminal offences

- The caregiver may fear the abuser

- The caregiver may be afraid that if the abuse is reported, the older person will deny it

What is the Role of the Parish Nurse?

Anyone in Ontario is required by law to report to a local regional office of the Ministry of Health and Long-Term Care any harm that *they see* being done to persons living in *nursing homes.* "This also applies where someone suspects that an older person is being harmed or might be harmed" (Wahl & Purdy, 2002, p. 11).

The Ministry of Health and Long-Term Care has the authority to investigate abuse in *municipal* or *charitable* homes, but at the present time people are not *required* to report abuse in private homes or in the municipal or charitable homes, as they are in *nursing homes.* The law is expected to change so that reporting of abuse in municipal and charitable homes will be mandatory. It is hoped that the revised law will also include *any* location that an abused older person inhabits. Anyone who suspects that an older person is being abused can express his/her concerns to police or to social or legal services.

Parish nurses should be well informed as to the legal requirements in the faith community's jurisdiction and be familiar with resources for safety, shelter, and financial assistance.

An abused older person may be determined to remain in his/her home. Assisting by contacting community support services (with the client's permission) to reduce the dependency on the abuser can be one way to sustain the client's wish to remain at home. If the older person is isolated, the parish nurse can offer ways for the individual to be more involved outside the home. *Baby steps* may be needed here.

A parish nurse can offer resources on counselling, the criminal justice system, opportunities for social activities, and linking with other isolated individuals.

Abuse of an elderly person is a very complex issue. We generally assume that adults are capable of making their own decisions. That does not mean that individuals always make the best decisions. Decision-making can be off-centre because of other factors such as being abused by a member of one's own family. People may tolerate abuse thinking (or hoping) that it will get better. When someone like a parish nurse confronts the older person with the notion that the abuse does not have to be endured, it gives the person permission to consider different options. Sometimes, when someone else verbalizes what an individual has been mulling over, those thoughts are validated. Great comfort can be derived from that validation!

> *Although the world is full of suffering,*
> *It is also full of overcoming it.*

Helen Keller

One of the real challenges for nurses, and others involved with individuals who are being abused is recognizing that the perpetrator is also a child of God. How do we show love and compassion for a person who has committed such objectionable acts? We should be willing to assist that person to get the help that is needed, whether it be counseling, anger management or help for addiction problems.

Principles That Should Guide the Development of Plans for Intervention

- An abused older adult should be presumed to be competent. Interventions should be based on voluntary and informed consent after the individual has been presented with all the appropriate alternatives.

- Intervention is necessary when abuse is life threatening or when the abused older adult is incompetent to make decisions.

- Interventions should be based on a skilled, multi-disciplinary assessment. The assessment and plan should be documented in the event that the case proceeds to court.

- All interventions should be culturally sensitive.

- Any criminal actions must be reported to the appropriate authorities (Hawranik & McKean, 2004).

Elder abuse is never right, and it seems that strategies aimed at prevention would be superior to *picking up the pieces* after the fact. Education is the most frequently mentioned approach in a prevention plan. The focus of education programs is to change values, attitudes, and behaviours and should be aimed at various audiences (Hawranik & McKean, 2004).

Education for potential abusers (e.g. family caregivers) can help them recognize the danger signals in their own feelings and behaviours. Learning should include education on coping strategies and how to get help before abuse happens.

Lectures, presentations for seniors by seniors, and visits by police officers are useful strategies for encouraging older persons to be less accepting of abusive behaviours. Increasing awareness of fraud and potential scams has resulted in increased reporting of crimes (Hawranik & McKean, 2004).

Prevention strategies should also be aimed at families and friends of seniors, professionals, caregivers, policymakers, the media, institutions, community groups, and youth. Prevention involves developing a *critical mass* that will use influence and available resources to advocate for funding for education programs. Prevention programs are only effective if they reach the most vulnerable, as well as the general population. Culturally sensitive and non-threatening workshops should be developed with the knowledge that in some areas, attending a program on abuse may have a stigma attached. Empowering seniors' groups to support one another is essential in preventing abuse and neglect.

Empowerment Involves:

- learning and understanding what constitutes abuse and one's rights.

- becoming aware of possible choices and the consequences of each one.

- having one's privacy, right to live with dignity, and right to live at risk respected.

- being respected for one's decisions and eventual actions.

Faith communities and other influential groups can, over time, have an impact on elder abuse. Starting with our young people, promoting respect and dignity for people at all ages is a beginning.

You cannot do a kindness too soon
because you never know how soon
will be too late.

Ralph Waldo Emerson

Part Seven:

Grief and Loss

Forty-three
Grief and Growth

Carry each other's burdens and in this way you will fulfill the law of Christ.

Galatians 6:2

Grief is a journey, one that most of us dread and would rather avoid. The process of grief may begin gradually, as when watching a loved one slowly die. Or it can begin instantly when there is a sudden death or loss. Whatever the case, grief is a major life event.

Lawrence Langer (as cited in Pulleyblank Coffey, 2004), in his book *The Holocaust* suggests that there are two kinds of time: chronological time and durational time. He says that we expect to live in chronological time where there is a past, present, and future.

When a significant event such as the death of a loved one occurs, Langer suggests that this pain becomes the norm of life, and we live in what he calls *durational time.* Durational time has no past or future, just a disturbing, recurring experience of the present. This experience of the present is disorienting and overwhelming. Self-care is not usually a high priority when one exists in durational time.

Hundreds of books have been written about loss and grief, so I will not focus on the grieving process but will identify specific strategies that I have found useful through personal experience and learning from a variety of sources (education, books, observation, and interactions with people experiencing grief. Most people want someone else to recognize the magnitude of their loss. It seems that when others make an attempt to understand, it validates the significance of the loss. When walking with people through their grief, we must take our cues from them. Each will have a different way of dealing with his/her loss. If they want to talk, listen. If they want to be alone, respect that.

> *No greater burden can be borne by an individual than to know that no one cares or understands.*
>
> Arthur H. Stainback

All people experience losses in their lifetime. Loss of friends, health, and independence affect many people. Some live through the death of a child, a divorce or separation, death of a beloved pet, or a geographical separation from family. These experiences can cause grief responses, and if they are not resolved, over time they tend to accumulate.

Many years ago Dr. Stephen Fleming (1984), a professor at York University, said that the goal of the grieving process is to experience the pain and suffering in order to move through the grief. He spoke of the *Wall of Pain.* When we invest in a relationship and lose it, we are tossed into that wall of pain. In order to come out the other side, we have to work hard in that wall. He stated that we have to experience the emotions associated with the loss. In *the wall* we must work at withdrawing our emotional investment in the person we have lost. We must try to recover our *self* from that relationship. People suggest that we will be our *old self* soon. That is not true because we are different as a result of the loss. We will not be the same person, but we can be healed. Dr. Fleming (1984) described the desired outcome as the *legacy*, the comfort of having loved that person and having a new relationship with that person. The person is no longer with us, but we have the memories of who he/she was in our lives.

So how do we get through the wall of pain? We must change! It takes courage to face that pain and begin to come to terms with the new realities. Some people do not have the courage to deal with the pain and run away from it because it hurts too much. We will probably have to renegotiate the loss several times as our perspective changes. We may feel panic as we move deeper into the wall of pain, realizing that our lives have changed forever. We may have to look back and reconnect with the past, in order to move on. It is important for people to be given permission to grieve. There is no prescribed time for grief to be finished, though some people will get stuck in the wall of pain and never recover. Others will bury their grief and learn later in life that the unresolved grief has caused emotional or physical illness.

As Parish Nurses How Can We Help Those Who Grieve?

- Allow people to have time alone. (Miller, 1994). Some people want to talk; others just need time and space to begin to make some sense of their lives. I always ask permission to call occasionally, leaving the door open for more involvement if that is wanted and/or needed.

- Offer material for reading if people want to understand the grieving process better. It can be reassuring to learn that their experiences are normal.

- Inquire as to what might be of help: a support group, a person with a similar experience, or a trusted person to help with sorting priorities.

- Remind people that grief is not a solitary activity. Others do care, but they may be awkward and embarrassed and say *the wrong thing.*

- Educate other people on ways to *walk alongside* those who grieve.

- Acknowledge a person's anger toward God, the doctors, and others, without judgement. This can be empowering for the individual. (Mitsch & Brookside, 1993). The use of prayer can help people express these feelings.

- Include people in your personal prayers. Prayer chains and healing prayer services can be comforting for those who grieve. When visiting, the parish nurse can offer prayer if the grieving person wishes it. You should ask.

- Let people know that others are praying for them. This can be a comfort itself.

- Inquire as to specific needs such as child-care, meal provision, or just time spent in a different place other than home (Miller, 1994). Taking someone for a cup of coffee in a coffee shop can provide a glimpse of normal or *chronological* time.

- Sensitively remind the bereaved person that our faith in God can help us to work through these tough times. People fear that if they feel grief, they are not being *faithful*. There are many examples in the Bible speaking of grief and mourning; for example, Joseph grieving the death of his father, Jacob. Sackcloth and ashes are mentioned as signs of mourning.

- Encourage talk about the loved one who has died. People tend to avoid the topic as the bereaved person may cry. You can be sure that there is crying on the inside, so why not let it out? By speaking of the deceased, you are affirming a life that was lived. The significance for the bereaved person is immense.

Strategies To Avoid

- Do not say *call me if I can help you...* People will not usually call. Call them.

- Do not say that you understand. We cannot know how it is for somebody else.

- Do not use clichés: *It's God's will* or *God will never give you more than you can handle.* That may be your belief, but do not assume that others want to hear it. I have heard these expressions and others, and have seen, and personally experienced, negative reactions to them.

- Do not treat the person as a victim. The individual is still a person, albeit a person who has had a significant loss.

- Do not ask *how are you?* If a person has suffered a significant loss he might react strongly; for example "My wife just died, how do you think I am?"

- Do not use words like *should, could,* and *ought.* These words cause feelings of guilt. People are usually aware of what they should do, and if they could, they would.

The journey of grief is a search for meaning; learning how to say goodbye and let go of the relationship as it was. Showing that you care and are willing to listen is the greatest gift that you can offer. Sharing the burden lightens the load.

Forty-four

A Program For Those Who Grieve

*Teach me how to know death and
go on with life.
Teach me how to love life and not
fear death.*

Judith Viorst
Necessary Losses

We experience losses throughout our lives, and the losses can accumulate. When we are very little, we begin to lose our innocence as we learn the harsh realities of the world: things like not everyone is nice, people fight with each other and do mean things, mommies cry, and people take things that don't belong to them. Our parents experience loss when we are first able to ride our bikes to the corner, instead of just three doors away. A pet dies, a friend moves away, an engagement is broken, a favourite object is lost... the list of losses grows. In most cases, we grieve the loss of the small things and move on. When a BIG loss occurs, we may feel that our world has ended! Our world as it once was has ended, and we are changed because of that event. The death of a person close to us has a major impact on our lives. The loss of a job, the loss of independence resulting from a stroke, and the loss of dreams because of a chronic illness are other examples of life-changing events that cause us to experience grief.

To address these issues, the clergy and I developed an education/support program, presented in four ninety-minute sessions, a week apart. On the fifth week we have a *Service of Remembrance and Hope* that is open to anyone who wishes to attend. The clergy and the parish nurse are involved in that worship service.

The program is open to anyone who has suffered a loss. We send letters to parishioners that we know have had a loss during the previous year. Notices are posted on church bulletin boards, in the Sunday bulletin, on the website, and in the church newsletter. We suggest that people invite family, friends, and neighbours.

The Objectives Of The Growing Through Our Losses Program Include:

- providing a safe, supportive environment for people to express their pain.

- helping people understand the normal grieving process.

- offering resources to assist people to move through their grief.

- helping people see that what they are experiencing is normal.

- dispelling the myths of grieving.

- learning how to use scripture, prayer, and meditation as tools to work through the grief process.

First Session

- Welcome and introduction – (10 minutes)

- Opening exercise - an icebreaker – (10)

- Setting group norms, hopes, and dreams for the program – (10)

- Overview of normal grief process – (15-25)

- Break – (15-25)

- Journaling – (10)

- Assignment for next week – (10)

- Meditation, scripture, prayer – (10-15)

In the first session we outline our objectives and ask if these are consistent with group expectations. We adjust each program to meet the needs of that group. All allotted times are flexible when good discussion is occurring. We invite input from the group on behaviour expectations. As leaders, we outline our hopes: respect for one another, listening to others' stories without interruption, non-judgement of other persons' feelings or experience of grief.

One of the leaders gives an outline of the normal grief process. Questions and discussion are welcome. We recommend that each person keep a journal through the four weeks of the program (and longer, if desired), and each is given a notebook for this purpose.

We Encourage Journal Writing Because It:

- helps people to work through issues that may be difficult to communicate.

- is personal and confidential.

- is a safe place to express anger or other powerful emotions.

- provides a record of where a person has been, change, and progress.

- is therapeutic to vent emotions and actually name the feelings.

We inquire each week as to how the writing is going. We encourage people to share what they have learned through writing. Before our closing devotions, people are invited to speak about the session or anything meaningful coming out of the session. We light a candle to create a peaceful atmosphere and close with a reading, from scripture or other source, and prayer. (We have a break in the first session, as we find that people begin to share one-on-one and then feel more comfortable talking in the group).

Second Session

- Welcome and review of previous week – (5-10 minutes)

- View and discuss objects representing people's grief – (10-20)

- Discussion about how journaling is progressing – (5-10)

- Hand out and discuss resources – (5-10)

- View and discuss video on working through grief – (35) or do a case study identifying different losses experienced by a person, sample included

- Assignment for next week – (5)

- Four Key Facts About Grief– (5)

- Devotion, prayer – (5-10)

The assignment for the second week is to select an object that reflects people's grief (Deits, 1992). We ask "what does your grief look like, feel like, sound like?" People choose something that represents their grief: a poem, a painting, music, a sculpture, and we place them all on a table. We ask people to talk about the object, if they are comfortable doing that, and tell how it represents their grief. People have chosen a wilted flower, a dried up leaf, an empty ring box, an empty vacuum bag, a large blank sheet of paper with a tiny image of a person in the centre. When people look at what represents their grief, they have something concrete to focus on rather than just a nebulous feeling of pain.

The agenda for this session is quite heavy, but we work around what people need to talk about. We light a candle and put a cloth on the table where people place the objects representing their grief. These items are treated with respect and people do ask each other about them. Some of the handouts we use include ideas for writing in their journal, a booklet prepared by a local hospital (used with permission), *Credo* written by John Kennedy Saynor (included), and *The Myths of Grieving* by Cathy-Lee Benbow (included). *The Recent Life History Survey* (Deits, 1992) gives people a picture of recent *loss* events in their lives and helps them determine which of those are still causing some problems. The Four Facts about Grief (Deits, 1992) are very practical reminders about the work of grief:

THE WAY OUT OF GRIEF IS THROUGH IT.
THE VERY WORST KIND OF GRIEF IS YOURS.
GRIEF IS HARD WORK.
EFFECTIVE GRIEF WORK IS NOT DONE
ALONE.

Third Session

- Welcome and seek feedback on journaling, impact of second session – (10 minutes)

- Revisit *Four key facts of grief;* discuss *Wall of Pain-* (5-10)

Please see Chapter 43 on Grief and Growth.

- Work on life history survey (from second session) with another person. Examine responses using the suggestion sheet – (20)

- Return to group... debrief – (5-10)

- Discussion about common feelings, for example anger, guilt – (20)

- Introduce concept of "writing a letter of goodbye" – (5-10)

- Scripture and prayer – (10)

By the third session, people are feeling more comfortable as a group and are willing to tell their story to another person. Discussing the life survey provides some opportunity for that. It is important to provide chances for people to express the strong emotions they experience. Participants are often reassured to hear that others are having, or have had, similar feelings.

Writing a letter of goodbye to the person who has died, or even entertaining the idea, can be shocking for some people. We introduce the tool and supply a handout, giving some tips on writing that letter. We make it clear that there are no expectations. People can do what feels right for them, or not do it at all.

Fourth Session

- Welcome and feedback on their journey through grief – (10-15 minutes)

- Reconciliation, moving on, steps to take – (15)

- Faith help – (15-20)

- Guided meditation – (15)

- Affirming Credo, asking for what we need. – (10)

- Introduce concept of writing a letter to your grief and writing a letter from your grief in response. – (5)

- Devotions, closing prayers – (10)

In the final session we are summing up, and offering tools for people to continue their grief work. We talk about how our faith can help in these difficult times.

Ways Our Faith Can Help

- Utilizing prayer for acknowledgement of pain, and anger towards God – get the feelings out and face them

- Using prayer as listening to God, hearing supportive friends as God speaks through them

- Struggling with feelings about God but learning to accept the simple comforts of faith; resurrection after the cross can be a pattern for our life's losses

- Through scripture, learning to let go and forgive (e.g. Jesus forgave his murderers); new relationships start with forgiveness of old hurts

- Accepting the faith community's offers of support through worship, visiting, and listening

- Reading the Psalms that validate human feelings (e.g. Psalm 69 shows how feelings can be turned around, and we can again learn to hope)

We ask people what they think they need in order to move on. We offer suggestions for setting goals, supply a bibliography for further exploration, and remind participants of our availability to listen. We ask them to fill out an evaluation form to determine if they felt their needs were met.

Some Questions We Ask

- What were your expectations of the program? Were these expectations met?

- Tell us what was most helpful in the program.

- Were the leaders effective in running the program?

- What would have been more helpful for you?

- Was there anything about the program that made you feel uncomfortable?

- What specific changes would you suggest?

- Would you recommend this program to others?

Growing Through Our Losses - Program Resources

Credo

1. *I believe grief is a process that involves a lot of time, energy, and determination. I won't "get over it" in a hurry, so don't rush me!*

2. *I believe grief is intensely personal. This is my grief. Don't tell me how I should be doing it. Don't tell me what's right or what's wrong. I'm doing it my way, in my time.*

3. *I believe grief is affecting me in many ways. I may be being affected spiritually, physically, emotionally, socially and mentally. If I'm not acting like my old self, it's because I'm not my old self and some days I don't even understand myself.*

4. *I believe I will be affected in some way by this loss for the rest of my life. As I get older, I will have new insights into what this death means to me. My loved one will continue to be part of my life and influence me until the day I die.*

5. *I believe I am being changed by this process. I see life differently. Some things that were once important to me aren't anymore. There are some things I used to pay little or no attention to that are now important. I think a new me is emerging, so don't be surprised and don't stand in the way.*

©*John Kennedy Saynor, GENESIS Bereavement Resources (Used with permission)*

The Myths of Grieving

TO GRIEVE IS A SIGN OF WEAKNESS.

Too often we are told *you have to be strong for others*. This statement insinuates that to acknowledge grief is to be weak. Although it does take considerable emotional strength to deny a loss, it takes considerably more emotional strength to allow ourselves to grieve, to feel the pain, the anger, and to work at dealing with it.

I SHOULD GET OVER MY GRIEF QUICKLY, ACCEPT THINGS, AND GET ON WITH MY LIFE.

Grief is hard work and it takes time. Do we ever *accept* a loss? I never use that word in relation to loss. In time we adjust to the loss. We adjust to the emptiness that the loss has left, but I do not think that we ever accept a loss – particularly one of major significance to us. Accepting, sounds as if it was offered to us, and we gladly took it.

IT IS ABNORMAL TO GRIEVE FOR AN EXTENDED PERIOD OF TIME.

Everyone's experience of grief is unique. Kubler-Ross gave much to the literature of grief work, but the stages of grief she outlines are simply guideposts. Do not judge the appropriate nature of your grief based on another's experience. After the death of my father, I caught myself questioning my own grief and had to remind myself that it is a process and we all do it differently.

CHILDREN DO NOT GRIEVE; THEY HAVE NO CONCEPTION OF GRIEF.

We begin to experience loss from the time we enter this world. Our first loss is being ejected from the womb, a warm, perfectly suited environment. Too often children's behaviours labelled as "acting out" are attributes of grief reaction. Parents need to understand this.

CRYING WILL GET YOU NOWHERE.

Crying will get you everywhere! We are given tears for more reason than to wash our eyeballs. We need to cry. It relieves tension and relaxes us.

LIFE WILL BE THE SAME AGAIN

I seriously question if after a major loss, life can ever be the same again. Many people set themselves up for further losses with their expectations that all will return to what it was. Life can be good again; life can be worth living again, but after a major loss, part of grief work means coming to terms with the reality that life will *never* be the same again.

Adapted from an article written by Cathy-Lee Benbow

Sample Case Study: TED

Ted first picked up a golf club at five when his grandfather gave him a junior set of clubs for his birthday. In high school Ted played golf every chance he had and dreamed of becoming a golf pro. Though he pursued a career in advertising, he continued to play golf in his spare time. Ted made some good friends at the club he joined.

When he retired, Ted spent a lot of time at the club, teaching junior members and enjoying playing golf. And then, at the age of 69, he had a stroke that left one side of his body paralysed. He was diligent in his rehabilitation, but the harsh reality was that he was never going to play golf again. His golf buddies were good to him and took him to the club, so he could be part of what was going on. Club newsletters reflected his presence and spoke of how well he seemed to be dealing with the stroke.

A few months later, Ted's daughter moved a great distance away, as her husband was offered a fantastic job. After that, Ted seemed to lose interest in going to the club. He had no interest in seeing his friends and finally asked them to stop calling him. He spent most of his time just staring into space.

Part Eight:

Life Challenges (Supporting Individuals And Families)

Forty-five
Life Crises

Compassion is the quality shown by people who can freely express kindness.
It is by nature never effortful, never on the surface merely.

Deepak Chopra (1991)

Generally we assume that life is going to turn out as we expect. If we have learned a skill or trade, have established a career, married the *right* person, had children and raised them responsibly, life should work out for us. On the outside it may appear that for some people this is true. I have learned that we all have wounds. Whether they are raw and open, or hidden and healed, everybody has a story! That is part of life, but some people, it seems, have more challenges than others. Consider a caregiver who has tended another until that person's death and can finally see a clear path, only to face a diagnosis of cancer. How do we explain, or ever come to terms with the death of a child? And what happens to our faith when continuing challenges arise?

Spiritual doubt often occurs when people are facing difficult situations. We try to find a reason. Questions like "Why did God allow this to happen?" "What did I do to anger God?" "What am I supposed to learn from this?" are common. As parish nurses, how do we minister to people in pain? We don't have answers to the questions that theologians have sought answers to for centuries. Rabbi Harold Kushner asks the question, "Can we accept the idea that some things happen for no reason and that there is randomness in the universe?" (Kushner, 1983. p.46). Grappling with the possibility that there is nobody to blame causes even greater stress. If one can be angry with God and blame Him for an earthquake, a freak accident, or a sudden loss, it seems easier to accept.

People may feel uncomfortable when someone is suffering and *turn a blind eye*, as they do not know how to respond. Others have become immune to tragedy or focus on their own issues. The church (the ministers, the people, and the parish nurse) can provide emotional and spiritual support to one another as people face the challenges of life. The parish nurse models and teaches caring for others.

> *We are here to awaken from the illusion of our separateness.*
>
> Thich Nhat Hanh

A parish nurse should remember that the church may not be the only support available for people. Families, friends, neighbours, and other professionals have a role to play as well. The clergy may be contacted initially in a tragic situation, but the parish family can offer a consistent, supportive presence over a longer period. It can be helpful to have the parish nurse organize appropriate support for families and individuals so that coordinated, unobtrusive assistance is provided as needed. It has been said that an "economy of words" is more often helpful than a lot of chatter to people in crisis (Shelley & Fish, 1988. p.121). We tend to talk too much because of our own discomfort. We should spend more time listening.

An excerpt from Joseph Bayly's book, *The View From a Hearse,* describes how he felt after the death of a son:

I was sitting, torn by my grief. Someone came and talked to me of God's dealings, of why it happened, of hope beyond the grave.
He talked constantly; he said things I knew were true. I was unmoved except to wish he'd go away. He finally did.
Another came and sat beside me. He didn't talk. He didn't ask leading questions. He just sat beside me for an hour and more, listened when I said something, answered briefly, prayed simply, left.
I was moved. I was comforted. I hated to see him go.

(Shelley & Fish, 1988, p.121).

An Example From My Practice

People usually appreciate the help of others in times of critical illness, loss, or tragedy. Helen, a woman whose young daughter died tragically, had the support of friends, neighbours, and family members who ensured that meals were provided, errands carried out, and details managed. There seemed to be a constant whirlwind of activity at Helen's home. While she was grateful for that help, Helen was most thankful for the people who just sat with her without doing anything. In those times of questioning, pain, and tears, Helen felt safe expressing her anger at God. She vocalized her incredible heartache and her fear of a future without her beloved child. She wasn't really expecting answers. She didn't want platitudes. She just needed acceptance without judgement while she struggled to make sense out of something so senseless.

A parish nurse should verify what assistance is appropriate in different circumstances. Some people would feel smothered by having others sitting with them. Many would feel abandoned without people. A wise parish nurse will check with family members when considering what role the congregation might have. Ultimately, the desires and needs expressed by the individual, even though they may change several times, are always to be respected. There is no room for paternalistic or *the nurse knows best* behaviours. Prayer support may be all that the individual or the family want. In some situations, it may be apposite to offer methods for dealing with changes and crises in life.

Potentially Beneficial Strategies Include:

- keeping a journal expressing hopes and dreams. Address the magnitude of the losses. Revisit months later to see the growth.

- working   at rebuilding self-esteem. Note positive things that people have said and things that have promoted a change in thinking.

- joining a support group, or speaking with people dealing with similar circumstances.

- practicing meditation and relaxation techniques.

- using the foundations of your faith; this can be an important aspect of healing. Psalms 23, 56, 62, and 139 are Psalms of hope (Miller, 1997).

  A 400-year-old prayer

  Lord, be thou within me, to strengthen me;
  without me, to keep me;
  above me to protect me;
  beneath me, to uphold me;
  before me, to direct me;
  behind me, to keep me from straying;
  round about me, to defend me.

Forty-six
Coping With Dementia

Courage is as often the outcome of despair as hope.
In one case we have nothing to lose, in the other, all to gain.

Diane De Poitiers

Author's note:

While this chapter is written from a professional perspective, the author has considerable personal experience in her own family.

Dementia is one of the most devastating classes of illness that affects family congruency and stability. Near the beginning, the individual with dementia tries, often fairly successfully, to cover up the deficits. Close family members may notice some early symptoms, but they may be fleeting or may not be severe. As time progresses and symptoms worsen, families may be embarrassed by their loved one's behaviour and withdraw from social interactions. In other instances, family members might deny the reality of the loved one's declining abilities. Frequently the affected person becomes quite defensive, and angry at any suggestion that something is amiss. Helping the person with dementia and family members to develop coping mechanisms and adapt successfully to changing and painful realities is an ongoing challenge for the parish nurse.

Dementia is a medical term used to describe a group of symptoms, including those caused by Alzheimer Disease, Parkinson's Disease, Lewy-Body Dementia, Multi-infarct Dementia, Huntington's Chorea, Pick's Disease, and Creutzfeld Jacob Disease (Mace & Rabins, 1991). These conditions each have complex behaviours associated with them.

Alzheimer Disease

Alzheimer Disease is a progressive degenerative brain disorder causing short-term memory loss and a decreasing ability to reason and use logic and judgement (Hart, 1997). As the disease progresses, the individual becomes less able to carry out the normal tasks of conversation, eating, and dressing. Personality changes, volatile eruptions, wandering, and aggression may develop over time. In later stages of the disease, the person becomes incontinent, unable to say more than a few words, and physically unstable, with frequent falls. Family members have a difficult time, as the person believes he/she is always right. The person with the disease can be so pleasant with strangers that people wonder what the caregiver is talking about. People will say that the person with dementia appears normal, while the caregiver is experiencing a totally different reality (Hart, 1997).

Multi-infarct Dementia

The second most common cause of dementia is characterized by a gradual progression of losses (Zarit, Orr, & Zarit, 1985). This condition can be misleading, as some memories can be quite clear while others are very poor. The area of the brain affected by the ischemia determines the type of deficit. After each ischemic attack there can be some loss, and possibly a partial regaining of memory. There can be permanent loss as well (Hart, 1997). It is possible for people to have both Alzheimer disease and multi-infarct dementia (Mace & Rabins, 1991).

Parkinson's Disease

Dementia in Parkinson's disease can be overshadowed by the physical symptoms, such as the mask-like expression and staccato speech (Hart, 1997). Forming words can be a very slow process with this disease and careful assessment is important. Cognitive deficits may be presumed but, given enough time, the person might demonstrate clear thinking (Hart, 1997).

Lewy-Body Dementia

This condition is similar to Alzheimer disease, but also presents with physical symptoms similar to Parkinson's disease (Hart, 1997). The disease can progress rapidly in some cases. Other symptoms include periods of deep coma-like sleep, with incontinence and then sudden awakening. The appearance of a *forward propulsion gait*, consistent with the gait often seen in Parkinson's, may be present (Hart, 1997).

There Are Treatable Causes Of Dementia!

Treatable diseases and conditions can also cause the symptoms of dementia. Depression, metabolic disorders, infections, toxic substances and trauma can present with cognitive impairment. Thorough assessment and diagnosis is imperative to uncover potentially treatable conditions (Mace & Robins, 1991).

Challenges for Families Dealing With Dementia

Delay in Diagnosis

The caregiver and family members may attribute early memory problems to stress, grief, or depression. When a diagnosis is made, the family members often feel guilty because they did not seek diagnosis earlier. People should not be judged for what they did, or did not do. They are usually so overwhelmed by the agitation and anxieties of the loved one that they do not know what to do.

Caregiver is Not Believed

Caregivers may detect a problem that others do not see. This can cause tensions in families, because nobody really wants to face the truth, and the caregiver feels hurt because the family does not believe him/ her. The caregiver observes the fears, paranoia, angry outbursts, confusion, and inappropriate behaviours (e.g. putting on several layers of clothing) that family members do not see.

Difficulties at Work

The individual with early dementia may blame problems at work for personal difficulties. When having problems at work, people with dementia may blame others.

An example from my practice

An accountant in his 40's began to have difficulties at work. He made mistakes in areas where he had previously excelled. At home he was withdrawn, angry, and restless. His colleagues at work covered for him for a while, as they believed he must be under stress at home. When they asked him about his mistakes, he said he was having a bad day. His *bad days* became a frequent occurrence and the supervisor was called in. The supervisor told the man to take some time off, and see a doctor. When the accountant returned to work, after having seen his doctor, with a diagnosis of *stress* he was given assignments that he could handle. Eventually when the man became too ill to function at work, he was put on long-term disability. His wife took a part-time job to bring in some money and to preserve her sanity. The man started dashing into the streets without his clothes, and his children were horrified! The man was angry with everyone, and the woman feared for the safety of her children. He was admitted to a safe care facility. The family was wracked with pain about this decision, but there was no choice.

Personality Change

Some people with dementia experience changes in mood and personality (Hodgson, 1995). The person *who used to be* is no longer there. Families have said, "It is like living with a stranger". A polite, pleasant person can become combative and shriek obscenities without being aware of what is happening.

An example from my personal experience

A *proper* professional woman had a long and successful career as a dietician. After she retired, her siblings began to notice some changes in her memory, and her deficits became more apparent when she entertained. This woman, who was an expert in food preparation, had difficulty coordinating a meal at home for her siblings and their families. She lived alone and began drinking. She could not remember how many drinks she had had and began to fall and injure herself. She was moved to a retirement facility but soon, because of her increasing dementia, was moved to a more protective area of the facility. She became quite combative and often struck other residents when they wandered into her room. This woman would have been horrified had she been aware of what she was doing.

Frustration Due to Inability to Perform Simple Tasks

The person with dementia may find simple tasks difficult and frustrating, reacting with angry outbursts, which often cause fear in the caregiver. One can only imagine what it must be like to become afraid of someone that has been the love of your life!

An example from my practice

A man did not remember how to tie his shoes and threw them across the room with a great out-burst of profanity. When his wife offered to help him, he burst into tears. His wife felt so sad about what was happening to her husband that she was unsure how to respond. She distracted him by talk-ing about a pleasant trip in their past, and before long he had forgotten about the shoes. The wife helped him put on shoes with Velcro straps, and he seemed satisfied with the situation. She grieved the loss of yet another skill!

Paranoia And Accusations

Some people with dementia develop paranoia and accuse closest family members and friends of stealing and/or deliberately hiding things (per-sonal experience). The person with dementia may have hidden something and then forgotten where he put it. Another manifestation can be frequent closing and locking of doors and windows. This behaviour may occur because of fears that the person with dementia cannot verbalize.

Loss of Sense of Time

One of the early signs of dementia is loss of the ability to sense the passage of time (Hodgson, 1995). A family member could be out of sight for a few moments, and to a person with dementia, it may feel like hours have passed. In order to sense the passage of time one has to remember what happened in the past few minutes (Mace & Rabins, 1991).

An example from my personal experience

A man became very upset when he could not find his wife in the house. He called the police to say that his wife was missing! His wife had left notes in the kitchen *to* remind him that she had gone to have her hair done. At that time, he could understand the message, but he did not remember that she always left him a note in the kitchen. The police had received calls from him before, so were compassionate and listened to him. When his wife returned home, he remembered where she had been and did not remember calling the police.

Worsening In The Evening

People with a dementia often have behaviour problems in the evening. The cause is not known, but there is speculation that dim light increases the likelihood that a person misinterprets what is being seen (Hodgson, 1995). *Sundowning* is the term used to describe this phenomenon. People that have been calm during the day may become agitated and restless in the evening. Leaving lights on, and planning for quiet evenings may help to some degree. Family members can become very frustrated with this behaviour and dread the ending of the day.

An example from my practice

An older man with a dementing illness lived

with a family member and they managed quite well during the day. As soon as the family member went to bed, this gentleman would get dressed (or not!) and leave the house. Sometimes he would get on a bus and stay on it until the driver called the police. This man would also run naked around the neighbourhood in the evening and frighten people. These behaviours were draining for the caregiver. The older man needed to be in a safer environment.

> *The voice of one crying in the wilderness, Prepare ye the way of the Lord, make his paths straight.*
>
> St. Matthew 3:2

How A Parish Nurse Can Be Supportive

It is important for a parish nurse to understand dementia and the impact on families. Discover what resources are available in the community and become familiar with what assistance can be provided. Your local Alzheimer Society has literature, support groups, social workers, and possibly a *day away* program that gives the family caregiver respite. In Ontario, Community Care Access Centres have information lines. Health Canada and disease specific sites on the Internet offer background information. (Keying in *Alzheimer Society* brings up local, national, and international sites). Books and videos are usually available on loan from the Alzheimer Society in many countries.

Do not fail to recognize the impact of the illness on the caregiver and other family members. In many cases, the family caregiver becomes ill due to the unrelenting responsibility. Take time to listen to the caregiver. Family members are likely dealing with their own painful emotions, and may not be able to support the caregiver. An empathetic listener can validate the caregiver's feelings. This is a first step for the caregiver to accept assistance and guidance from outside the family unit.

If there are support groups available in the community, offer to go to the first meeting with the caregiver. Some family caregivers will never attend a support meeting because they are embarrassed, or choose not to discuss personal issues in public. Caregivers may appreciate having some information about dementia, but the parish nurse should always ask if they would like to have it. In the early stages, family members may not be ready to face the magnitude of the condition. Try to build a solid relationship with the caregiver and family members. People still believe that there is a stigma in having a brain disorder that causes unpredictable behaviours. When the parish nurse accepts the person with dementia, that person's worth is validated.

When visiting the person with dementia, use a quiet, gentle approach, as rapid movements and loud voices may be misunderstood. Catastrophic reactions can result if the person with dementia feels threatened. In some cases, a person may not understand the words but reacts to tone of voice or body language.

A parish nurse can help caregivers and family members face the realities. For example, a person who has lost the ability to make a meal is not going to relearn that skill so alternative arrangements (e.g. meals-on- wheels) for meal provision will have to be initiated. A parish nurse can identify possible options for the family members to consider when faced with their loved one's increasing disability. If the person with dementia provided transportation and there are no other drivers in the home, different choices will need to be established.

An informed parish nurse can *walk alongside* the family caregiver and family members offering successful strategies learned from other sources. Caregiver burnout is inevitable and the nurse can offer options for keeping the caregiver healthy. Respite care in the home, so the caregiver can go out, or respite in the community so the caregiver can be at home if desired, are choices. A person may enjoy gardening but be unable to do it with the ill partner around. Encourage the caregiver to maintain a sense of humour. Some of the happenings are quite funny. A good laugh shared by the ill person and the caregiver is of benefit to both people.

The spiritual dimension of the caregiver may be suffering when living with the daily struggles of care giving. Encourage church attendance if this was important to the people prior to the illness. Remind them that we are all God's children regardless of our limitations. A friend, family member, or lay pastoral visitor can be of assistance in orchestrating this. If getting out to church is too difficult, the minister can arrange to go to the home when family members are there. It is important to remember that each person in the family will have developed his/her own way of coping. Some may choose to talk about the issues and some may not.

I learned a great deal from families caring for a person with dementia. When my own father was diagnosed with Alzheimer disease, I had knowledge of useful strategies that I could model for my siblings. This was not always appreciated which can be distressing! It is impossible for people to comprehend the emotional devastation of watching a loved one disappearing before one's eyes, unless they have experienced it.

If I were to offer one piece of wisdom, I would advise people to *be with the person where he is*. It is not about accuracy of information. The person with dementia will not remember anyway.

My final memory of time spent with my father before his death, was standing at his bedside in hospital with one of my brothers, helping Dad plan his gardens for next year. We knew that he would not plant those flowers but that didn't matter. Being with him where he was gave us a sense of peace as we shared with him one of his greatest joys, his garden. He died two days later.

Forty-seven

Promoting Mental Health (While Acknowledging Mental Illness)

*As the hand is made for holding
and the eye for seeing,
Thou has fashioned me for joy.
Share with me the vision that shall
find it everywhere.*

Gaelic Prayer

It has been difficult for people to come to grips with the necessity for mental health promotion because we do not like to acknowledge that mental illness exists. We talk about preventing mental illness by developing better eating patterns, managing stress, staying out of trouble, and getting lots of exercise, but we do not attend to the fundamental principles of mental health promotion.

The World Health Organization (WHO) has recognized that there are countless burdens on society as a result of mental illness. These burdens are difficult to measure and quantify, and so they have remained hidden and undefined, with far-reaching negative results (WHO Fact sheet # 218, Nov., 2001).

Examples Of Undefined Burdens (WHO Fact Sheet #218, Nov., 2001)

- The economic and social burden for families and communities because of lost production from people with mental illness who are unable to work

- The cost of supporting dependents of a person with mental illness

- The underemployment, alienation, and crime associated with young people whose childhood mental health problems were not identified and/or addressed

- The diminished quality of life for family

members and, possibly, poor cognitive development in the children of mentally ill parents

Hidden Burdens Associated With The Stigma Of Mental Illness
(WHO Fact Sheet #218, Nov., 2001)

- Rejection by friends, neighbours, family members, and employers can lead to aggression and feelings of isolation and loneliness.

- Deterrence from equal participation in social networks, family life, and community activities can result in further isolation.

- Stigmatization can be detrimental to recovery from mental illness.

- Ostracism of family members because of the lack of understanding of mental illness and the myths surrounding it can be humiliating

Of course, with the paucity of effective mental health services around the world, the challenges facing countries attempting to promote mental health on both individual and societal levels are enormous.

In Canada: *(Health Canada, 2002)*

- 20 % of Canadians will experience a mental illness in their life span.

- Suicide accounts for 24 % of all deaths among 15-24 year olds and 16 % among 25-44 year olds.

- 8 % of adults will experience a major depression during their lives.

- 1% of Canadians (that's nearly 321,000 people) live with schizophrenia.

- The economic burden of mental illness on the health care system (1998) in Canada was estimated at $7.9 billion. ($4.7 billion in care and $3.2 billion in disability and early death).

- An additional $6.3 billion was spent on uninsured services and time away from work because of depression and distress.

- And these are the reported cases. Almost 50 % of those who stated they had suffered depression or anxiety disorders did not seek medical attention!

- In 1999, 1.5 million hospital days, that's 3.8 % of all admissions to general hospitals, were due to depression (major), bi-polar disorders, schizophrenia, eating disorders, anxiety disorders, personality disorders, and suicidal behaviour.

While these Canadian statistics are staggering, this phenomenon is mirrored worldwide. The World Health Organization (WHO) has announced its first-ever global forum on community health services. During the first phase, which is to be completed by

September 30, 2005, individuals, families, health care professionals, mental health providers, and other non-governmental organizations are invited to tell about the scope of their mental health experiences (WHO, 2005). The objective is to compile data on people's experiences of what does and doesn't work in community-based services for the prevention and treatment of mental illness. WHO will publish a report that highlights issues and concerns with a focus on projects successful in developing psychosocial rehabilitation services in the community. With the reduction of hospital beds worldwide and an increasing dependence on community services, more effective strategies to reduce mental health problems and homelessness are needed. A future international conference is planned as part of this forum.

Light tomorrow with today.

Elizabeth Barrett Browning

When we speak about mental health, what do we really mean? There are many variations of the definition of mental health, and when asked that question, people often think of mental health problems rather than mental wellness.

Mental Health Definitions

- "What helps us to enjoy life, cope with life, and make the most out of life" (NWHB, 2000)

- "Mental health is the emotional and spiritual resistance which enables us to enjoy life and to survive pain, disappointment, and sadness. It is a positive sense of well-being and an underlying belief in our own and other's dignity and worth". (Mentality, 1997).

- "It is a state of well-being in which the individual realizes his or her own abilities, can cope with the normal stresses of life, can work productively and fruitfully, and is able to make a contribution to his or her community". (WHO, Fact Sheet # 220).

Mental Health Promotion

Internationally, there is a growing awareness of the interrelationship between the care and nurturing we receive when we are young, the social environment in which we live, our interactions with others and a sense of inclusion, and our emotional well-being and mental health. Issues such as education, housing, town planning, employment opportunities, and transportation all have a role to play in determining the mental health of a population (Queensland Health, 2001).

Health Canada has a more detailed list of the mix of social and psychological determinants that affect overall health in general and mental health in particular.

Health Canada's List Of Determinants Of Mental Health Includes:

- Personal health practices
- Coping skills
- Genetics
- Income and social status
- Education
- Social support and networks
- Physical environment
- Social environment
- Healthy child development
- Access to health services
- Resilience – how we bounce back from difficulties
- Sense of control over one's life

Effective mental and emotional health promotion should aim to meet the needs of the *well* population and the *at risk* population on an individual, community, and structural/policy basis (Dept. of Health, 2004). Mental health promotion is an approach that views all humans as holistic beings. It encourages building strengths, knowledge, and resources. It does not distinguish between healthy and sick, able-bodied and those living with disability, but strives for improved quality of life for all people (Public Health Agency, 2003).

The World Health Organization, in a news re-lease in September 2004, showed evidence to sup-port the notion that public health interventions and social programs do promote and enable good mental health. Some top researchers working in both developed and developing countries brought together this report (WHO, 2004). Dr. Catherine Le Galès-Camus, WHO Assistant Director-General, Noncommunicable Diseases and Mental Health, cautions that planners and professionals often get so caught up in treating the ill and dealing with immediate problems that they overlook the lon-ger-term needs of those who appear well but may be on the cusp of developing a problem. Dr. Le Galès-Camus welcomes a report that provides sol-id evidence for mental health promotion and pre-vention of mental disorders (WHO, 2004).

Parish nurses and faith communities need to be selective in health promotion strategies, as it is impossible to address all areas of the determi-nants of health. Some, such as physical and social structure of the community, are beyond the scope of faith communities. Advocacy, education, and support are appropriate roles for addressing the structural issues. That does not mean that com-munities cannot lobby for needed improvements. Health committees and the parish nurse can iden-tify the main stressors in a particular population and develop health promotion programs to ad-dress those concerns.

Examples From My Practice

Situation # 1

One effective intervention is a support group that provides a forum for expressing the pain and anger that can be a result of job loss. The format for a program for unemployed may be reinvented several times to respond to the needs of the group at the time. An effective facilitator will be able to offer new approaches as people move through their grief and begin to look at next steps. In our community there was a general slowdown of manufacturing. People came from a variety of industries and brought expertise with them that was of benefit to others. The facilitator encouraged all participants to work on communication and writing skills and recruited professionals to help, or utilized those in the group who had a high skill level in those areas. In the early stage of development, group members expressed how shattered they felt by losing their jobs. They articulated that they had lost confidence in their own abilities. As time went on, members were able to envision a future. The support and encouragement of this group promoted mental health through difficult times in their lives.

Situation # 2

It can be advantageous to provide a forum for agencies already addressing major stressors and educate people about ways to deal with issues, and places to go for help. Our staff team became aware of more occurrences of mood disorders in our congregation, other faith groups, and in the community. Depression seemed to be the most-often mentioned mood disorder, so the Health and Wellness committee and I organized a mental health promotion workshop on this topic. We worked with the Canadian Mental Health Association (CMHA) and the Mood Disorders Association of Ontario (MDAO) and advertised in the community. The workshop was well attended. A consumer/survivor told her story of managing mental illness, which, in turn, encouraged others to tell their stories. There was a clear message that one is not alone and that there are resources out there to help. We had very positive feedback from attendees. An unintended consequence was that two other organizations utilized these resources to offer programs as well.

For More On Planning An Educational Event Please See Chapter 26.

Situation # 3

There are times when mental health promotion occurs on an individual basis. When a nurse provides information on available community resources for dealing with the stress of a family situation, an illness or financial crisis, the nurse is empowering individuals to take control of their own lives. Giving this information does not mean that the nurse should then abandon the people. The nurse can help people to develop a framework of strategies for next steps without taking away control.

A young woman was struggling with her self-esteem, her weight, and many put-downs from her mother. She felt depressed, and ate for comfort. Her grades at school were dropping, and she was becoming angry and bitter. She became pregnant and was determined to keep the child, even though she had no way of providing a home for the baby. Her own mother was a single mom so she could not help her out, as she could barely support herself. This young woman needed more than a framework within which to work! That did not mean that I took control of her life. She needed a friend to listen without judgement while she worked through some of the issues. I identified community resources that might be useful and offered to go with her if she made appointments. We met twice a week at the beginning but reduced it when she utilized other community services.

One can see from the above examples that mental health promotion does not have to be a large, community-wide activity. Small steps and interventions can indeed begin to *light tomorrow with today*, as suggested by Elizabeth Barrett Browning.

There are many other ways to promote mental health. I have not addressed specific interventions for children and youth. Early childhood education, support for parents, and home visits to new moms can help promote mental health. Children's school programs that encourage respect, caring, and dignity when dealing with other children (and adults) teach children that they should treat others as they would want to be treated.

Mental Health promotion through education can serve dual purposes. Addressing the determinants of mental health is one purpose. Another, equally important role for parish nurses is to help to erase the stigma by providing the facts about mental illness. As with any other illness, there are numerous reasons for a mental illness to develop. Some possible causes include genetic factors, abuse as a child, loss, torture, poverty, and abandonment. There are usually interventions to help people to improve their health and live productive lives (CMHA, ON). There will always be a small percentage of people whose mental illness will be debilitating, but that can be true of any illness.

Parish nurses have an opportunity to help to dispel the myths about mental illness and, hopefully, reduce the stigma. The nurse can educate staff, committees, and other groups within the faith community to expand the understanding of mental illness and demonstrate breaking down the barriers that have long shrouded mental illness.

> *Take the first step in faith.*
> *You do not have to see the whole staircase, just take the first step.*
>
> Martin Luther King, Jr.

Forty-eight

Living With Terminal Illness

The capacity to care is the thing that gives life its deepest meaning and significance.

Pablo Casals

People living with a terminal illness are doing just that – LIVING! It is tragic how often when that diagnosis is rendered, family and friends scatter because they are uncomfortable or don't know what to say.

Palliative care conjures up images of a bedridden person, maintained on high doses of narcotics for pain control, just waiting to die. In some cases, that can be true, but it is not the norm. In reality, "dying is that process a few minutes before death when the brain is deprived of oxygen; everything else is living" (Adams, 1998, p. 82).

Paul Chidwick, a minister and teacher in pastoral theology, spent ten years working with terminally ill people. He sensed that terminally ill people were concerned about spiritual issues but help in that area was left to a *particular professional group* (Chidwick, 1988). Rev. Chidwick wanted to understand if his perception of the spiritual needs of critically ill people was correct and wondered if ministers were the only ones addressing those spiritual needs. As part of his research he sent letters to some of the world experts in the field of palliative care and focused on Canadians as much as possible. Through his discussions he learned that spiritual matters were of vital importance to people living with a terminal illness.

His Findings Revealed Some Consistent Themes
(Chidwick, 1988)

- Palliative care requires a holistic approach.

- To practice holistic palliative care, there needs to be a deep awareness of "life and the spiritual needs of fellow men and women" (Chidwick, 1988, p. 10).

- Effective palliative care usually involves very caring individuals.

- For Christians caring for those who are terminally ill, Christ is found to be part of the team, and is "lying in bed in the heart of suffering and standing by the bedside as a loved one engulfed in grief" (Chidwick, 1988, p.10).

- He quotes Dr. Derek Doyle of St. Columba's Hospice in Edinburgh who says "that religious people, of any faith, have a deep innate sense of sacrifice in the service of others" (Chidwick, 1988, p.10). Dr. Doyle believes that people who have deep religious convictions of any faith have a sense of the *non-finality of death.*

- A search for meaning is a common theme. Dame Cicely Saunders of St. Christopher's Hospice in England believes "that the connection between spirituality and palliative care would be a perpetual search for meaning which, in a Christian field, means a perpetual discovery of the compassionate vulnerability of God" (Chidwick, 1988, p.11).

Consensus Between Practitioners And Critically Ill People?

These were the views and opinions of the practitioners in palliative care. But what about those people living with terminal illness? What do they want?

Patch Adams was trained as a doctor but did not have any lectures on dealing with persons whose lives would be shortened by a serious illness. He interviewed patients with terminal illness who were living out the remainder of their lives in a hospital. He found that, for the most part, those people were lonely and felt estranged from life. All that kept them connected to the world was visitors, and a few keepsakes in the room (Adams, 1998). In contrast, family and friends and all the familiar treasures of their lives surrounded people who were choosing to die at home. These people experienced joy and gratitude, and had less fear about impending death.

Patch Adams asked people to imagine what kind of a death they would want to have. Replies included "I don't want it to be painful"; "I want it to happen in my sleep". Patch asked patients in hospital if they would prefer a miserable anxious death, alone in hospital, or a *fun death*. What he means by fun death is whatever would be considered ideal and feasible within the individual's limitations (Adams, 1998).

Jerome Groopman (2005) has spent three decades working in haematology and oncology. He has been willing to be taught by his patients. He has learned techniques to determine what patients need in the way of emotional and spiritual care, along with the management of their physical illnesses. He discovered that hope could exist in desperate situations. He defines hope as "the elevating feeling we experience when we see – in the mind's eye – a path to a better future" (Groopman, 2005, p. xiv). Hope can be confused with optimism, which arises from being told to think positively or from hearing an overly rosy forecast. Optimism, in his view, has a prevailing attitude that things will turn out for the best. With hope, there is the acknowledgement that there are significant obstacles along the way, and that there is no room for delusions. "Hope, unlike optimism, is rooted in unalloyed reality"; he believes that "clear-eyed hope gives us the courage to face our circumstances and conquer them" (Groopman, 2005, p. xiv).

From my experience working with people living with a terminal illness, I have learned that the most important issue for them is being able to maintain a sense of control. When caring professionals, family, and friends start making decisions for ill people, self-esteem is diminished in an already fragile being. Ill people should be consulted on all issues concerning their care and their life, if well enough to handle them. They need to be asked!

A parish nurse is usually just one member of a team of people involved in the care of a person choosing to die at home. As in any situation, the nurse should determine the appropriateness of his/her involvement and what needs, if any, can be met.

When A Person Is Choosing To Die At Home, Important Considerations For The Parish Nurse

- Ask the individual with terminal illness what is wanted or needed. Inform the person that there is no judgement on wishes or desires. No wish is too insignificant, or too silly.

- Offer possible solutions to concerns that have been mentioned. Be sensitive to the feelings of the family and the individual.

- If others seem to be avoiding spiritual issues, inquire whether the person wants to talk about thoughts and feelings.

- Ask the caregiver or close family members if they need to talk about what is happening to their loved one. There is usually support for the ill person, but there may not be a listener for the family.

- If the person is asking questions regarding faith issues, attend to the concerns and ask if it would be helpful to have a minister come to discuss them.

- Ask whether the individual or family would like prayer with the nurse. If not, pray privately for them.

When an individual with a life-threatening illness is still able to make choices about how the remaining days will be spent, we must do everything that we are able to do to honour those wishes.

> *God has infinite treasures to bestow, and*
> *we take up with a little sensible devotion,*
> *which passes in a moment.*
> *Blind as we are, we hinder God and stop*
> *the current of His graces.*
> *But when He finds a soul penetrated with*
> *a lively faith,*
> *He pours into it His grace and favours*
> *plentifully.*
> *There they flow like a torrent...*
> *which spreads itself with impetuosity and*
> *abundance.*
>
> Brother Lawrence (Popov, 2004, p. 205.)

Forty-nine

Caring for Caregivers: Education and Support

Be of good cheer. Do not think of today's failures, but of the success that may come tomorrow.
You have set yourself a difficult task, but you will succeed if you persevere; and you will find a joy in overcoming obstacles.

Helen Keller

Care giving can become an all-consuming task. Caregivers need to establish objectives and to set limits. This may sound very harsh. After all, in the real world how can you do that? Once the caregiver accepts the need for setting limits, the nurse can help that person find a way.

Working with caregivers in the forty-plus age group is particularly important as they are often balancing caring for children and working outside the home while trying to provide support and/or care for aging parents. The *sandwich generation,* as it has been labeled, is being pulled in all directions and as a result has no time for personal needs. The result is burnout!

Signs Of Excessive Stress Levels Include:

- Anger at the person being cared for

- Exhaustion

- Social withdrawal – no time for friends

- Depression – feeling sad and hopeless

- Overreacting emotionally – irritable, crying a lot

- Sleeplessness

- Health problems such as chronic backaches, headaches, weight gain or loss

- Anxiety - not really looking forward to another day

- Inability to concentrate

When caregivers are suffering high levels of stress, intervention is necessary. It is better if we can prevent their getting to that state at all. A parish nurse should learn to identify people at risk and try to help them avoid a crisis situation. Failing that, a parish nurse can work one on one with individuals in crisis to help them set more manageable goals for themselves. Brainstorming and exploring the merits of different ways of reaching objectives, or lowering expectations of themselves and others, can lead to more balance in clients' lives.

I've developed a new philosophy...
I only dread one day at a time.

Charlie Brown

In some circles people talk about role reversal, *parenting the parent.* I have a problem with this analogy. There is a change in what assistance is given and who is giving the assistance. But to speak of parenting a frail elderly person is not the same as parenting a three-year-old child without any life experience. We are <u>not</u> attempting to raise our parents as we raise our children. They are not our children, and they don't need us to control their lives. What they probably need is some assistance along the way.

With the very old there is wisdom; and in length of days comes understanding.

Job 12:12

In my practice I learned that education and support groups work very well for some people. In response to a need, I offer a program called *You and Your Aging Relatives.* Depending on the numbers of participants and their particular objectives for the program, it runs from four to six evening sessions.

Full-time caregivers may require someone to stay with the family member so that the caregiver can attend the program. Trained lay pastoral visitors could be called for this ministry.

The First Session Includes:

- building a comfort level within the group using group-building activities, and small group discussions about personal objectives for the program.

- asking people to talk about what they hope to get from taking the course.

- outlining my objectives for the program, which are to meet the needs of the group. I stress that I will be dealing with the aging process and communication strategies.

- giving a quiz on the facts and myths of aging. It is a good way to debunk some myths that people believe to be truths.

The Second Session Includes:

- discussing the aging process. Looking at

the quiz from the previous week and seeking to understand the truths about the aging process. I use role-plays to help people get a sense of the realities of being older and having less control over their lives.

- discussing the emotions felt during the role-play (see below).

- talking about new insights as a result of the role-pay (see below).

- setting topics for discussion for next session.

A Sample Role-Play

I ask people to put themselves in the role of an older person.

I ask them to imagine:
You have lost the use of your dominant hand. It is totally paralyzed. You cannot move it.

I have them repeat:
I have lost the use of my right/left arm. It is totally paralyzed. I cannot move it.

I ask:
What does the loss mean to you?
How do you see yourself?
How do you think others will see you?
And treat you?
What can you now not do for yourself?

Now, make me your caregiver:
   I am going to make sure that you get all
   the help you need.
   I will help you exercise.
   I will give medication.
   I will teach you how to compensate with
   the other arm.

   Would that solve your problems?
   Would that resolve for you the impact of a
   dead arm?

Now you are 84 years old.
   Your spouse of 60 years dies.
   You still have one side that doesn't work.
   How are you feeling, and how will you
   manage?

Your only child and his family have been
transferred to another part of the country.

   What do you feel now?
   How might your child be feeling?

It is important at this point to have a dialogue
in a quiet reflective manner about what people are
thinking and how they are feeling.

The above is an emotional scenario, but it
demonstrates what some people face and illus-
trates why people might react in certain ways. As
the facilitator I am the one piling on the losses,
so each person in the group gets to experience
the individual emotions, and they can discuss their
feelings as a group. This is a very effective way to
promote discussion! It is also useful to show how
the offers of assistance do not mean a lot when a

person is trying to come to terms with some overwhelming new realities. Helpers sometimes do not understand why a person lashes out when assistance is offered.

The Third Session Includes:

- asking for feedback on the previous session.

- discussing emotions associated with their aging relatives (their own and their relative's).

- asking people to identify the issues associated with those emotions.

- meeting with a funeral director to discuss pre-planning funerals, costs, options etc. Many people have had no experience with funerals so having a funeral director who is willing to answer questions is a great service for caregivers.

- talking about the grief process.

Examples of issues and emotions

- Older adult showing anger and impatience (may fear losing control of life)

- Younger adult feeling sad and helpless (may be grieving the losses of older adult or may not know what to do to help a loved one)

- Younger adult feeling guilty because the

older adult feels lonely (may wish to give more help but has other responsibilities)

The Fourth Session Includes:

- getting feedback from the previous session. What was helpful? What was not?

- talking about services available in the community:

  - How do you gain access?
  - What do you have to pay for?
  - What are the costs?
  - How do you qualify for long-term care?
  - What are the different levels of care?
  - How does the system work?
  - Waiting lists?
  - What if my parent or relative cannot afford the services?
  - Does being a veteran have any benefits?

Needless to say this fills up the whole session. People with some experience can offer hints to others. I stress the importance of advocacy as individuals may need someone to speak on their behalf.

The Fifth Session Includes:

- Communicating with our aging relatives:

  - Good listening skills

- What do I mean versus what do they hear?
- Body language inconsistent with the older adult's verbal language. Body language inconsistent with the younger adult's.
- Sharing opinions with older adults
- Giving advice to older adults – welcomed or not?
- Collaborating for decision-making

The Sixth Session Can Include: (depending on group needs)

- *Ways to reduce caregiver stress:*

  - Have healthy meals – get adequate exercise and rest
  - Take time to relax everyday!
  - Keep in touch with family, friends, and church
  - Set priorities – what can you let go of?
  - Enlist help from others
  - Use the available community services
  - Link with others dealing with similar issues
  - Attend support group meetings; meet at a coffee shop!
  - Use relaxation techniques – prayer, meditation, and massage
  - Do not make promises that will be difficult or impossible to keep
  - Educate yourself and others about the situation of your loved one

- Don't *beat yourself up* for what you cannot do
- Do as Charlie Brown does – "Dread only one day at a time."

Other Topics Could Be:

- Difficult behaviours

- Memory loss - normal

- Dementia

- Self-esteem issues

- Grief of younger adult- anticipatory grief

- Powers of Attorney

- Executorships

- Care giving at a distance

- Depression in the elderly

It is most important to meet the needs of the group. Have solid plans for the first session and then have options that can be addressed in other sessions. A wonderful quotation by Johann Wolfgang Von Goethe (1749-1832) is still an excellent guideline for balanced living today.

Nine Requisites For Contented Living

Health enough to make work a pleasure
Wealth enough to support your needs
Strength to battle with difficulties and overcome them

*Grace enough to confess your sins and
forsake them
Patience enough to toil until some good is
accomplished
Charity enough to see some good in your
neighbor
Love enough to move you to be useful
and helpful to others
Faith enough to make real the things of
God
Hope enough to remove all anxious fears
concerning the future*

Fifty

How Complex
Can Situations Be?
– A Story

*Sometimes you have to take a step
back, in order to move forward.*

Unknown

Many situations involving elderly people are complex, and it may seem nearly impossible to preserve both autonomy and safety. For the purpose of this story, I will use *husband* for the partner who is mentally competent but physically ill, and *wife* for the physically well person diagnosed with an early dementia.

The husband, a man in his 80's, was taken to hospital with breathing difficulties, in addition to numerous other chronic physical ailments. The wife, of similar age, consistently demonstrated that her judgement and short-term memory were failing, but was adamant that she was managing at home on her own. There was evidence that she was not capable of making decisions about financial matters or determining which mail was important, as she took piles of paper and mail to her husband in hospital. This activity overwhelmed the husband whose health was failing. Because the wife could not remember recent conversations, she continued the same behaviours. Things appeared to be on a downward spiral!

Prior to this hospitalization, the home situation had been tenuous, as the husband had suffered many injuries from falls, due to his progressive illness. His wife was usually able to find someone in the building to help him get up. Several times the ambulance was called when he required medical care. The family doctor and the family were encouraging the couple to look at alternative living arrangements, but they were not willing to consider any other options and felt that people were trying to run their lives.

I encourage people to plan ahead and think about options when they are well, but I find that most people do not make changes until they are in crisis and have fewer alternatives. That is unfortunate, as being autonomous means, "acting or existing independently or having the power to do so" (Oxford, 2000, p. 54). Most often, families are genuinely concerned about their older relatives and want to keep them safe, but their efforts can cause friction between themselves and the older people.

Important Questions to Consider

- What happens to the spouse when the person who is mentally competent is in hospital?

- What if the person with dementia believes that she is competent but repeatedly demonstrates otherwise, and refuses help?

- How do you deal with the husband's denial of the severity of his wife's memory problems, while not worrying him needlessly?

- What if there is no family available to stay with the spouse at home?

- How do you respect the autonomy of the mentally competent person in hospital while protecting the spouse living at risk at home?

What is the role of a parish nurse?

It is always difficult to shift gears from a supportive role to one of intervention. I had been visiting this couple that, despite all their infirmities, had been able to remain reasonably safe and autonomous. Together, by using their individual abilities, they were able to manage. When one required hospitalization and *the team* fell apart, new and different strategies had to be initiated. This situation would have been even more difficult if the couple had not followed my recommendation when they were well enough to make good decisions, and appointed substitute decision makers for health and property.

Please See Chapter 16 On Advance Directives.

In any complex situation, it is important to stop and look at the whole picture and keep clear objectives in mind. Band-aid solutions may seem to be the answer in the short term but often get in the way of the long-term objectives. The role of the parish nurse is to be an advocate for the couple. It can be useful to bring together all the people involved, including the couple, and discuss possible actions that may alleviate some of the difficulties. In this particular case, I was in touch with the wife on a daily basis and reassured the husband of my support. Increasingly, it was evident that the wife was losing touch with reality. She did not dress appropriately for the climate (e.g. no boots or winter coat even though there was snow and the temperature was −10 C). She wore the same dress every day, could not manage her medications, and exhibited signs of poor nutritional status.

As the husband was unable to confront and deal with the fact that due to his worsening condition he could not return home to live, I contacted his son, who was the designated power of attorney. I recommended meeting with his father at the hospital to explore the possibility of his taking over the financial matters until his father was again able to do it. I made a point of saying *when*, not *if*, as it left the door open for later, should his father's condition improve to a point that he was interested in, or capable of managing the finances. I spoke with the social worker on this man's ward, and suggested that it might be helpful to have a discussion with this gentleman and his son. The social worker, a physiotherapist, a case manager from the home care program (CCAC), and I met with the husband to consider his future options. It was important to have the initial discussion without the wife being present, as the husband needed to face his own limitations.

I Confirmed Our Objectives:

- To investigate long-term care options through Veterans Affairs for, and with, the husband

- To facilitate the involvement of the designated substitute decision maker to help manage his father's financial affairs

- To determine what immediate interventions could support the wife's safety

- To identify resources to enhance the quality of the wife's life, taking into account her precarious condition

- To look at potential long-term solutions that would allow for husband and wife to be near to one another while receiving appropriate levels of care

Early Outcomes

- The husband agreed that it would be helpful to have his son assist with managing his finances.

- The application process for long term care was to be initiated with inquiries about benefits for Veterans.

- I called the man's doctor with whom I had maintained contact, and informed him of the hospital meeting. The hospital was out of our area but we were able, eventually, to have the man transferred back to our local hospital, where his own doctor could care for him.

- I took the wife to see her doctor, at the doctor's request. Arrangements were made for an assessment with a geriatrician, with a view to determining if memory-enhancing medication might be helpful and appropriate.

The wife's physician again broached the subject of long-term care, where both could receive the care they needed and be together. With being close to one another as the main focus, the wife, for the first time, entertained the idea of leaving her home. The wife asked the doctor for medication to help her sleep. The doctor was concerned about the lady's ability to manage her medications. The physician had previously ordered the medication to be administered in *blister packs* so that medications for specific times were packaged together, to reduce confusion, and also to determine whether the lady was taking the medication appropriately.

There was no evidence of *blister packs* in the home and pills were in wine goblets with pieces of paper in the glasses. Some had three medications and one label; one had three labels and one medication. The husband's medications were all mixed up with hers. With the lady's permission, I took the husband's medications and the remainder of hers, with the new prescription, to the pharmacist, and told him what I had seen. He had personally been delivering the medications on a weekly basis so was shocked!

Immediate Next Steps

- The pharmacist contacted the physician to clarify what medications the wife should be taking.

- Consent of power of attorney (POA) was required before CCAC could intervene.

- The pharmacist again delivered medication in blister packs.

- I contacted the CCAC coordinator to determine if a nurse could visit on a regular basis to monitor the medications.

- The son was overwhelmed and wanted to delay the assessment by the geriatrician. The son was informed by the social worker of his liability if he refused, and if the lady was then injured in a preventable event.

It is impossible to document all the challenges in a situation such as this, but I will outline a few of the more significant ones. When dealing with a couple, one in hospital and the other in the community, who both require placement, it is almost unattainable to have everyone on the same page at the same time.

The doctor told the man, who was about to be discharged from hospital that his health had deteriorated to the point that he needed to go to a long-term care facility. He was also informed of his wife's deteriorating mental status. When both husband and wife met with a geriatrician, they agreed that being together was the most important thing, and they would go (reluctantly) to a long-term care facility. Because the husband was in hospital, his need to be placed was seen as a higher priority, as his bed was needed. This meant that he would have to take a bed that was not necessarily his first choice. He could wait there until the selected facility was open, and he and his wife could both be admitted.

A meeting was arranged for the wife to meet with her doctor. Her POA for personal care was present, as was the parish nurse, a case manager, and a placement coordinator from the Community Care Access Centre, the home care program in Ontario. The doctor explained to the wife that she and her husband could be placed together in a soon-to-be-opened facility. In the meantime, some help at home would be provided to monitor and assist her until things could be arranged. Following this meeting, the POA said that she was meeting with a social worker at the hospital to talk about retirement homes for the couple. It had been clearly stated by the doctor that the husband's health care needs exceeded what could be provided in that type of facility. With both partners presenting with signs of dementia, trying to come to a consensus long enough to actually begin the process was something akin to *trying to nail jelly to the wall.* In the end, the husband went to a long-term care unit in the hospital, and the wife refused to leave her home. Being together did not seem to have the same priority it once did!

The doctors had been trying for about two years to get this couple to look to the future and make plans. As in most cases, they resisted. Now, when they needed to have a unified plan, it was impossible as they changed their minds, and often could not remember what they had agreed to do. The powers of attorney were trying to help but became frustrated, as their hands were tied.

The status at the time of writing

- The husband is in long-term care and his

health has improved, as he is eating well and getting his medications consistently. He is still very frail and displaying more memory loss.

- The wife is somehow managing at home with more involvement by the power of attorney. Is she living at risk? Yes! What can be done? Nothing, unless the doctor is prepared to declare this lady incompetent. She is not totally incompetent, but does have deficits.

- Some services are being provided, but until there is a crisis, nothing will change.

This story demonstrates the limits faced by a parish nurse or any health care professional. People have the right to make their own decisions, even if others disagree with their choices. Unless the wife is declared incapable of making her own decisions, she can live as she chooses, as long as she is not putting others at risk. The stove has been disabled so that there will be no more fires (there were two). It is difficult to stand back and wait until something happens to the wife, but that is the current situation. Meanwhile, the husband is pressing to go home from the long-term care facility.

The clergy are involved with both husband and wife. When it can be arranged, a minister takes the wife to hospital when Communion is being taken to the husband. This helps to keep both partners connected with the church and with each other. The clergy can remain neutral, as they are not directly involved in the chaos of trying to sort out appropriate, safe living arrangements for the couple.

> *True freedom lies in the realization*
> *and calm acceptance of the fact*
> *that there may very well be no perfect*
> *answer.*

Allan Reid McGinnis

Part Nine:

The Parish Nurse
As Role Model

Fifty-one
Taking Care of Ourselves

We are all substantially flawed,
wounded, angry, hurt, here on Earth.
But this human condition, so painful
to us, and in some ways shameful
- because we feel we are weak when
the reality of ourselves is exposed -
is made much more bearable when
it is shared, face to face,
in words that have expressive human
eyes behind them.

Alice Walker
Anything We Love Can be Saved

Consider for a moment the things in life that give you energy and lift your spirits; then think about what percentage of your time is spent doing those things. Are you running with a full tank or are you approaching empty? Nursing is a caring profession. Continually evaluating situations and interacting with people requires a great deal of energy. Because of the significant giving of self, it is even more important to keep self-care in mind. It is so easy to get caught up in giving that little bit more which may put the nurse's own health in jeopardy. When you work in an independent practice there are not the same opportunities for the day-to-day peer support as in a clinical setting. Building a network of support people is essential. Linking with other parish nurses and comparing notes on problem solving can be useful. Developing strategies for managing the challenges is an ongoing, dynamic process.

Set Priorities

I have learned, sometimes the hard way, that there are always more opportunities to serve than one person can handle. Setting priorities and re-evaluating them regularly helps to keep me focused on the most important tasks. Working with the ministers and having them give feedback helps me to prioritize. It is crucial to our well-being that we look within ourselves and become more aware of our strengths and weaknesses.

Develop Self-awareness

What does it mean to be self-aware? I believe that spending time with yourself in silence, meditation, and prayer; listening to your thoughts; being mindful of your breathing; and being in the *here and now* on a regular basis can fortify and strengthen you. It takes considerable discipline to maintain a regular prayer and meditation practice, but if managed, I find that clarity and serenity are the benefits.

Focusing on the present moment gives you the benefit of letting go of the past and not projecting into the future. Worry about the future and regrets about the past may not be useful and can be destructive. Over time we can become anxious and frustrated. While future planning is important, focusing our attention on the here and now can result in more energy and insight in dealing with current situations. A healthy balanced diet, regular exercise, and sufficient sleep are other essential components of well-being. Learning what it takes to keep well and balanced in all aspects of your life requires ongoing self-examination and reflection. Relaxation exercises, therapeutic massage, yoga, and Pilates are other tools for reducing stress and promoting healing within.

Letting Go

One reason for entering the helping professions is a need to be needed. Recognizing one's own desire to be needed helps to keep things in perspective. When faced with a new situation, it is useful to ask yourself *whose need is this?* When your life is beginning to feel out of control, it is time to stand back and examine what has tipped the balance. If you are unable to sort that out yourself, seek a trusted person to assist you. It is often easier for another person to be more objective about your life. It can be painful to accept the fact that we cannot be all things to all people, but recognizing that we cannot please everybody is an important step in taking care of ourselves. It is hard to admit that we sometimes need to distance ourselves from certain situations. Women, in particular, have been socialized to think that we have to do it all! Challenge the belief that others always come first!

Parish Nurses As Role Models

If a parish nurse is feeling completely drained, what is there left to give? If we listen to our bodies, there may be signals indicating the need for a change in behaviours. Backache, headache, gastric distress, and sleeping problems are just some of the warning signs of excessive stress. Ignoring those signs will sooner or later affect our health. If we manage our own health, we can be better examples for others.

There are times when I need to stop *doing* and direct my attention toward *being*. Jon Kabat Zinn and Saki Santorelli promote and teach *Mindfulness Based Stress Reduction*, a technique for meditation practice. Mindfulness, according to Saki Santorelli is "an inner discipline for learning to meet and enter with awareness the challenges inherent in taking care of ourselves and serving others" (Santorelli, 1999, p.1). When I am disciplined in following this program, I do feel healthier. I am more able to deal with the concerns of others when I have taken the time to care for myself.

Using the life of Jesus as a model for ministering to others while caring for self, Solari-Twadell (1990) outlines the steps Jesus took to keep well. He developed a strong team to work with Him; He developed a close network of friends to support Him; He prayed often; He slept and ate healthfully; He practiced solitude, and He did God's will. When problems arose, Jesus dealt with them and did not allow them to take Him away from His work. What better role model could we have?

Core Concepts

- Listen to your body.

- Take time for prayer and meditation.

- Work at developing and maintaining balance in your life.

- Build a network of support.

- Celebrate what you can do and let go of what you are not able to complete.

Fifty-two
Shattered, But Still Whole

*For, lo, the winter is past, the rain is
over and gone;
the flowers appear on the earth;
the time of singing has come,
and the voice of the turtledove is
heard in our land.*

Song of Solomon 2:11-12

You have multiple sclerosis... those words, and the implications of them changed my life, as I had known it. I was now different. I was set apart from others. I had an illness. I did not know how this was going to play out, but I was shattered by the possibilities. Images of dependency, assistive devices, and abandonment flashed through my mind. How could I be a support to others when I was feeling devastated? The fatigue, the stumbling, the exacerbations, dropping things, the anger, the fear! Each day when I awakened, I was reminded of the new status attached to me. I was a person with an illness. An illness that was here to stay. An illness for which there was no cure. This news reshaped my view of the world.

The medications used to reduce the symptoms and slow down the progression of the disease can cause unpleasant side effects. Flu-like symptoms, depression, weakness, and discoloured swellings at the injection sites challenged my resolve to stay on the medication. I was angry. I was profoundly saddened. I blamed myself when my body didn't function the way I wanted. This wasn't how my life was supposed to be. I was supposed to be healthy. How could I expect to have any credibility when I could not be a healthy role model, as parish nurse? I read everything I could find about the disease. I tried to find a reason. What did I do to cause this illness? There were no answers to those questions.

I read a book that was required reading for a meditation conference I was planning to attend.

The book title is *Heal Thy Self* by Saki Santorelli. He tells the story of a sculptor who lived with a disability and yet was able to carry on with his work. The artist created an imposing sphere out of marble. He worked hard to perfect this sphere, chipping and polishing until the surface was flawless. Upon completion of his masterpiece, he took a hammer and broke it into hundreds of pieces. He then, painstakingly, put it back together using a drill and screws and glue. When it was finished he named it *Shattered, But Still Whole*. Shattered, but still whole! Shattered I felt, but I certainly had not thought of myself as still whole. On the contrary I saw myself as damaged, broken. I read and reread that story.

As I reflected on the possibilities, the potential for being a victim of a serious chronic illness, I realized that I had some choices to make. I could let this illness take over my life, or I could manage my life while living with this disease. I made the decision to regain control and not be a victim. It was a bumpy and winding road back. With the support of family, friends, staff, and my doctors, I came to believe in myself again. Prayer, meditation, exercise and long discussions with my husband helped me through the tough times.

Some Things I Learned Along The Way

- Chronic illness is unpredictable. Expect that.
- There are good days and bad days.

- People do care.

- Life isn't over.

- There are many things you can still do.

- Coffee with a good friend helps a lot.

- You have to conserve energy and rest more often.

- You become more aware of how others are managing their conditions.

- You have more credibility when dealing with people who are unwell, as they know that you have some understanding of what it might be like for them. Using the words of Henri Nouwen, I felt like a *wounded healer.*

Once I realized that it was up to me how I perceived my new reality, I shifted my thinking to focus on what I have, rather than what I have lost. I have become healthier in spirit, mind, and yes, in body.

Disclosing the diagnosis proved to be an interesting study in human behaviour. Some people were empathetic and wanted to understand, and be helpful. Others found it necessary to reveal to me the worst case of multiple sclerosis they had ever encountered. There were those who pitied me. I found this type of situation the most difficult to handle. I felt that pity somehow diminished my status, while elevating the other person's.

The passage from the Song of Solomon at the beginning of this chapter speaks of hope. The winter and rain of our lives can pass; the flowers will bloom again and there will be singing. We can choose to see and hear the beauty in the world. We can choose our attitudes. Our choices do have an impact on our healing. We may have been shattered, but we can still be whole.

Part Ten:

Success Stories

Fifty-three
From The
Parish Nurse...

*It is only as we develop others
that we permanently succeed.*

Harvey S. Firestone

The presence of a nurse in a staff position in a church was unusual when I began my ministry. Increasing the profile of the role while educating people was a challenge. I submitted articles for the church newsletter and maintained a bulletin board with current faith and health issues. I wrote occasional articles in the Sunday service bulletin but I found that people were still somewhat baffled as to what a parish nurse really does.

When I created a weekly column *From The Parish Nurse...*for the Sunday bulletin, it was as if I had turned on a light. People began to really understand the scope of my role. As I imagine anyone writing a weekly column discovers, it is a challenge to create something with a weekly deadline. In spite of that stress, it was by far the best communication tool I developed.

Over the years I have written about countless health and faith issues and have made an effort to connect with all people by choosing topics pertaining to different *ages and stages*. I have been diligent at keeping in tune with current issues and specially designated weeks or months (e.g. Heart and Stroke month). In the autumn when children are returning to school, articles on appropriate backpacks, bullying, and compassion for others are met with great interest.

One story on compassion

An 8-year-old boy had kicked four of his team's five goals in a soccer game by half time, and the other team had failed to score. Near the end of the game he was in a position for another certain goal. To the amazement of all he weakly tapped the ball and failed to score. On the way home when asked by his father why he did that, the boy replied sadly, "But Dad, their goalie was crying".

A short article such as this serves as a reminder for parents, as well as children. Some articles are factual; others tug at the heartstrings. Prayers and meditations have been well received, and people have told me that they put them on their refrigerators. In fact, I believe many of the articles have been posted on refrigerator doors at one time or another. Not all articles are serious, as humour is needed too. "No excuse Sunday" that talks about having cots for all who need more sleep, having doctors and nurses present for those who plan to be sick, and having the church decorated with both Christmas poinsettias and Easter lilies for the people who have never seen it undecorated, gives people a chuckle.

My sources and resources are varied. I subscribe to several reliable online health newsletters that keep me current on physical and mental health issues. I borrow books from the clergy and the church library for some of the spiritual resources, but I have developed a fairly extensive parish nurse library as well.

Stress, depression, grief, and anger have been topics for an article, or series of articles. By introducing different themes, I show parishioners that I am willing to talk to them about whatever concerns them. I write a series of articles pertaining to an educational event for a few weeks prior to the event. I attempt to challenge people's assumptions and try to create a desire to learn more about that subject matter.

When health crises such as SARS, West Nile virus, and post traumatic shock in response to terrorist attacks occur, gathering data, doing first-rate research, and presenting a summary of information with references to reputable sources give people the opportunity to draw their own conclusions. Personal bias and scare tactics should be avoided.

I write *food for thought* articles that often include contradictory quotations on a particular subject. My objective is to increase awareness of specific issues and, hopefully, to foster discussion of the issues in the congregation. Some examples are relationships, mid-life issues, parenting, family meetings, talking with teens, and listening to teens.

Throughout the church year I write articles pertaining to Lent, Easter, mothers and fathers (around the times of the designated days), gratitude, Thanksgiving, Advent, Christmas, and the hopes and dreams of a new year. The scope is sizeable here so let the creative juices flow!

I enjoy writing the articles and do research to satisfy my own desire to learn. Having a venue for utilizing this valuable information challenges me to assimilate it and present it in a fashion that educates people, while encouraging them to come to their own understanding of the subject. An unanticipated and amazing outcome has been the response of parishioners: comments like "I read your article before I read anything else in the bulletin", and "I look forward to seeing what you will write about each week". A tool designed to increase the awareness and understanding of the role of parish nursing has far exceeded my expectations!

Keep in mind that there may be opportunities to send your articles by email to churches without a parish nurse on staff. Two other churches included some of my articles in their church bulletins for a year or two. Sharing resources among churches and denominations broadens the opportunity for health promotion in the community. It can also give the receiving congregations a beginning insight into the value of having their own health ministries. In a congregation with a fledgling parish nurse, having regular or occasional bulletin articles from an experienced parish nurse can be a great support. It can provide health information to the congregation, while modelling one aspect of the nurse's teaching role and reducing some of the strain on the new parish nurse. Since most parish nurses practice in independent settings, sharing resources and supporting each other are even more important than in most nursing practice settings. Sending articles that you have already written for your own congregation is an easy and wonderful way to share your experience.

Fifty-four
Tuesday Ladies and Men

The harvest of old age is the recollection and abundance of blessings previously secured.

Cicero

Being alone is in the deepest sense the human condition. Loneliness is the disease of feeling isolated, cut off from human contact and human warmth. Some people battle all their lives against this poignant emotion, struggling constantly to come to terms with the immutable fact of their existence: that all human beings are separate, one from another, and will remain so all their lives; each sealed within a thin veneer of skin. If this struggle is successful, the individual ultimately transcends his physical limitations and becomes most himself precisely because he is closely bound to others.

Eric P. Moss (*The Conquest of Loneliness*)

Loneliness and isolation can be a part of aging, but they do not need to be a way of life. We can choose to be isolated from others, but in the long run we lose our identity, self-esteem, and our ability to seek out others. In spite of the fact that each person is a self-contained entity, we do benefit and grow personally when we interact with others. As parish nurses we learn to identify the people who are isolated, and we should, if possible, find ways to bring those isolated, frail elderly people together if that is what they choose to do. Encouragement is acceptable; harassment is not!

A group of eight to ten persons seems to work very well. If there are regular meetings, one or two people will not attend for a variety of reasons. Health issues and doctor's appointments are often the rationale for absence. Small groups can foster closer connections among the members.

Robert Atchley (1980) states that some older people prefer to disengage from activities and roles they occupied in middle age. The term *disengagement* was coined by Cumming and Henry (as cited in Atchley, 1980) to refer to a process whereby an individual responds to aging by gradually withdrawing from others and focusing more on himself. This process is not inevitable, nor is it always a bad thing, as people recognize that there is a short time left in their lives, and they are content to live with their memories.

Dr. Michael Gordon, a noted geriatrician, emphasizes that the majority of older people do not have the psychological problems that the general public and many health care providers believe they have (1981). Significant changes are frequently the result of illness and should be investigated. Minimal changes in memory can occur but are most often related to the way a person has always been.

For parish nurses, identifying a need for a group of homebound people to come together for social interaction and purposeful activities can have a positive impact on the lives of some older people. The Tuesday Ladies' and the Tuesday Men's groups were a big success. The key to success is to have good leadership for the groups. As parish nurse, I worked with both groups during the start-up phase and then gradually involved others in a leadership role.

The Tuesday Ladies, as mentioned in Chapter

One, enjoyed a relationship with the children in the junior choir. Sharing activities such as having tea, singing together, making small gifts, and receiving thank-you notes from the children augmented the ladies' participation in the church family. Speakers on relevant topics such as planning a funeral, wills, estate planning, and safety were interspersed with lighter subjects like making teddy bears, flower arranging, and story telling. These activities provided opportunities to have fun while learning new things. Occasionally the Tuesday Men and Ladies met together for a special program.

The Tuesday Men originated as the result of a question from the Alzheimer Society about activities for men whose wives were in daycare. We did not have such a group, so we started one. One of the ministers and I identified potential members and spoke to them personally but also invited all older men in the congregation. We had ten men at the beginning, and the group learned about each other's lives. Sports, history, politics, and the changes they had noted in their lifetime were frequent topics of discussion. As in the Tuesday Ladies group, the participants learned that it was a safe place to share their pain. For the most part, in the early stages the men just enjoyed reminiscing but there was a need for repairing hymnbooks and prayer books so the men undertook the task. They could chat while they worked, and they felt good about providing a service to the church. Over time as the group became smaller, the men enjoyed cribbage games, stories, and jokes.

Over the years the focus of the groups changed,

and the Tuesday Men's group is no longer in exis-tence. Now we find other ways to have older men involved. For some older people, the Wednesday morning worship service provides spiritual and so-cial enrichment in a quieter atmosphere than Sun-day services. Once a month we organize a coffee hour for those attending the Wednesday worship service. We provide drives for those events as well as for the luncheons (in place of the coffee hour) four times a year. The Tuesday Ladies group still exists, and although these ladies are even frailer, they continue to meet to socialize and offer sup-port to one another. For those unable to come out to meetings, the parish nurse, clergy, and lay pas-toral visitors help to keep them connected to the church.

Please See Chapter 35 For More On Lay Pastoral Visitors.

The challenge for parish nurses, as in any nurs-ing position, is to engage with people but be able to grieve and let go when they become ill and die. As nurses, we are trained to care for people where they are and love them. We must recognize that we need that professional distance, or we will never be effective in this ministry of parish nursing.

> *Well, mythology tells us that where you stumble, there your treasure is....*
> *The world is a match for us and we're a match for the world.*
> *And where it seems most challenging lies the greatest invitation to find deeper and greater powers in ourselves.*
> Joseph Campbell

Fifty-five
Mentoring

The expert at anything was once a beginner.

Hayes

A registered nurse asked me, when starting a parish nursing ministry in her church, if I would consider acting as a mentor to her from September to June. I was delighted and flattered, but apprehensive. I did not see myself as an authority, but I was excited at the prospect of having a colleague with whom I could discuss concerns and strategies. I had been a *lone wolf* for many years. I had consulted with other nurses, helping to develop parish nursing in their churches, but none for an extended period.

I had met with this nurse and some of the team involved in developing a parish nursing ministry in her church, but I never expected to have an opportunity such as this. I say opportunity because I learned so much. When I was questioned about what I was doing and why I chose a certain strategy, it lead to formalizing the concepts so that I could communicate my reasons. I had started my program before there were guidelines so I had often worked *instinctively*.

It was a privilege to have an intelligent, accomplished nurse, who taught nursing as a profession, working alongside me as a member of our pastoral team. Fresh insights from a new person foster innovative ideas and validate strategies, programs, and ways of doing things that are functioning well. I believe we both felt that it was a win-win situation.

There is always potential for tension in new work situations, so why was this so successful?

We identified some points for others to consider when contemplating a mentoring relationship.

- Our personalities, although very different, complemented one another. That is an important consideration because if we were very similar, there would not be the same impetus for growth. It goes without saying that compatibility and mutual respect are essential.

- Both parties should be open and honest about their expectations.

- The mentor should be clear about what is manageable.

- The person being mentored ought to be aware of the appropriateness of his or her presence in certain sensitive situations, and act accordingly.

- The mentor is responsible for presenting opportunities for learning, while the person being mentored has to be willing to participate in the majority of tasks, not just preferred ones. The mentor is taking on extra responsibilities, so sharing the load provides more time for learning experiences.

In certain circumstances, it is beneficial to have two people involved in visiting a couple. An example is a caregiver situation where the caregiver needs someone to hear his or her story, while the other nurse visits with the person requiring care. Each is given one-on-one attention, reinforcing the worth of each person.

The nurse I mentored and I see other opportunities for parish nurses to share their experience. One option could be mentoring undergraduate BScN students in a community health rotation; another is mentoring RN's in post-graduate parish nursing programs. Mentoring validates the importance of this field of nursing to colleagues as well as to clients. We encourage experienced parish nurses to consider this different and valuable role for parish nurses.

Mentorship is a privilege to be honoured. When another person trusts you as a respected teacher and guide, you have a responsibility to share your knowledge and to be open to listening and learning from another professional.

Like the body that is made up of different limbs and organs, all mortal creatures exist depending on one another.

-Hindu proverb

Part Eleven:

The Voice Of Experience

Fifty-six
Little Things Mean a Lot...

Those who bring sunshine to the lives of others cannot keep it from themselves.

James M. Barrie

Little things mean a lot. How often have we heard that said? I have been amazed at how true it is. Countless times I have been surprised at feedback from parishioners about something that seemed such a small effort on my part, but made a big difference in someone's life. When we bring sunshine into a situation, the impact can be far reaching.

Examples From My Practice

Situation # 1

A man in his early eighties was living with the devastating effects of cancer on his face. The cancer was spreading to his bones as well. Mr. D. had been an avid golfer all his life and had managed a golf course at one time. He lived with his wife who was temporarily incapacitated because of surgery. Mrs. D. enjoyed walking with her husband but Mr. D. was feeling isolated, as he was not well enough to go alone. I asked a man who loved golf if he would walk with Mr. D. to the coffee shop, have a coffee with him, and talk about golf, once a week. The men enjoyed one another and the *golf chats*, and Mrs. D. felt better knowing that her husband was having some enjoyment. When Mr. D. was not well enough to walk to the coffee shop, the visitor picked up the coffee and went to Mr. D.'s home. This small act of kindness by one human being enriched the lives of both men.

Situation # 2

Older people who are in poor health and move to a new area to be close to a son or daughter frequently find it difficult to adapt to their unfamiliar surroundings. They have left their friends and their home behind and have no contacts other than family. If the adult children work outside of the home, the older person is alone all day. This can be disheartening for the older person. One woman, following her husband's death, came to stay with her daughter. The older lady had planned to return home after about a month but had a minor stroke while visiting the daughter. The daughter felt that it was safer for her mother to move closer to her, rather than returning alone to her home. The woman had been very active in her church and missed it a great deal. The daughter phoned our church to see what might be available to help her mother. I visited the woman several times and, after getting to know her, contacted another widowed woman who was a lay pastoral visitor and asked her to visit by phone. Connecting these two women did not require much effort on my part, but the two became close friends and supported one another. The new woman was welcomed into the Tuesday Group and became an active member in that group and others.

Please See Chapter 54 For More On The Tuesday Group.

Situation # 3

A person, who loves to bake and has nobody left to bake for, as her husband has died and children have moved away, is constantly reminded of that void. Mrs. O. offered to bake for a group of older men who met twice a month at the church. Mrs. O experienced great pleasure having people enjoy her baking. The men definitely loved it! They made contact with her to express their appreciation. When one of the men was not well enough to come out, the meeting was moved to his house. His wife was quite isolated now that her husband was less mobile, so I invited the *cookie lady* to visit with the wife while the men had their game of cribbage. This truly was a win/win situation. The two women who both were lonely developed a lasting friendship. The men were able to continue meeting at the couple's home. My cribbage skills improved too!

Situation # 4

Women who are in their 80's in the early 21st century have not, for the most part, been involved in filing income tax forms. In that age group, the men most often handled financial affairs. When these women are widowed, they are overwhelmed with the prospect of doing their tax forms. For many years, a retired chartered accountant helped the women with their income taxes. The gentleman was pleased to use his skills and was recognized for his contribution. The women were thankful to have a *man from the church* helping them.

Situation # 5

Many people who are no longer able to drive their cars do not know where to begin when faced with selling a vehicle. I recruited a parishioner who enjoys dealing in automobiles to take on the task of helping older people sell their cars. Imagine the relief when there is someone with expertise who is willing to help! The man shows great respect for the people and explains each part of the process. He shows them the *black book* suggested price for a car of their make and model. The client pays for advertising, and the transfer of ownership and the man does the rest. Ministry to others happens in many different ways.

It is more blessed to give than to receive.

Acts 20:35

Situation # 6

In some circumstances I find it helpful to visit with another person, usually clergy, in order to respond to individual needs. A 95-year-old man with severely impaired vision cares for his wife with advanced dementia in their home. He makes the meals and looks after for her with some help from the provincial home care program. His wife, who had studied to be a concert pianist but had a breakdown and never finished her studies, really enjoys music. In spite of not being able to speak with much clarity, the lady can read music and play the piano. In this instance I encouraged the lady to play the piano and the minister gave the man an opportunity to express his frustrations. The man took great pleasure in knowing that his wife was playing the piano and enjoying herself. It is gratifying to observe the devotion of this couple. The man has a deep faith and appreciates receiving Holy Communion at home with his wife.

Parish nurses have many opportunities to make an immense difference in people's lives. Finding *the right person* to stay with someone while the caregiver attends church, taking a non-driver for a ride in the country or to visit the local market, or offering to provide a lay pastoral visitor for an isolated individual does require some time but serves to remind folks that they are loved and not forgotten.

Fifty-seven

And the Greatest of These is Love...

And now faith, hope, and love abide, these three;
And the greatest of these is love.

1 Corinthians 13:13

When I decided to write this book, I could not envision how it would look. I had never written a book before, and I did not even know where to begin. I had scribbled notes, reminders, concepts, and situations, but believed I should start at the beginning. But where was the beginning? Was it when I wrote a proposal for the position to exist? Was it when I became a lay pastoral visitor? Was it when I completed a gerontology program at Ryerson? No, the real beginning was when I was born!

As I reflect on my journey down the road of life, I realize how important love has been in my life. Beginning with loving parents, extended family, friends, and neighbours, while growing up in a quiet community in a peaceful country, I took love for granted because I didn't know anything different. When I entered nursing school, I had no idea where that would lead me, except that I was in training to become a nurse.

As student nurses, we lived in a residence under the watchful eye of those trying to protect us from our immature, spontaneous behaviours and ourselves. We would not have identified love as being a significant aspect of that supervision, but those women were there to help *pick up the pieces* when we felt like our lives were falling apart. For most of us, it was our first experience living away from home. And for me, it was flying on my own, away from the loving protection to which I had become accustomed.

Each of us has a story, a journey influenced by

the joys and sorrows along the way. As we live out our stories we make choices, and they have consequences. In our youth we have great hope for our unrealized dreams. We have faith in ourselves that we will meet our objectives. Some things work out well; others prove to be more of a challenge, and some do not work out at all. Those life-forming experiences prepared us for the responsibilities we undertook when we pledged to be nurses.

Nursing in a faith community proclaims to the world that we are living out our faith in the care of God's people. Parish nursing is a relatively new specialty in the nursing profession. With any new vocation or career, there is a need for structure, guidelines, rules, and regulations. There may be debates about standards, legal issues, principles, and ethics to ensure accountability, and responsibility. The risk is that the true essence of the profession can be temporarily masked by the need for structure. Yes, we need that structure, but we must not lose sight of our faith in the vocation and the hope we hold for its future.

And now faith, hope, and love
abide, these three;
And the greatest of these is love.

Appendix

- Client Intake Chart
- Client Progress Notes
- Lay Pastoral Visitor Information
- Parishioner Information For Lay Visiting
- Parish Nurse Job Description
- Program Evaluation Form
- Tips For Making Life Easier For Families With Someone Critically Ill Either At Home Or In Hospital
- Tips For Visiting A Friend Or Family Member In Hospital

Client Intake Chart

Name of Individual and Date of Birth

Date of first contact

Circumstances of first contact (clergy or physician referral? self referral?)

Address

Phone

Email

Physician

Physician phone number

Next of kin (phone contact)

Power of Attorney for Personal Care designated?

Name

Phone number

Living alone or with others? (Use separate chart for each client)

Client Intake Chart (Page Two)

Areas of Concern (as expressed by client, family member, physician)

Areas of Concern as observed by parish nurse

Objectives for Care

Possible Interventions

First Steps (Strategies in response to objectives)

Communications (who needs to know and what permission do you require?)

Client Progress Notes

(Sample client progress notes)

Background

Mrs. M., in her mid eighties and living alone had been falling and was adamant that she was not prepared to leave her home. She was having more difficulty making her meals and up to this point had refused any assistance (bathing, meal preparation, light housekeeping). The daughter had asked me to visit.

Initial Visit

Using the client intake chart on the first visit in the presence of Mrs. M's daughter, Susan, Mrs. M. listened to her daughter's concerns. Susan also stated the doctor's concerns but Mrs. M. was not interested in hearing them. Client denied any concerns except that she was tired. There was a strong urine odour in the apartment.

At My Initial Visit I Identified The Risks.

- Falling and not being able to get up on her own and not able to contact someone.

- Mrs. M. appeared to be losing weight. Nutrition was an issue.

- It was winter and Mrs. M. was feeling lonely and isolated. (Her daughter lived out-of-town).

- She was at risk of injury in having a bath, as she was very frail and weak. Skin breakdown due to poor hygiene.

Objectives

- The main objective was to reduce the risk of injury.

- Improved nutrition was necessary.

- Discuss options at next visit.

- Have Mrs. M. begin to think about what she was prepared to do and what steps she might consider.

- Improve hygiene to reduce risk of skin breakdown and infection.

- Improve medication safety by having pharmacist help with her medications (blister packs).

Possible Interventions

- Contact Home Care (Community Care Access Centre) for assistance with bathing and dressing.

- Look at options for meal preparation (e.g. Meals on Wheels)

- Emergency lifeline for immediate access if Mrs. M. should fall.

- Pay for extra help for light housekeeping, social interaction, and meal preparation.

- Match Mrs. M. with a lay pastoral visitor to go into the home and/or take her out.

- Moving to a safer environment e.g. retirement home or assisted living facility.

First Steps

- Leave Mrs. M. with some notes on possible options

- Ask permission to return in a week to listen to her ideas and ask her some questions about staying at home and what would be required to stay there safely.

- Ask permission to explore possible options for interventions for discussion in a week.

Second Visit- Questions I asked

- What is the most important issue for you?

- What are you prepared to do to support the objectives we discussed at the first meeting?

- Why are you falling? Can you get up on your own?

- What if you cannot get up? Are you prepared to lie there until someone finds you?

- Do you have a *lifeline?* Would you object to using one?

- Do you have safety bars in the bathroom? A bath seat?

- Would you accept help with meals?

- Would you like a lay pastoral visitor?

- Would you accept help with bathing, meal preparation, cleaning, and laundry?

- Would you be prepared to pay for some services?

I deliberately did not ask these questions on the first visit, as Mrs. M. needed to think about why her daughter, doctor, and parish nurse were concerned. People need time to think about the discussion and formulate some ideas. The parish nurse can support the appropriate interventions identified by the client. Offer to assist in initiating some of them. Clients are more likely to accept help when the ideas for assistance are their own.

Once the suitable supports are in place, the parish nurse can keep in touch and check in with the daughter (with Mrs. M.'s permission) to see how Susan is feeling about her mother's condition. The parish nurse can be a supportive presence for the daughter, the caregiver.

Lay Pastoral Visitor Information

Date:_____

Name:_____

Address:_____

_____

Phone:_____

Why I would Like to be a Lay Pastoral Visitor:

_____

_____

_____

Training and/or experience related to visiting:

_____

_____

_____

Why I feel I would be a good Lay Pastoral Visitor:

_____

_____

Situation in which I would not feel comfortable:

_____

_____

Problems with an older person that I would find difficult:_____

_____

_____

Type of time commitment I am able to make:

Weekly Visit_____Twice Monthly Visit_____

Telephone Contact Only_____

I would be interested in driving an older person to:

Wednesday coffee hours
(once a month-mornings)_____

Tuesday ladies group (twice a month-after-noons)_____

Seniors' luncheons (four times a year)_____

Not available for driving_____

Parishioner Information
For Lay Visiting

Date:_____

Name:_____

Address:_____

Phone:_____Email:_____

Family / Friend Contacts:

1._____Relationship_____

      Phone:_____Email_____

2._____Relationship_____

      Phone:_____Email_____

3._____Relationship_____

      Phone:_____Email_____

Interests/Hobbies:_____

_____

_____

Frequency of Visits:

Occasional_____Telephone_____

Accompany you on outings?_____

Regular/How Often:_____

Able to attend church?_____

490

If not, why?_____

If accompanied, would you like to attend:

Wednesday Services_____Luncheons_____

Coffee Hours_____Tuesday Group_____

Other_____

_____

Observations/Recommendations:

Parish Nurse Job Description

Objectives For The Parish Nurse

- To assist people in improving the quality of their health related decision-making

- To increase the health and health resource knowledge base of the parish

- To assist people in understanding the interrelationship of the spirit, mind, and body and the effects on healing, health, and wellness

- To help the faith community become a place of healing and wholeness through education, discussion and linking to community resources

Education and Personal Resources

- Registered Nurse with a current license to practice in applicable geographical area

- Education and/or experience in pastoral ministry

- Active in a faith community

- Demonstrate spiritual depth and maturity

- Ability to understand and communicate the concept of the interrelationship of the spirit, mind, and body to health, wellness and healing

- Good listening and communication skills

- Sensitivity to people and their concerns

- Ability to communicate well in written form

- Skill in, and commitment to working in collaboration with all stakeholders including clergy, congregation leadership, congregation members and community

Practical Experience in Nursing

- A minimum of three years with experience in teaching and community health

Responsibilities

- Maintaining a practice consistent with the guidelines of the College of Nurses for particular geographical area

- Maintaining a practice consistent with parish nursing guidelines

- Maintaining accurate and confidential records consistent with professional guidelines

- Maintaining a practice that is accountable to the faith community and the nursing profession

Professional Development

- Assumes responsibility for professional development and contributes to the professional growth of others

- Complies with the Quality Assurance Program as prescribed by the nursing associations in the particular geographical area

- Keeps informed of current theory and practice in parish nursing by membership in an association, independent reading, conferences and networking

The Parish Nurse As A Health Educator/Facilitator

- Provides relevant and current health-related information in bulletins, newsletters, bulletin board and in communication with individuals and groups

- Encourages self-care and understanding of the link between physical, spiritual and mental health

- Provides education and support for caregivers

- With a supportive body of members within the *congregation*, organizes educational events on topics of interest and relevance

The Parish Nurse As An Integrator Of Faith And Health

- Helps to broaden the definition of illness to include spiritual conditions such as loneliness, despair and fear

- Expands the perception of professional caring and healing to include forgiveness and hope

- Connects congregation members with appropriate spiritual resources within the faith community

The Parish Nurse As Health Counselor

- Listens!

- Respects confidentiality

- Applies theoretical and scriptural concepts as a basis for decision-making in practice

- Documents according to parish nursing guidelines

- Uses the nursing process of assessing, planning, evaluating and documenting according to professional guidelines

The Parish Nurse As A Liaison To Community Resources

- Becomes a visible expression of Christ-centred caring in the community

- Collects data on community resources and helps people gain access to these services

- Links with other professionals in the health-care field

- Advocates on behalf of faith community members with other health professionals for better and more appropriate and consistent care, when necessary

The Parish Nurse As Coordinator of Volunteers

- Finds opportunities for others to participate in the ministry of parish nursing

- Encourages others to reach out to those in need

- Recognizes the different skills of prospective volunteers and assists those willing to serve to find appropriate roles

- Explores alternative ways of encouraging volunteer ministry in changing times

- Links parishioners in need with those who are willing and able to provide support

Program Evaluation Form

Program Title:
Date: Location: Phone #:
Presenters:
1. Please evaluate each of the following aspects of the program by circling a number on the scale below.

	Excellent	Good	Fair	Unsatisfactory	Not applicable
Achievement of program objectives	4	3	2	1	N/A
Achievement of my personal objectives	4	3	2	1	N/A
Relevance of content to my needs and interests	4	3	2	1	N/A
Organization of the program	4	3	2	1	N/A
Usefulness of handouts	4	3	2	1	N/A

	Excellent	Good	Fair	Unsatisfactory	Not applicable
Instructors' knowledge	4	3	2	1	N/A
Match between content and my questions	4	3	2	1	N/A
Instructors' ability to explain content clearly	4	3	2	1	N/A
Instructors' ability to respond well to questions	4	3	2	1	N/A

2. The length of the program was:
   ❑ Too long
   ❑ Too short
   ❑ Just right

3. The level of material covered was:
   ❑ Too high. I felt overwhelmed.
   ❑ Just right. I got just what I needed.
   ❑ Beneath me. I needed something more.

Please leave name and address/ email if you wish to be notified of next workshop.

_____

_____

_____

_____

Further comments:

_____

_____

_____

Other topics you would like us to cover:

_____

_____

_____

Thank you very much for your input.

Tips For Making Life Easier For Families With Someone Critically Ill Either At Home Or In Hospital

- Take an older relative, who may not be able to visit independently to visit the person who is ill.

- When preparing food for families, instead of taking in one large meal, consider making individual meal packets to put in the freezer, as meal times are often irregular. Inquire as to food preferences and allergies and provide meals in disposable containers so families do not have to wash and return containers.

- Offer to help with the care of children and other dependents. Spend time with them on a regular basis, providing some stability in their lives when their world seems to be in chaos.

- Offer practical help: taking clothes to the dry cleaners, responding to calls about appointments. Take children to their appointments and activities such as hockey or swimming classes.

- Set up a network of supporters who can help to keep the family system working through a difficult period, keeping in mind that you on your own cannot do it all!

- The family member closest to the ill per-

son may need someone to listen to him/
her. There is usually support for the person
who is ill but it may be lacking for the family.

- Sometimes being in the home to field phone
  calls and visitors can provide relief for family members. People are well intentioned
  but their calls and visits can be a burden to
  stressed family caregivers.

- Assisting with routine chores like laundry
  and shopping can be helpful. If the person
  who routinely does these chores is ill, the
  other family members may appreciate the
  assistance. Some may feel that laundry is
  a personal activity and decline assistance.
  Accept that.

Developed by the Health and Wellness Committee
Amended by Barbara Caiger

Tips For Visiting A Friend
Or Family Member In Hospital

- Visit for 15 or 20 minutes. Remember the person is there because of illness and your visit should be supportive, not exhausting. Patients may need to rest but feel that their role is to *entertain* you.

- Ask a patient: "would you like" rather than asking, "what would you like." People want to know what range of assistance you are offering. Once the patient determines what you are offering, it may be easier to ask you for something specific.

- If a family member is keeping watch at the bedside an offer of staying there so the person can have a break might be welcomed.

- Check in with the patient to see if your time for visiting is appropriate. If not, leave gracefully. Ask yourself whose needs are you meeting?

- Thoughtful gifts to take to someone in hospital include: a small teddy bear; a walkman or CD player with relaxation tapes; a small soft pillow to place under a tender area; fragrance-free body lotions; a magazine with lots of pictures; photos of family members; pictures drawn by children.

- Cut-up melon pieces, grapes and mints might be a welcome gift.

- Taking care of a patient's flowers and plants can be helpful if the person is not able to care for them.

- A small notebook and pen, note cares, stamps and labels might be useful.

- If a person is very ill, send a note rather than make a phone call or visit. Your objective should be to let the person know that you care.

- If someone is receiving chemotherapy, plants may not be permitted in the room. Fragrant flowers may not be welcome. Check with hospital re policies before taking or sending them.

- For long-term and terminal illness, take in sheets and/or pillows from home to provide comfort.

- New pajamas or nightgown may be appreciated (or laundering of current ones).

- Taking in ethnic meals for patients may be fitting.

- Offer to read cards, notes or other mail to individuals if they are not able. Offering to write notes might be welcomed as well.

Developed by Health and Wellness Committee
Amended by Barbara Caiger

References

References

Adams, P., & Mylander, M. (1993). *Gesundheit!* Rochester, VT: Healing Arts Press.

Albom, M. (1997). *Tuesdays with Morrie: An old man, a young man and life's greatest lesson.* New York: Doubleday.

American Psychological Association. (2002). *Publication manual of the American Psychological Association.* (5th ed.). Washington, DC: Author.

Anglican Church of Canada. (2001). *Sexual misconduct policy.* Toronto, ON: Diocese of Toronto. Retrieved Nov. 10, 2004 from http://www.toronto.anglican.ca

Anglican Church of Canada. (2003). *Responsible ministry: Screening in faith.* Toronto, ON: Diocese of Toronto. Retrieved Feb. 15, 2004 from http://www.toronto.anglican.ca

Arnold, E., & Boggs, K. (1995). *Interpersonal relationships: Professional communication skills for nurses.* (2nd ed.). Philadelphia: Saunders.

Atchley, R.C. (1980). *The social forces in later life: An introduction to social gerontology.* (3rd ed.). Belmont, CA: Wadsworth.

Ateah, A., & Mirwaldt, J., (Eds.). (2004). *Within our reach: Preventing abuse across the lifespan.* Manitoba: Fernwood / RESOLVE, co-publishers.

Avery, B. (1996). *The pastoral encounter: Hidden depths in human contact.* Glasgow: HarperCollins.

Backlar, P. (1994). *The family face of schizophrenia: Practical counsel from America's leading experts.* New York: Putnam.

Ban Breathnach, S. (1998). *Something more: Excavating your authentic self.* New York: Warner Books.

Baumohl, A. (1987). *Grow your own leaders: A practical guide to training in the local church.* London: Scripture Union.

Beers, M. H, & Urice, S. K. (1992). *Aging in good health: A complete, essential medical guide for older men & women & their families.* New York: Pocket Books.

Beinfield, H., & Korngold, E. (1991). *Between heaven and earth: A guide to Chinese medicine.* New York: Ballantine Books.

Bennett-Goleman, T. (2001). *Emotional alchemy: How the mind can heal the heart.* New York: Harmony Books.

Bennett, H.Z. (2001). *Write from the heart: Unleashing the power of your creativity.* (Rev. ed.). Novato, CA: Nataraj.

Bentley, J. (1992). *Elder abuse: The hidden crime.* Byesville, OH: Area Agency on Aging Region 9 Inc. Retrieved July 29, 2005 from http://seniors-site.com/fraudm/elder1.html

Bibby, R. (2004). *The future families project: A survey of Canadian hopes and dreams.* The Vanier Institute of the Family. Retrieved Feb. 16, 2005 from http://www.vifamily.ca/library/publications/futured.html

Birren, J. E., & Schaie, K.W., (Eds.). (1977). *Handbook of the psychology of aging.* Toronto: Van Nostrand Reinhold.

Bisset, A. (Ed.). (2000). *The Canadian Oxford paperback dictionary.* Canada: Oxford University Press.

Borysenko, J. (1988). *Minding the body, mending the mind.* New York: Bantam Books.

Borysenko, J. (2001). *Inner peace for busy people: 52 simple strategies for transforming your life.* Carlsbad, CA: Hay House.

Brandon, N. (1971). *The psychology of self-esteem.* New York: Bantam Books.

Buckman, R. (1988). *I don't know what to say: How to help and support someone who is dying.* Toronto, ON: Key Porter.

Caiger, B. (1997). Homily given in Kingston, Ontario.

Canadian Association of Critical Care Nurses. (1999). *Advance directives: Canadian Association of Critical Care Nurses: Position statement.* Retrieved Sept. 12, 2004 from http://www.caccn.ca/advance_directives.htm

Canadian Association for Parish Nursing Ministry. (2003). *Standards of practice and core competencies.* Retrieved Sept.18, 2004 from http:// www.capnm.ca/standards.html

Canadian Health Network. (2004). *Why adults still matter to teenagers (even if they won't admit it).* Public Health Agency of Canada: Author.

Canadian Mental Health Association. (2003). *Mental health: Scope of the April issue.* Canada: Citizens for Mental Health.

Canadian Mental Health Association. (2005). *Your mental health.*

Canada: Author. Retrieved June 8, 2005 from http:// www.cmha.ca

Canadian Mental Health Association, Ontario. (2005). *Stigma and mental illness.* Ontario: Author. Retrieved June 16, 2005 from http:// www.ontario.cmha.ca

Canadian Nurses Association. (1994). *Joint statement on advance directives.* Ottawa, ON: Author.

Canadian Nurses Association. (1998). *Ethics in practice: Advance directives: The nurse's role.* Ottawa, ON: CNA Policy Regulation and Research Division.

Canadian Nurses Association. (2002). *Code of ethics for registered nurses.* Ottawa, ON: Author.

Canfield, J., Hansen, M. V., Augery, P., & Mitchel, N. (1997). *Chicken soup for the Christian soul: 101 stories to open the heart and rekindle the spirit.* Deerfield Beach, Fla.: Health Communications.

Carlson, R. (1997). *Don't sweat the small stuff and it's all small stuff.* New York: Hyperion.

Carlson, R. (1998). *The don't sweat the small stuff workbook.* New York: Hyperion.

Carlson, R. (2002). *What about the big stuff: Finding strength and moving forward when the stakes are high.* New York: Hyperion.

Carpenito, L. J. (1997). *Handbook of nursing diagnosis.* (7th ed.). Philadelphia: Lippincott.

Chidwick, P. (1988). *Dying yet we live: Our responses to the spiritual needs of the dying.* Toronto, ON: Anglican Book Centre.

Chopra, D. (1990*). Quantum healing: Exploring the frontiers of mind/body medicine.* New York: Bantam Books.

Chopra, D. (1991). *Creating health: How to wake up the body's intelligence.* Boston: Houghton Mifflin.

Clark, M. B., & Olson, J. K. (2000). *Nursing within a faith community: Promoting health in times of transition.* Thousand Oaks, CA: Sage.

Clinebell, H. (1991). *Basic types of pastoral care & counselling: Resources for the ministry of healing & growth.* (Rev. & enl.). Nashville, TN: Abingdon Press.

Clinebell, H. (1992). *Well being: A personal plan for exploring and enriching the seven dimensions of life: mind, body, spirit, love, work, play, the earth.* San Francisco: Harper.

College of Nurses of Ontario. (1996). *The ethical framework for nurses in Ontario.* Toronto, ON: Author.

College of Nurses of Ontario. (2002). *Core standards for documentation.* Toronto, ON: Author.

College of Nurses of Ontario. (2002). *Professional standards for registered nurses and registered practical nurses in Ontario.* Toronto, ON: Author.

College of Nurses of Ontario. (2004). *Confidentiality and privacy – personal health information.* Toronto, ON: Author.

Cook, J. (1999). (Comp. & arr.). *The book of positive quotations.* New York: Granmercy Books.

Cruden, A. (N.D.). *A complete concordance to the Holy Scriptures of The Old and New Testaments.* (New ed.). New York: Revell.

Davidson, G. W. (1990). *Living with dying: A guide for relatives & friends.* (Rev. ed.). Minneapolis, MN: Augsburg Fortress.

Davis, M., Eshelman, E.R., & McKay, M. (2000).

The relaxation and stress reduction workbook. (5th ed.). Oakland, CA: New Harbinger.

Demaray, D.E. (1984). *Watch out for burnout: A look at its signs, prevention, and cure.* Grand Rapids, MI: Baker Book House.

Dembe, E. (2000). *Use the good dishes: Finding joy in everyday life.* Toronto, ON: Macmillan, Canada.

Department of Health. (2001). *Making it happen: A guide to developing mental health promotion.* London: Department of Health. Retrieved May 14, 2005 from http:// www.helh. nhs.uk/nsf/mentalhealth/whatworks/intro/models.html

Department of Justice Canada. (1985). *Privacy Act (R.S. 1985, c.P-21).* Ottawa: Author. Retrieved Jan. 3, 2005 from http://www.laws. justice.gc.ca/en/P-21/94799.html

Department of Justice Canada (2005). *Child abuse: A fact sheet.* Ottawa: Author. Retrieved June 5, 2005 from http://canada.justice. gc.ca/en/ps/fm/childafs.html

DePaulo, J.R. Jr., & Horvitz, L.A. (2002). *Understanding depression: What we know and what you can do about it.* New York: Wiley.

Doherty, D. (on behalf of the Muriel McQueen Fergusson Centre). (2002). *Health effects of family violence.* Fredericton, N.B.: Centre for Family Violence Research. Retrieved June 18,

2005 from
http://www.hc-sc.gc.ca/nc-cn

Durbin, N. L. R. (1998). *Valuing the gifts you bring: Developing those gifts into an effective parish nurse practice.* Paper presented at the Twelfth Annual Westberg Parish Nurse Symposium, Itasca, Ill.

Edelstein, S. (1999). *100 things every writer needs to know.* New York: Berkley.

Edinberg, M.A. (1987). *Talking with your aging parents.* Canada: Random House.

Egan, G. (1986). *The skilled helper: A systematic approach to effective helping.* (3rd ed.). Monterey, CA: Brooks/Cole.

Eiben, T., & Gannon, M., with the staff of Poets and Writers Magazine. (2004). *The practical writer: From inspiration to publication.* London: Penguin Books.

Erikson, E. (1963). *Childhood and society.* (2nd ed.). New York: Norton.

Evans, M.A., & Maney, A. (1998). *IWISE Leadership program.* (International Women in Science and Engineering) Ames, IA: Iowa State University. Retrieved Aug. 7, 2004 from http://www.iwise.com

Fast, J. (1971). *Body language.* Canada: Simon and Schuster.

Fennell, P. A. (2001). *The chronic illness work-*

512

book: Strategies and solutions for taking back your life. Oakland, CA: New Harbinger.

Ferguson, B. (2000). Identifying the risks. *Network, 6-7.* Canadian Mental Health Association, Ontario Division.

Fleming, S. (1984). Presentation on Grief at Hospice King. King City, ON.

Fontaine, K. L. (2000). *Healing practices: Alternative therapies for nursing.* Upper Saddle River, NJ: Prentice Hall.

Foskett, J., & Lyall, D. (1988). *Helping the helpers: Supervision & pastoral care.* London: Anchor Press.

Frank, M. O. (1986). *How to get your point across in 30 seconds - or less.* New York: Simon & Schuster.

Freedman, Z. (1990). *Pleased to see you: A guide to visiting your doctor; you have a right to ask.* Ottawa, ON: ElderRights Communications.

Freel, W. (2000, Fall). Helping students succeed. *Network, 12-14.* (Canadian Mental Health Association, Ontario Division).

Gerard, P. (2000). *Writing a book that makes a difference.* Cincinnati, OH: Story Press.

Gladwell, M. (2000). *The tipping point: How little things can make a big difference.* London: Little, Brown.

Gladwell, M. (2005). *Blink: The power of thinking without thinking.* New York: Little, Brown.

Glasser, M., & Kolvin, I., et al. (2001). Cycle of child sexual abuse: Links between being a victim and becoming a perpetrator. *The British Journal of Psychiatry.* 179: 482-494. Retrieved June 25, 2005 from http://bjp.rcpsych.org/cgi/content/full/179/6/482

Goldberg, N. (1986). *Writing down the bones; freeing the writer within.* Boston: Shambhala.

Goldsmith, T. D., & Vera, M. (2000). *What causes domestic violence?* Retrieved July 16, 2005 from http://psychcentral.com/library/domestic_causes.htm

Gordon, M. (1981). *Old enough to feel better: A medical guide for seniors.* Toronto: Fleet Books.

Government of Canada (2005 a). *Spousal abuse: A fact sheet from the Department of Justice Canada.* Ottawa: Author. Retrieved June 11, 2005 from http://www.justice.gc.ca/en/ps/fm/spouseafs.html

Government of Canada (2005 b). *Abuse of older adults: A fact sheet from the Department of Justice of Canada.* Ottawa: Author. Retrieved July 26, 2005 from http://canada.justice.gc.ca/en/ps/fmadultsfs.html

Government of Ontario (1996). The *Advocacy, Consent and Substitute Decisions Statute Law*

Amendment Act (1995). Dept. of Justice of Ontario. Toronto: Author. Retrieved July 14, 2004 from http://www.attorneygeneral.jus.gov.on.ca/english/family/pgt/pgtsda.pdf

Government of Ontario. (2001). *Healthy babies, healthy children program.* Ministry of Health and Long-Term Care: Author. Retrieved Jan. 4, 2004 from http:// www.gov.on.ca/health

Government of Ontario. (2003). *Child and Family Services Act.* Ministry of Children and Youth Services: Author. Retrieved June 26, 2005 from http://www.children.gov.on.ca/CS/en/programs/ChildProtection/

Publications/repChAbuse.htm

Grigg, R. (1989). *The tao of being: Lao Tsu's Tao Te Ching adapted for a new age.* USA: Humanics.

Groopman, J. (2005). *The anatomy of hope: How people prevail in the face of illness.* New York: Random House.

Guinan, Sister St. M., & MacPherson, J. A. (Eds.). (1984). *Where life's harvest mellows: A guide for volunteers preparing for pastoral care visiting.* Toronto, ON: Canadian Institute of Religion & Gerontology.

Halley, H. H. (1964). *Halley's Bible handbook: An abbreviated bible commentary.* Grand Rapids, Michigan: Zondervan.

Halpern, J. (1988). *Helping your aging parents: A*

practical guide for adult children. New York: Ballantine Books.

Hanson, P. G. (1986). *The joy of stress.* (Rev. 2nd ed.). Islington, ON: Hanson Stress Management.

Harris, J. G. (1987). *Biblical perspectives on aging: God and the elderly.* Philadelphia: Fortress.

Hart, S. (1997). *The lady from the centre: A guide to the professional caregiver's universe.* Newmarket, ON: The Alzheimer Society of York Region.

Hart, T. N. (1980). *The art of Christian listening.* Ramsay, NJ: Paulist Press.

Health Canada, & Queen's University (Social Program Evaluation Group). (2001-2002). *The health behaviour in school aged children (HBSC).* Canada: Author.

Health Canada. (2002). *The report on mental illness in Canada.* Health Canada Editorial Board Mental Illnesses in Canada: Ottawa, Canada.

Health Canada Online. (1986). *Health Canada – Health care - achieving health for all: A framework for health.* Retrieved Sept. 20, 2004 from http://www.hc.sc.gc.ca/english/care/achieving_health.html

Herman, J.L. (1997). *Trauma and recovery.* New York: Basic Books.

Hodgson, H. (1995). *Alzheimer's, finding the words: A communication guide for those who care.* Minneapolis, MN: CHRONIMED.

Hogan, R. (1976). *Personality theory: The personological tradition.* New Jersey: Prentice Hall.

Huber, C. (1990). *That which you are seeking is causing you to seek.* Mountain View, CA: A Centre for the Practice of Zen Buddhist Meditation.

Hurley, K., & Dobson, T. (1993). *My best self: Using the enneagram to free the soul.* USA: HarperSanFrancisco.

Jarvie, G. (1993). *Bloomsbury grammar guide.* London: Bloomsbury.

Jarvik, L., & Small, G. (1990). *Parentcare: A compassionate commonsense guide for children and their aging parents.* Toronto, ON: Bantam.

Johnson, S. (1998). *Who moved my cheese?* New York: Putnam.

Justice, B. (1987). *Who gets sick: How beliefs, moods, and thoughts affect your health.* Los Angeles: Tarcher.

Kabat-Zinn, J. (1991). *Full catastrophe living: Using the wisdom of your body and mind to face stress, pain, and illness.* New York: Dell.

Kabat-Zinn, J. (1994). *Wherever you go there you are: Mindfulness meditation in everyday life.* New York: Hyperion.

Kahn, S., & Saulo, M. (1994). *Healing yourself: A nurse's guide to self - care and renewal.* Albany, N.Y.: Delmar.

Keegan, L. (1994). *The nurse as healer.* Albany, N.Y.: Delmar.

Kemper, D.W, The Healthwise Staff, & Stilwel, D. (Ed). (1995). *Healthwise handbook* (Cdn. ed.). Boise, Idaho: Healthwise.

Kirsta. A. (1986). *The book of stress survival: Identifying and reducing the stress in your life.* New York: Simon & Schuster.

Korenblum. M. (2000). Recognizing the warning signs. *Network, 8-10.* (Canadian Mental Health Association, Ontario Division).

Kornfield, J. (1993). *A path with heart: A guide through the perils and promises of spiritual life.* USA: Bantam Books.

Kunz, D. (1990). *Visual aspects of the healing arts.* Wheaton, Ill: The Theosophical Wheaton Publishing House.

Kushner, H. S. (1983). *When bad things happen to good people.* New York: Avon Books.

Lazar, M., Greiner, G., Robertson, G., & Singer, P. (1996). Bioethics for clinicians: Substitute decision-making. *Canadian Medical Association Journal.* Retrieved October10, 2004 from http://www.cmaj.ca/misc/bio_substitutes.html

Lee, R. S. (1980). *Principles of pastoral counselling.* London: William Clowes (Beccles).

Lieb, S. (1991). *Principles of adult learning.* Arizona: Dept. of Health Services. Retrieved Aug. 8, 2004 from http://www.honolulu.hawaii. edu/intranet/committees/FacDevCom/ guidebk/teachtip/adults-2htm

Lukawiecki, T. (1999). *Financial abuse of older adults.* Ottawa: Public Health Agency of Canada. Retrieved July 25, 2005 from http://www. phac-aspc.gc.ca/ncfv- cnivf/familyviolence/ html/ agefinancialab_e.html

Mace, N. L., & Rabins P.V. (1992). *The 36-hour day: A family guide to caring for persons with Alzheimer's disease, related dementing illness and memory loss in later life.* (Rev. ed.). New York: The Johns Hopkins Press.

Maddocks, M. (1992). *Twenty questions about healing.* (3rd impression). Great Britain: BPCC Hazells.

Manning, D. (1999). *Don't take my grief away from me.* (26th ed.). Oklahoma City, OK: In-Sight Books.

Manning, D. (2000). *The gift of significance: Walking with people through a loss.* (3rd printing). Oklahoma City, OK: In-Sight Books.

Marmot, M.G. (2004). *Creating healthier societies.* Bulletin of the World Health Organization,

82 (5). Retrieved May 12, 2004, from http://www.who.int/bulletin

Martin, John D., & Ferris, F. (1992). *I can't stop crying: It's so hard when someone you love dies.* Toronto, ON: Key Porter.

Marty, M., & Marty, M. (1995). *Our hope for years to come: The search for spiritual sanctuary.* Minneapolis: Augsburg Fortress.

Maslow, A. H. (1962). *Toward a psychology of being.* (2nd ed.). New York: D. Van Nostrand.

Maté, G. (2004, December 18, 2004). Are violent teens suffering 'the rage' of the unparented? *The Globe and Mail.*

Mayo, P. E. (2001). *The healing sorrow workbook: Rituals for transforming grief and loss.* Oakland, CA: New Harbinger.

McCreary Centre Society. (2003). *Highlights from the 2003 adolescent health survey III.* McCreary Centre Society, 2004: Author.

McGraw, J. (2001). *Life strategies for teens workbook.* New York: Simon & Schuster.

McKay, M., & Fanning, P. (1995). *Self-esteem.* (Rev. ed.). Oakland, CA: New Harbinger.

McKee, K. J. (2000). Notes from a lecture: *Meaning of illness,* given Apr. 26, 2000. Retrieved Sept.18, 2004 from http:// www.shef.ac.uk/~smtw/2000/bs/bs0426e.htm

McPherson, B. D. (1983). *Aging as a social process*. Toronto, ON: Butterworths.

Mentality. (1997). *What is mental health promotion?* UK: Health Education Authority. Retrieved May 16, 2005 from http://www.mentality.org.uk/services/promotion/whatis.htm

Millar, R., Crute, V., Hargie, O. (1992). *Professional interviewing*. New York: Routledge.

Miller, J. E. (1994). *How can I help? : 12 things to do when someone you know suffers a loss*. Fort Wayne, IN: Willowgreen.

Miller, J. E. (1997). *Welcoming change: Discovering hope in life's transitions*. Minneapolis: Augsburg.

Ministry of the Attorney General. (1996). *Powers of attorney*. Toronto, ON: Author.

Ministry of Health. (1999). *Parenting today's teens: A survey and review of resources*. Ottawa, ON: Author.

Miriam Dobell Healing Centre (2002). Brochure.

Mitsch, R. R., & Brookside, L. (1993). *Grieving the loss of someone you love: Daily meditations to help you through the grieving process*. Ann Arbor, MI: Servant.

Molloy, W., & Mepham, V. (1992). *Let me decide: The health care directive that speaks for you when you can't...* Toronto, ON: Penguin Books.

Molloy, W. (1993). *Vital choices: Life, death and the health care crisis.* Toronto: Penguin Books Canada.

Moore, T. (1994). *Care of the soul: A guide for cultivating depth and sacredness in everyday life.* New York: HarperCollins.

Moyers, B. (1993). *Healing and the mind.* New York: Doubleday.

Nhat Hanh, T. (1990). *Transformation & healing: Sutra on the four establishments of mindfulness.* New York: Parallax Press.

Nhat Hanh, T. (2002). *Anger: Wisdom for cooling the flames.* New York: Riverhead Books.

NiCarthy, G., & Davidson, S. (1997). *You can be free: An easy-to-read handbook for abused women.* New York: Seal Press.

Nijenhuis, E., van der Hart, O., & Steele, K. (2004). *Trauma-related structural dissociation of the personality.* Posted at Trauma Information Pages website by permission. The Netherlands: Mental Health Care Drenthe. Retrieved June 18, 2005 from http://www.trauma-pages.com/nijenhuis-2004

Nilson, J. (1997). *The Health Care Directives And Substitute Health Care Decision Makers Act.* Saskatchewan: Executive Council. Retrieved Oct. 21, 2004 from

522

http://www.gov.sk.ca/newsrel/releas-
es/1997/05/09-222.html

Nouwen, H. J. M. (1990). *The wounded healer:
In our own woundedness, we can become a
source of life for others.* New York: Doubleday.

Novak, M. (1997 a). *Aging & society: A Canadian perspective.* (3rd ed.). Scarborough, ON:
Thomson Canada Ltd.

Novak, M. (1997 b). *Successful aging: The myths,
realities and future of aging in Canada.* Toronto: Penguin Books Canada.

Oates, W. E., & Oates, C. (1985). *People in pain:
Guidelines for pastoral care.* Philadelphia: The
Westminster Press.

Ontario Community Support Association. (1974-
2004). *Through other eyes.* Ontario Ministry of
Health: Author.

Oxford University Press. (1964). *The concise Oxford dictionary of quotations.* London: Glaren-
don Press.

Peck, M. S. (1978). *The road less travelled: A new
psychology of love, traditional values and spiritual growth.* New York: Simon and Schuster.

Peel, D. (1980). *The ministry of listening: Team
visiting in hospital and home.* Toronto: Anglican Book Centre.

Pearsall, P. (1998). *The heart's code: Tapping the*

wisdom and power of our heart energy. New York: Broadway Books.

Popov, L. K. (2004). *A pace of grace: The virtues of a sustainable life.* New York: Penguin Books.

Powers, M. F. (1996). *The footprints book of prayers.* New York: Harper Collins.

Prather, H. (2000). *The little book of letting go: A revolutionary 30-day program to cleanse your mind, lift your spirit and replenish your soul.* Berkley, CA: Conari Press.

Pratt, T. K. (1998). *Gage Canadian thesaurus.* Toronto: Gage Educational.

Psychologist 4therapy.com. (2005).*The youngest victims of domestic violence.* (2005). Retrieved July 8, 2005 from http://www.4therapy.com/consumer/conditions

Public Health Agency of Canada. (1998). *The consequences of child maltreatment: A reference guide for health practitioners.* Ottawa: Author. Retrieved July18, 2005 from http://www.phac-aspc.gc.ca/nc-cn

Public Health Agency of Canada. (2003). *Mental health promotion: Promoting mental health means promoting the best of ourselves.* Ottawa: Author. Retrieved June 13, 2005 from http://www.phac-aspc.gc.ca/mh-sm/mental-health/mhp/faq.html

Public Health Agency of Canada. (2005). *Youth*

and violence. Ottawa: Author. Retrieved June 21, 2005 from http://www.phac-aspc.gc.ca/ncfv-cnivf/familyviolence/html/nfntsyjviolence_e.html

Public Safety and Emergency Preparedness Canada. (2005). *Bullying in Canada.* Retrieved July 16, 2005 from http://www.prevention.gc.ca/en/library/features/bullying/index.html

Pulleyblank Coffey, E. (2004). *Family therapy with families facing catastrophic illness: Building internal and external resources.* Retrieved January 8, 2005 from http://www.4therapy.com NETWORK

Putnam, R. D. (2000). *Bowling alone: The collapse and revival of American community.* New York: Simon & Schuster.

Queensland Health. (2001). *Social determinants of health: Mental health fact sheet.* Australia. Southern Public Health Unit Network, West Moreton Public Health Unit, Ipswich.

Quigley, D. (2000). *Notes on meaning of illness.* Retrieved September 8, 2004 from http://www.alchemyinstitute.com/explore.htm

Redman, B.K. (1984). *The process of patient education.* (5th ed.). St. Louis, Missouri: Mosby.

Registered Nurses Association of Ontario. (2002). *Enhancing healthy adolescent development.* Nursing Best Practice Guidelines: Author. Retrieved Nov. 4, 2004 from http://

www.rnao.org/bestpractices/completed_
guidelines/bestPractice_firstCycle.asp

Roberts, D. J. (1991). *Taking care of caregivers: For families and others who care for people with Alzheimer's disease and other forms of dementia.* Palo Alto, CA: Bell.

Room, A. (1994). *Dictionary of confusible words.* Great Britain: Helicon.

Ruiz, D. M. (1997). *The four agreements: A practical guide to personal freedom.* San Rafael, CA: Amber-Allen.

Rybarczyk, B., & Bellg, A. (1997). *Listening to life stories: A new approach to stress intervention in health care.* New York: Springer.

Sampson, E. E., & Marthas, M. (1981). *Group process for the health professions.* (2nd ed.). New York: Wiley.

Santorelli, S. (1999). *Heal thy self: Lessons on mindfulness in medicine.* New York: Random House.

Santorelli, S., & Kabat-Zinn, J. (Eds.). (2002). *Mindfulness-based stress reduction professional training: Integrating mindfulness meditation into medicine and health care.* Boston: University of Massachusetts Medical School.

Shelly, J. A., & Fish, S. (1988). Spiritual *care: The nurse's role.* (3rd ed.). Downers Grove, Ill: Intervarsity Press.

Shipway, L. (2004). *Domestic violence: A handbook for health professionals.* New York: Routledge.

Shulman, B. H., & Berman, R. (1988). *How to survive your aging parents so you and they can enjoy life.* Chicago, Ill: Surrey Books.

Simmie, S., & Nunes, J. (2001). *The last taboo: A survival guide to mental health care in Canada.* Toronto, ON: McClelland & Stewart.

Simmie, S., & Nunes, J. (2002). *Beyond crazy: Journeys through mental illness.* Toronto, ON: McClelland & Stewart.

Simonton, O. C., Henson, R., & Hampton, B. (1994). *The healing journey: Restoring health and harmony to body, mind, and spirit.* New York: Bantam.

Singer, P.A., & Sperling, D. (2002). *University of Toronto, Joint Centre for Bioethics: Living Will.* (rev.2002)

Retrieved February 2, 2004 from http://www.utoronto.ca/jcb/outreach/document/JCP_Living_Will.pdf

Skidmore, R. A. (1983). *Social work administration: Dynamic management and human relationships.* Englewood Cliffs, NJ: Prentice-Hall.

Smith, M. (2005). *Commitment to care: A plan for long-term care in Ontario.* Ottawa: Ministry of Health and Long-Term Care. Retrieved July 30,

2005 from http://www.cleo.on.ca/english/
pub/onpub/PDF/seniors/elderab.pdf

Smucker, C. J. (1997). *Spiritual assessment: Hearing the story of the soul.* A paper presented at the Eleventh Annual Westburg Parish Nursing Symposium: Itasca IL.

Smucker, C.J. (1998). *In the garden of good and evil: The meaning of illness.* A paper presented at The Twelfth Annual Westberg Parish Nurse Symposium: Itasca, IL.

Solari-Twadell, A., McDermott, M.A., Ryan, J.A., & Djupe, A.M. (1994). *Assuring visibility for the future: Guideline development for parish nurse education programs.* Park Ridge, IL: Lutheran General HealthSystem.

Solari-Twadell, P. A., Djupe, A. M., & McDermott, M.A. (Eds.). (1996). *Parish nursing: The developing practice.* Oak Brook, IL: Advocate Health Care.

Stephens et al. (2001). *The report on mental illness in Canada* (2000). Canadian Mental Health Association Fact Sheet.

Stephens, T., & Joubert, N. (2000). *Measuring population mental health in Canada: An overview.* Ottawa: Health Canada & Universities of Toronto & Ottawa.

Swanson, S.M. (1999). *Abuse and neglect of older adults.* Ottawa: Public Health Agency of Canada. Retrieved July 24, 2005 from http://www.

phac-aspc.gc.ca/ncfv/familyviolence/html/
agenegl_e.html

Switzer, D. K. (1986). *The minister as crisis counselor.* (Rev. & enl.). Nashville, TN: Abingdon Press.

Tammet, B. (2001, Fall). The value of family meetings. *Mental Health Matters*: Canadian Mental Health Association, York Region Branch.

Tatelbaum, J. (1980). *The courage to grieve: Creative living, recovery & growth through grief.* New York: Harper & Row.

Tennstedt, S. (2002). *Commentary on "research design in end-of-life research: State of science".* Watertown, MA: Institute for Studies on Aging, New England Research Institutes.

The Canadian Red Cross Society. (1984). *The friendly visitor's handbook.* Ontario: Author.

The Holy Bible*: New revised standard version.* (1990). Nashville: Nelson.

The National Clearinghouse on Family Violence (2005). *Health effects of family violence.* Canada: Author. Retrieved June19, 2005 from http:// www.hc.sc.gc.ca/nc-cn

The North Western Health Board. (2005). *Promoting positive mental health.* Ireland: Health Promotion Service. Retrieved May 4, 2005 from http://www.nwhb.ie/files/healthpromotion/topics/mentalhealth.shtml

Thompson, W. (1987). *Aging is a family affair: A guide to quality visiting, long-term care facilities and you.* Toronto, ON: NC Press.

The Ontario Community Support Assoc. in partnership with the Ontario Ministry of Health. (1974-2004). *Through other eyes: A program for creating a better understanding of the challenges of persons with impairments.* Retrieved Jan 18, 2005from http://www.ocsa.on.ca

Tolle, E. (2003). *The power of now: A guide to spiritual enlightenment.* Vancouver, BC: Namaste Publishing Inc.

Topf, L. N., &. Bennett H.Z. (1995). *You are not your illness: Seven principles for meeting the challenge.* New York: Simon & Schuster.

Tourles, S. (2000). *365 ways to energize mind, body, & soul.* Pownal, VT: Storey.

Tournier, P. (1987). *A listening ear: Reflections on Christian caring.* Minneapolis: Augsburg.

Trowbridge, B. (2002). *The hidden meaning of illness: Disease as a symbol & metaphor.* Virginia Beach: A.R.E. Press.

Truss, L. (2004). *Eats, shoots and leaves: The zero tolerance approach to punctuation.* Toronto, ON: Penguin Books.

Tubesing, N. L., & Christian, S. S. (Eds.). (1995). *Structured exercises in wellness promotion: A handbook for trainers, educators & group lead-*

ers. (Vol.5). Duluth, MN: Whole Person Associ-
ates.

Tutty, L. (1999). *Husband abuse: An overview of
research and perspectives.* Ottawa: Family
Violence Prevention Unit, Health Canada. Retrieved June 18, 2005 from http://www.hc.sc.
gc.ca/nc-cn

United States Dept. of Justice (2003). *Statistics
reported on family violence in the United States
between 1998 and 2002.* Retrieved June 22,
2005 from http://www.ojp.usdoj.gov/bjs/ab-
stract/fvs.htm

Valent, P. (1998). Introduction to survival strategies. *From survival to fulfillment: A framework
for the life-trauma dialectic.* Philadelphia:
Brunner/Mazel. Retrieved June 18, 2005 from
http://www.trauma-pages.com/valent98.htm

Vanier Institute of the Family. (2005). *Core values.* Retrieved April 5, 2005 from http://www.
vifamily.ca/about/values.html

Vella, J. (1990). *Learning to listen, learning to
teach: The power of dialogue in educating
adults.* San Francisco: Jossey-Bass.

Virtue, D. (1994). *Losing your pounds of pain:
Breaking the link between abuse, stress, and
overeating.* Excerpt reprinted with permission
from publisher, Hay House. Retrieved Feb. 22,
2005 from http:// www.advocateweb.org/
hope/frametop.asp

Wahl, J., & Purdy, S. (2002). *Elder abuse: The hidden crime.* (7th ed.). Toronto: Advocacy Centre for the Elderly & Community Legal Education Ontario. Retrieved July 25, 2005 from http://www.cleo.on.ca/english/pub/onpub/PDF/seniors/elderab.pdf

Walker, K. (1995). *Loss of soul: Burnout.* Toronto, ON: KW Publication.

Watt, J., & Calder, J. (1981). *I love you but you drive me crazy: A guide for caring relatives.* Vancouver, BC: Fforbez.

Waxler-Morrison, N., Anderson, J., & Richardson, E. (Eds.). (1990). *Cross-cultural caring: A handbook for health professionals in western Canada.* Vancouver: UBC Press.

Weber, T. (2005, June 15). A day in the life of Canada's abuse shelters. For *The Globe and Mail.*
Retrieved June 15, 2005 from http://www.globeandmail.com/ servlet/story/RT-GAM.20050615.wshelter0615

Weber, T. (2005, July 14). Spousal violence affects almost 1.2 million: Statscan. For *The Globe and Mail.*

Retrieved July 14, 2005 from http://www.globeandmail.com/ servlet/story/RT-GAM.20050714.wviolen0714

Webster, B. (1998). *Grief journey: Finding your*

way after a loss. Mississauga, ON: Greenleaf Consultants.

Westberg, G. W., &. McNamara, J.W. (1990). *The parish nurse: Providing a minister of health for your congregation.* Minneapolis: Augsburg.

Wilkes, J. (1981). *The gift of courage: How pain and suffering can be confronted, understood, and met...with courage.* (2nd ed.). Toronto: The Anglican Book Centre.

World Health Organization. (1986). *Ottawa Charter.* Geneva: (Glossary). Retrieved June 12, 2005 from http:// www.who.int/hpn/NPH/docs/hp_glossary_en.pdf

World Health Organization. (2004). *Preventing mental disorders and promoting mental health is possible.* Geneva: Author. Retrieved June 17, 2005 from http://www.who.int/mental_health/evidence/en/

Wyllie, B. J. (1996). *Life's losses: Living through grief, bereavement and sudden change.* Toronto: MacMillan Canada.

Yalom, I. D. (2002). *The gift of therapy: An open letter to a new generation of therapists and their patients.* New York: HarperCollins.

Yount, D. (1997). *Breaking through God's silence: A guide to effective prayer with a treasury of over one hundred prayers.* New York: Simon & Schuster.

Zarit, S.H., Orr, N.K., & Zarit, J.M. (1985). *The hid-*

den victims of Alzheimer's disease: Families under stress. USA: New York University.

Zinsser, W. (2001). *On writing well: The classic guide to writing non-fiction.* (25th Anniversary ed.). New York: HarperCollins.

Index

Index

ISBN 141205385-4